W9-AUZ-012

11/03

Geneva Public Library District
127 James St.
Geneva, Illinois 60134

3 0052 00283 3007

GENEVA PUBLIC LIBRARY DISTRICT

RED★
WHITE
& LIBERAL

RED WHITE &LIBERAL

HOW LEFT IS RIGHT & RIGHT IS WRONG

ALAN COLMES

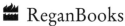 ReganBooks
An Imprint of HarperCollins*Publishers*

GENEVA PUBLIC LIBRARY DISTRICT

The author has included e-mail correspondence from some viewers. All names, e-mail addresses, and cities from which the e-mails were sent have been changed to protect the individuals' privacy.

"God Bless the USA" by Lee Greenwood on page 297. Copyright © 1984—Universal—Songs of PolyGram International, Inc. All rights reserved. Used by permission.

RED, WHITE & LIBERAL. Copyright © 2003 by Alan Colmes. All rights reserved. Printed in the United States of America. No part of this book may be used or reproduced in any manner whatsoever without written permission except in the case of brief quotations embodied in critical articles and reviews. For information address HarperCollins Publishers Inc., 10 East 53rd Street, New York, NY 10022.

HarperCollins books may be purchased for educational, business, or sales promotional use. For information please write: Special Markets Department, HarperCollins Publishers Inc., 10 East 53rd Street, New York, NY 10022.

FIRST EDITION

Designed by Kris Tobiassen

Printed on acid-free paper

Library of Congress Cataloging-in-Publication Data has been applied.

ISBN 0-06-056297-8

03 04 05 06 07   BVG/RRD   10 9 8 7 6 5 4 3 2 1

For Fay and Louis,
who gave me life,
and
For Jocelyn,
the love of my life

CONTENTS

ACKNOWLEDGMENTS

There is no way I would able to go through my daily paces without the love, help, and dedication of wonderful friends, family, and colleagues. Writing this book was one of the most rewarding experiences of my career. I've always talked into a microphone for a living, my words evaporating into the air; now seeing the tangible fruits of my labors in book form is a genuine thrill.

Were it not for the vision Roger Ailes had for the Fox News Channel and the confidence he's shown in me, I might never have achieved the level of success I now enjoy, and this book would likely never have been written. Roger sees things mere mortals overlook. Not only does he surround himself with the best and brightest people in the business, he also trusts them to do their jobs. The result is a superior product created by a focused, motivated group that each day reaches a little higher than the day before. If Chet Collier, one of television's great and legendary programmers, had not believed in me at the inception of *Fox News*, I have no idea where my career might have gone. Producers Fred Farrar and Roberta Dougherty were also responsible for encouraging a union between *Fox News* and me, and I will never forget their kindness. Kathy Ardleigh, our first senior producer of prime time, was also an early believer in my ability to do television. And many thanks to Sean Hannity—he was hired first and suggested me as a co-host. I hope this answers, once and for all, why his name comes first in the title of our show. Kevin Magee, who oversees programming at the channel, helps make *Fox* a wonderful place to be. He is always willing to listen, a rare commodity in the hustle-bustle world of broadcasting. And forget every joke you ever heard about lawyers. None of them apply to Dianne Brandi, *Fox*'s legal counsel, and the nicest attorney with whom you'll ever negotiate. Bill Shine, executive producer of *Fox News*, was the first producer of *Hannity and Colmes*, a fortuitous twist of fate that allowed me to learn how to do television from a master of the form. Bill's friendship and guidance has helped me maintain a much greater level of sanity than I ever could without him.

Monica Crowley brought my ideas to Judith Regan and helped me make them into a book. Monica is a true renaissance woman whose growing radio and television careers, along with her writing talents, make her a triple threat. Monica also gave me one of the greatest gifts anyone can give: she introduced me to my wife. In the interest of full disclosure, let me say that Monica isn't only a fabulous editor, she's also a wonderful sister-in-law. Were it not for the confidence Judith Regan showed in me, I'm not sure I would have believed myself capable of doing this in the first place. Thank you, Judith, for your support. Aliza Fogelson at Regan Books was amazing in her dedication to this project, helping me whip this book into shape. Aliza, you've made this book many times better than it would have been without your valued assistance. Lauren Clabby and John Finley, two members of the *Hannity and Colmes* staff, approached me early on and asked if they could participate, and I'm so glad I agreed. Their help with research and sourcing was invaluable.

There is no better personal manager than Rory Rosegarten. He has been both my friend and my professional support system through thick and thin, and the list of thin days is thicker than you might imagine. Thank you, Rory, for always being there for me, for always doing the right thing, and for always encouraging me to do the same.

Hannity and Colmes is the most successful debate show on television because of an incredible staff. Our senior producer, Meade Cooper, has been with the show since its inception, starting as a production assistant. Now she runs the show and has shepherded it to the top of the ratings. I'm very proud of her. The rest of our staff is similarly superb: Maureen Murphy, Erin McKenna, Jack DeMarco, Matt Linder, Tara Nicaj, John Finley, and Lauren Clabby. Our director, Chet Lishwa, has been with us since day one. If you've ever been in a television control room during a live broadcast, you know that anything can happen. I've never seen anyone able to stay so calm in the midst of such chaos. The unsung stars of *Hannity and Colmes* are the behind-the-scenes technical staffers who deserve far more acknowledgment than they ever receive: Helena Hernandez, Ray McKinney, Barbara Bazarnicki, Omar Coley, Erin Killman, Melissa Zomack, James T. Whelan, Kim Walker, Chuck Cuneo, Matt Harrington, Gabrielle Lavalle, Ed Schetting, Todd Maycher, and Kevin Pinckney. Karem Alsina's make-up skills make it possible for me to go on television without scaring people too much, and Mary Cicero and Linda Giambrone do a wonderful job making sense of my hair.

My nightly radio show, *Fox News Live with Alan Colmes*, has a brain trust unequaled in radio today. I'm grateful for Jack Abernethy's encouragement, support, and vision. Mark Masters, a proud conservative, always believed that I was one liberal who might survive on talk radio. He arranged to get my program heard on an impressive group of incubator stations before there was even a show, an almost unheard of feat in the world of radio syndication. Robert Finnerty, Jennifer Lingua, Doug Murphy, and Dave Manning have been instrumental in the growth of the program and in *Fox News Radio*. My day-to-day production staff is unparalleled, beginning with my executive producer, Joel Kaufman, who has been a key presence through the entire growth of the channel on both the radio and television sides, and whose expertise and enthusiasm are appreciated by all who work with him. Jon Costantino, who has been with me in a few radio incarnations, is a terrific producer, as is Joel Morton. Lisa Magalnick Jacknow and Mark Walsh round out an exceptional radio team.

Inspiration has come from diverse corners of the universe. I am fortunate to have grown up listening to radio greats Long John Nebel and Barry Gray, and blessed to have known Barry, whom I miss terribly. Chuck Zlatkin, a lifelong activist and passionate liberal, has a website called rightiswrong.com, a domain name that helped inspire the subtitle of this book. Michael Harrison has been a source of wisdom and guidance during my entire career. *P.S. You Are Ugly Too!* was his concept, and is incorporated into this book. For almost twenty years, my great friend Sanford Teller has been chiding me, with uncontainable glee, about all the things I lacked in my life: from a computer, to a fax machine, to a kitchen equipped with actual forks, to a wife and, finally, to a book I could call my own. Sandy, this must be killing you. Paul Guercio was always there to assure me that, no matter how dark it was, light would eventually appear. I am lucky to have not only a wonderful nuclear family: my sister, Susan Braitman, and her husband, Steve, but also a terrific extended personal and professional one. Among those who have made a difference along the way are Carl Grande, who gave me my first full-time radio job, Dale Parsons, John Hayes, Peg Kelly, and the late Bob Mounty, who brought me to WNBC, Tom Bird of WEVD, Nick Verbitsky and Andy Denemark of United Stations, Ed Salamon, Mark Mason, Jay Clark, Barry Farber, Michael Castello, Miguel Laboy, Julia Heath-Gil, Natalie Vacca, Charles Alzamora, Patricia Greenwald, Jon Moonves, and the G.B. Thank you for believing in me.

Finally, but most significantly, I wish to extend my deep gratitude to my wife, Jocelyn. She endured dozens of my lost weekends while I was buried in the preparation of this book, during both our engagement and the first couple of months of our marriage. Her support for my work and belief in me is a great source of strength always.

—ALAN COLMES
New York City
August 2003

Why You
Need This Book

Thank you for buying this book. If you're borrowing it from a friend or, even better, the public library, you're more than welcome to pony up what you would have otherwise spent to the ACLU, one of my favorite groups. If the ACLU rubs you the wrong way (although it shouldn't; even Bob Barr is with them now), how about People for the American Way, The Southern Poverty Law Center, or the NAACP? If you're of modest means, or you're a conservative who is already nauseous at the mention of these groups, I'll be happy just that you read the darned thing. In fact, I'm especially grateful if you're a nonliberal reading this. It shows a willingness to hear another point of view, even if you gnash your teeth while doing so.

For years, many on the left have ducked the "L" word. While characterized by the right as pink, the letter, unfortunately, has become tainted as scarlet. The right wing in America has been trying for years to claim ownership of God, family, and country. With the horror of September 11, 2001, came their attempt to seal that deal. The very first, knee-jerk reaction came from the far right wing in America, which blamed gays, the ACLU, and those who are pro-choice for making America vulnerable to attack. Ironically, just as

Reverend Jerry Falwell was claiming this to Reverend Pat Robertson, many of Falwell's defenders were pointing fingers at those on the left who expressed concern about our foreign policies and angrily labeling them "the Blame America First crowd." The first blame for September 11 was put squarely on liberals. When some liberals questioned the confluence of events that resulted in our vulnerability to terrorism, certain Americans who should know better have branded us as some kind of anti-American treason lobby. Those of us who have spoken out against the status quo have been told to keep our mouths shut and do our patriotic duty to support our country. Well, keeping our mouths shut is the opposite of our patriotic duty to our beloved country. As Thomas Jefferson said, "Dissent is the highest form of patriotism."

Conservatives love to quote our forefathers to argue that they are the natural progenitors of the founders of this nation. But did our forefathers keep their mouths shut and not speak out against what they saw as egregious wrongs? Were they compliant followers of regimes? Or were they, indeed, radicals, who could not and would not bear life as it was? In fact, it was their outrage at the no longer acceptable status quo that inspired them to found their own government. Our founding fathers held dear individual liberty and the empowerment of the state to protect those liberties. Sounds a lot like liberal thought to me. It's hard to find a landmass on which to found a new government these days, but our experiment in democracy is working quite well. Our system doesn't require the founding of a new one, but it does need strong, courageous voices who aren't cowed by a very loud and angry right wing, smug in its new assumption of power, and unwilling to give its fellow Americans on the left much credit for what we've achieved, together, as a nation.

One of the seminal liberal philosophers, John Rawls, described some of the fundamentals of liberalism in *A Theory of Justice*. Rawls's "veil of ignorance" theory was that if you didn't know your own circumstances and had the ability to make public policy, you'd make policy that benefited the greatest number of people. The poor, the weak, the infirm, and the needy have few advocates, few who will fight for them, but many who try to make political hay from their plight.

Red, White & Liberal: A User's Guide

My comments here about other pundits, congressmen and congress-women, senators, and President Bush are never personal. My differences are on policy and vision, on how we interpret where we are and how to get to where we should be. President Bush, for example, to whom I refer throughout this book as 43 (to distinguish him from the forty-first POTUS, President George H. W. Bush), is one of the most charming politicians (and people, not that they're mutually exclusive) I've ever met. I've liked him better the few times I've spent a couple of minutes with him than I've liked many on my own side politically, regardless of the amount of time I've spent in their company. I don't even know where many of my friends stand politically. My friendships are based on mutual caring and trust, and those qualities are not confined to one side of the political spectrum (although, if we kept score, liberals would win; but we're not keeping score; but we'd win if we did; but we're not).

You'll see passionate e-mails in *Red, White & Liberal* from some very angry conservatives who have automatic distrust of liberals, along with occasional antipathy for grammar, spelling, and the English language. As the cohost of Fox News Channel's *Hannity & Colmes*, I'm constantly under the looking glass. It's surreal to be in a profession in which people watch you do your job, and then feel no compunction about telling you off any time they don't like the job you're doing. Can you imagine having a job where the general public gets to respond to you like this?

From: ethinker
Sent: Wednesday, January 29, 2003 9:55 PM
To: colmes@foxnews.com
Subject: Ground teeth

Mr. Colmes,

On any given night, I cannot watch this broadcast past your
second comment. If I could reach through the screen, I'd crush
your throat. You are a walking example of why spewing leftist BS
ought to be a capital crime. Fortunately for you, you live in a
society where stupidity is tolerated and that I don't act on
impulse. But if I saw you dying in agonizing pain and by lifting a
finger I could save you, after spitting in your face I'd rush to find a
video camera so I could relive the pleasure of those treasured
moments again and again. Go join your pal in Baghdad; I hope you
both catch the first bomb.

Most sincerely yours,
ethinker

Sometimes these responses provide a good laugh; other times, some
frightening insights. Although most Americans don't look at life
through the prism of left versus right, there are enough who do, and
that subculture, on both sides of the political spectrum, represents a
soft bigotry that rarely gets addressed in our culture. Thankfully, in
life, we don't know how most of the people around us vote. There
are, however, some rabid ideologues on each side who will be introduced to you at a luncheon and then right after "Hello" comes,
"Where do you stand on *Roe versus Wade*?" Thanks for asking, but
I'd rather just enjoy my salad.

When I attended a Christmas party at the White House in 2001,
I thanked President Bush for inviting me, especially in light of my
ardent criticisms of his policies. My exact words were, "Thank you
for inviting a liberal to the White House." Without missing a beat,
he looked me in the eye and said, "We're all Americans." He
couldn't have said it more succinctly or more profoundly. There are
so many in this country who are just as moral, just as ethical, and just
as *American* as those who believe that they alone own these characteristics. I hope and pray (and I can say "pray" because I am not writ-

ing this on public property) that conservatives who read this will understand the commitment, the passion, and the Americanism of the other side.

All the noise the conservative camp is making tends to obscure the truth about how Americans see themselves politically. A Harris poll conducted during the entire year of 2002, involving more than thirteen thousand phone interviews, showed that 34 percent of those polled considered themselves Democrats; 31 percent, Republicans; and 24 percent, Independents. Forty percent said their political philosophy was "moderate," 35 percent said "conservative," and 18 percent said "liberal." This means that half don't consider themselves firmly in either camp; it also means that 65 percent don't consider themselves conservative.

I hope conservatives who read this book do so with a desire for a better understanding of the other side. Conservatives: I'd feel much better if you loathe liberals *after* reading this. Then, at least, you'll have a good reason to loathe us. I'm especially grateful to you for taking a chance, as you probably feel you should have this book covered in a brown paper bag. I hope you find in its pages valuable insight into how someone can think differently than you and not qualify for an insane asylum.

If you're politically independent or moderate, I value your ability to look objectively at all sides, and thank you for considering my side. If your political leanings are undefined, I ask that you read with an open mind and a desire to understand how and why a fellow American may feel so strongly about life in these United States in the early part of the twenty-first century.

For liberals who are reading this book, it's my wish that it gives you a sense of hope that you are not alone, that many Americans agree with you, and that not only is it healthy to speak out and stand up for what you believe—regardless of the political climate—it's also your patriotic duty to do so. There is no lack of conservatives out there loudly and sometimes belligerently voicing opinions, but I wouldn't mind a few more liberals jumping into the fire.

I hope some of what you read here offends you; not enough to propel you to take a match to these pages and engage in book-burning, but enough so that you'll really question me, and yourself. Writing this greatly helped me refine my own views, and I'm sure rereading it will make me wish they were even more refined in some cases. I hope some of what's written here irks you, too. That's good. That means I'm doing my job.

One more word to my fellow liberals: Take hope! You're *more* American than those who would run you out of your country for having the temerity to stand up for what you believe. It's time to paint that "L" word in its true colors: red, white, and blue.

From: James
Sent: Friday, February 14, 2003 6:59 PM
To: colmes@foxnews.com
Subject: Alan's Aspirations

Alan, your probably pretty jealous of Sean's success and his book sales, but please do not attempt to write your own book. Really, don't.

James
Hammond, IN

Sorry, James. As evidenced by what you hold in your hands, your warning has come much too late.

ONE

Red, White & Liberal

I'm proud to be a liberal. In my spare time I hug trees. I'd rather hug a tree than embrace a tax cut we can't afford. Ever try to hug a tax rebate check? Bark burn is so much more pleasant than paper cuts. I believe there is a role for government. So do conservatives, in spite of the fact that they love to shout about getting government off our backs. They love government, too. They just use government differently than liberals do. Conservatives want government to tell you what you *can't* do. In fact, the Republican view of legislation is "Just Say No." I am a liberal because I believe in what government *can* do as a force for good. I believe that, when used properly, government can create opportunity, equality, and equity. I agree with Ron Brown, the late Commerce secretary and former chairman of the Democratic National Committee, who stated, "The common thread of Democratic history, from Thomas Jefferson to Bill Clinton, has been an abiding faith in the judgment of hardworking American families, and a commitment to helping the excluded, the disenfranchised and the poor strengthen our nation by earning themselves a piece of the American Dream. We remember that this great land was sculpted by immigrants and slaves, their children and grandchildren."

I Am Not a Party Animal

The more I learned about the Democratic Party and its rich history, the more I felt at home with its ideals. This is not to say I agree with every Democratic politician, policy position, or pronouncement. And I'm often more critical of my own party than of the opposition. When I'm critical of Democrats or liberals on *Hannity & Colmes*, it drives my fellow liberals crazy because they feel I should be an ideological cheerleader. This is not something I can do while maintaining my intellectual honesty. I'm not a Democrat because I love political organizations (I am a loner, not a joiner), and I don't agree with much of the inside baseball that gets played within and between our American political parties. I'm a Democrat because the progressive ideas in which I fervently believe are closer to what the Democrats stand for than what the Republicans profess, and those two parties are the only viable infrastructures for electing candidates to office.

That being said, I heartily identify with the roots of the party. "The party of the common man" was founded by Thomas Jefferson in 1792 to fight for the Bill of Rights and stand up to the elitist Federalists. In the next century, William Jennings Bryan, known as the "Great Commoner," was considered the conscience of the nation. As a two-term congressman and three-time presidential nominee, Bryan fought for and won women's suffrage, direct elections of senators, and a progressive income tax. As President Woodrow Wilson's secretary of state and a peace advocate in the early part of the twentieth century, Bryan won the approval of thirty nations to agree to investigations of disputes before going to war. Wilson, that century's first Democratic president, brought us the League of Nations, the Federal Reserve Board, and the first child and welfare laws. President Franklin Roosevelt brought our country out of the Great Depression with his New Deal, Works Progress Administration, and the creation of Social Security. President Harry Truman integrated the armed forces. President John F. Kennedy created the Peace Corps and brought a new optimism to America. President Lyndon Johnson's administration heralded the civil rights movement with the Civil Rights Act and the Voting Rights Act. It was Johnson's Great Society that declared war on poverty and created Medicare and Medicaid.

In short, Democrats don't need to add the word *compassionate* to further define what they are: the notion is already built in to the philosophy. Liberals are the ones who have fought to move forward while conservatives have done what their name implies: conserve the past. That's why I'm proud of the "L" word and what it represents. And that's why I'm committed to fight for and uphold its ideals.

Liberal, Literally. Are You One?

The conservatives' tactic of making the word *liberal* seem as though it should be one of the seven words you can't say on the broadcast media has been brilliant. The word drips off the tongue, as though if it's said too often, the speaker will have an aneurysm as it parts the lips. (Conservatives also love to use the diminutive "lib" to marginalize the left.) When Congresswoman Nancy Pelosi was running for and then became leader of the House Democrats, the words *San Francisco liberal* were spit out of conservative mouths as though the pronouncers were trying to dispel toxic bile from their systems. The last time I checked, San Francisco is part of the very same America that conservatives claim to love so much. Or maybe they only love those parts of America that got colored red on the Bush/Gore maps of 2000. Sixties conservatives said, "My country: Love it or leave it." I say: "My country: Love it all or don't love it at all."

Liberal is a very nice word. Say it a few times. Let it roll off the tongue. Say it loud and there's music playing. Say it soft and it's almost like praying. Wait a minute . . . that's "Maria" from *West Side Story*. Actually, it wouldn't be such a bad idea if liberals could embrace this word with the same kind of glee with which Maria embraced her beauty:

> *"I feel liberal, oh so liberal. I feel liberal and witty and bright*
> *And I pity those conservatives who think they're right."*

Honestly, doesn't "liberal" sound nicer than "conservative"? "Liberal" has a lilt to it. "Conservative" has those hard sounds. And more syllables. Given what "conserve" means, does it make sense that conservatives would have more syllables than they really need?

Liberal is not, as some seem to believe, a word that must always be modified by the far-less-glamorous word *scum*. The *American Heritage Dictionary of the English Language* offers these definitions:

lib·er·al (liberel, librel) *adj.*

1.

    a. Not limited to or by established, traditional, orthodox, or authoritarian attitudes, views, or dogmas; free from bigotry.

    b. Favoring proposals for reform, open to new ideas for progress, and tolerant of the ideas and behavior of others; broad-minded.

    c. Of, relating to, or characteristic of liberalism.

    d. **Liberal** Of, designating, or characteristic of a political party founded on or associated with principles of social and political liberalism, especially in Great Britain, Canada, and the United States.

So we're not "traditional." Sometimes we wear earrings, even if we're male. Authoritarian dogmas tend to be fascist in nature, and fascism is on the right side of the political spectrum, not the left. Freedom from bigotry—now there's something worth mocking! This isn't to say that conservatives are bigoted, but we'll get to that definition in a moment.

Reform, progress, tolerance. Is there a problem here? The right loves to accuse the left of intolerance of conservative ideas, and if you point out to conservatives that liberals *are* tolerant, they don't want to hear it. Of course conservative tolerance for gays, the needy, and drug-dependent Americans is legendary, isn't it? Oh, and liberals. They're very tolerant of liberals. As for "broad-minded," okay, hold the Clinton jokes.

Here's the tolerance level of one *Hannity & Colmes* viewer who copied me on an e-mail he sent to Sean declaring that he would never be my friend because I am a liberal. He takes great issue with a passage in Sean's book, *Let Freedom Ring*. (You're welcome for the plug. It's published by ReganBooks, a division of HarperCollins.) This e-mail begins with the offending quote from Sean's book:

From: bill k
Sent: Tuesday, October 01, 2002 11:03 PM
To: Hannity; Colmes
Subject: Let Freedom Ring

"I certainly don't have any personal beef with my Fox News partner-in-crime, Alan Colmes. he is a great guy and a great American. . . ."

I can no longer take you seriously and will probably never finish your book. . . . Liberals are to be pitied or despised. This is far too serious to be reduced to a TV show.

Now, if that isn't worrisome enough, here comes the really scary part, and I don't think this guy is kidding:

I have no Liberal friends because I do not want to be their friend. I laid my life on the line for twenty years in the USAF defending the rights for Liberals to be stupid or subversive, which ever the case may be. I do not and will not ever consider them to be great Americans, and I will not lend credence to their destructive beliefs by saying they are.

Before I show you my reply to Mr. K, and his response to that, let me say a word about Sean Hannity. He is passionate in his beliefs, articulate, and persuasive. And I'm sure there are nights when he would rather be home with his beautiful wife and two darling children than on a stage somewhere debating a liberal. But Sean is also a great American who realizes that the great ongoing national debate as epitomized on *Hannity & Colmes* is integral to democracy. The give-and-take we offer nightly has caught on because people do want to see both sides of an argument, even if they strongly oppose one of them, or both of them.

From: Colmes
Sent: Wednesday, October 02, 2002 12:18 PM
To: 'bill k'
Subject: RE: Let Freedom Ring

It's really a pity that you want to shut yourself off from a huge number of fellow Americans just because they don't share your political beliefs. How do you know whether or not your doctor, dentist, dry cleaner, or grocer is liberal? If you needed emergency medical care would you make sure that the person giving you mouth-to-mouth resuscitation was a conservative? Do you want only one political party in America like they had in communist Russia?

If you want a political litmus test for every person you know and actively shut yourself off from other points of view, you are really shutting out most of the world.

Alan

From: bill k
Sent: Wednesday, October 02, 2002 12:42 PM
To: Colmes
Subject: RE: Let Freedom Ring

I usually don't reply to stupid people who make ridiculous statements but for you I will. Yes I would gladly shut myself off from anyone who I know is a Liberal. I would never let a Liberal dentist or doctor treat me if I know they are a Liberal. . . . They are the enemy of the United States and I don't have time to waste listening to their poppycock bullshit.

From: Colmes
Sent: Wednesday, October 02, 2002 1:15 PM
To: 'bill k'
Subject: RE: Let Freedom Ring

Bill,
Let me know next time you're in NY and I'll buy you a beer.
Alan

Amazingly, Bill never took me up on that offer. And I'd even buy him a domestic brew. I hope that Mr. K realizes that there are many Americans on my side, Americans who want and need a voice to combat what they see as the rising tide of conservatism in America.

From: beth
Sent: Wednesday, February 05, 2003 6:10 AM
To: colmes
Subject: Hang In There

Hi Alan—I know you have a tough job—but keep fighting for us liberals. We need a voice so badly. I pull for you every night.

Thanks. Beth

Beth, I'm there for you. And I'm there for Bill, too, whether he knows it or not.

It amazes me that some Americans can't for the life of them believe that there is such a thing as a liberal in America. It is beyond their imagination that there are a lot of people who think differently than they do. Some of my favorite e-mail is from people who believe that what I do is an act, that I'm a conservative at heart. But, hey, you have to pay the bills, right?

> **From:** Dan & Ellen S.
> **Sent:** Tuesday, October 01, 2002 9:57 PM
> **To:** colmes
> **Subject:** The Show
>
> Come on Colmes. You have got to be a plant on the show to play the devils advocate. I have to admit that it is working. BUT, you either love to be hated or you a very very dumb. I do not believe that you are that dumb and therefore have concluded that you are a plant to be the opposite and maybe boost the ratings. I am right aren't I?

Shhh, Mr. or Mrs. S. Please don't tell anyone our little secret. And when you see me raise my left eyebrow, that's a sign that I know I'm a conservative saying liberal things. It will be our little code.

I'm actually flattered when people are convinced that I'm a conservative just playing a liberal on TV. What they're really saying is, "I really like you, but I can't for the life of me figure out how someone I like could be a liberal; therefore, you must be a conservative. I want you to know I'm on to your amusing game."

> **From:** jami
> **Sent:** Wednesday, March 05, 2003 5:07 PM
> **To:** colmes
> **Subject:** (no subject)
>
> dear mr colmes,
> your secret is safe with me—you are a conservative at heart.
> jami
> Smyrna, GA

Conservative, Literally. Are You One?

So what does *conservative* mean? Our friends at *American Heritage* have this to say:

con·ser·va·tive (kən-sû'və-tĭv) *adj.*
1. Favoring traditional views and values; tending to oppose change.
2. Traditional or restrained in style: *a conservative dark suit.*
3. Moderate; cautious: *a conservative estimate.*
4.
    a. Of or relating to the political philosophy of conservatism.
    b. Belonging to a conservative party, group, or movement.
5. **Conservative** Of or belonging to the Conservative Party in the United Kingdom or the Progressive Conservative Party in Canada.
6. **Conservative** Of or adhering to Conservative Judaism.
7. Tending to conserve; preservative: *the conservative use of natural resources.*

So conservatives like to retain the status quo, are generally opposed to change, and are into preserving things as they are. It's the liberals who have traditionally fought for progress and advancement. Liberals realize that the world changes, that change can be for the good, and that legislation needs to keep pace with those changes. Conservatives wax poetic about "the way things were." Liberals talk about where we are and where we're going, and the way things could be in a better world. Conservatives have been successful in the marketing of bumper-sticker phrases that have sold well to their constituencies, but are really meaningless. You often hear conservatives talk about "taking my country back." Back from whom, the American Indian? Whom do they think "took" their country? The people who fought for equal rights, for gender equality, for decent wages, and for living conditions for the poorest among us? The only ones who can literally and realistically take this country back are ones to whom it originally belonged: the Native Americans. I believe it was the comedian Steve Martin who once said of Ronald Reagan, "He wants to make this country what it once was: a landmass filled with glaciers."

Conservatives have done a wonderful job appropriating words that have the same root as *liberal* and making them their own. According to *Merriam-Webster*, the word *liberal* has a rich background: "Etymology: Middle English, from Middle French, from Latin *liberalis* suitable for a freeman, generous, from *liber* free; perhaps akin to Old English *lēodan* to grow, Greek *eleutheros* free." We're free, we're generous, and we like to grow. That doesn't seem all that controversial. *Liberty* and *liberal* are cousins.

My friend and cohost wrote a book subtitled *Winning the War of "Liberty" Over "Liberalism."* (You're welcome again for the plug. By the way, did I mention that it's published by ReganBooks, a division of HarperCollins?) But, wait! Since when does one preclude the other? Liberals have fought to give liberty to the poor, the sick, the homeless, and minorities. I contend that it was liberal ideas that liberated many in our society. I further contend that we have a long way to go. *Liberate* comes from *liberal*. Bush 43 wanted to "liberate" Iraq. I say, if you want to use a word that is an offspring of "liberal" to apply for your own nonliberal political ends, find your own words. I wish there were a word adoption agency. Anyone who wanted to use a word for his or her own agenda would have to go to this agency, fill out forms, and prove that the word in question would not be misappropriated. Linguistic social workers would visit homes, schools, and libraries to make sure that there is no misuse going on once a word is formally adopted. The punishment for malfeasance would be that conservatives would not only have to find their own words, but stick to them.

A Friendly Word to Right-Wing Extremists

Let me take this moment to disabuse some conservatives of some of the liberal stereotyping that is all too rampant in America today. I write this paragraph not to most conservatives, but to some on the right (and the left) who have no tolerance for the other side. I dedicate these words to *those* Americans:

I unabashedly love my country and my family. As for God, my view of Her is none of your business, but I love Him, too. Don't you dare tell me that you are more patriotic than I, a better parent than I, a truer husband, a more loyal son, brother, friend, or any other category you wish to invoke with your smug anti-American comments. Yes, *you* are being anti-American if you think you are superior because of political party affiliation, because of religious affiliation, or because you think your views trump mine in any way. This is America, the land of the free and the home of the brave. We are *one nation*, and it is *you* who want to divide us by attacking anyone who doesn't share your narrow view of America. I have no obligation to worship your God, any more than you have to share my religious views. I am not obliged to blindly agree with a man just because he happens to be the president of the United States and the commander in chief of our armed forces. It is my right to speak as forcefully and as passionately about what I believe as you do. I am especially blessed to have a forum in both the print and broadcast media to do it, and I don't for a second take that for granted. Wars have been fought and Americans have died so I can write this and you can read it, unworried by a knock at the door that would delete these words from my computer as I write them or rip this page from your hands as you read them. The brave men and women who made sacrifices didn't do so to promote a political party or agenda. Some of them actually had Democrat registration cards in their wallets. And I don't need to have served in the military to voice any opinion about war, peace, the government, or any other issue. You are not better than I because you are a conservative; you are not smarter than I because you speak louder; you are not specially placed in God's firmament because you're more pious. If you truly want to live up to the ideals our forefathers had in mind, if you sincerely care to embody the spirit of Jesus, Buddha, or Mohammed, stop hating and start loving. Love even when you don't really feel it, even when you think you're faking it. Soon, you won't be faking it anymore, and you'll be a better parent, a better friend, a better American, a better person.

From: Ronnie
Sent: Wednesday, July 24, 2002 10:28 PM
To: Colmes
Subject: you

I just want you to know that I honestly hate you! I would never really do this, but, when you talk I fantasize about shooting you. I pretend I have a pistol in my hand and I shoot you all over. I pretend to shoot you in the head and in your torso. I despise you because of the way you think as evidenced by your line of questioning. If you died I would celebrate!

What Made Me Liberal?

I wonder if I'd grown up in a different time or in a different family whether I would have many of the views I have today. I had an iconoclastic mother who was critical of all politicians, regardless of party or ideology, and a father who was completely apolitical. My sister worked for many years as an assistant district attorney on Long Island, where we grew up. Although she's solidly Republican, she's not quite as far right as her husband, who each year serves up a healthy side of political debate with the Thanksgiving turkey. Sean Hannity likes to joke that all of the members of his family are conservative because there are no defective genes in his family. Although his family's influence shaped his views considerably, my views had more to do with the events of the day as I became more interested in the world around me. Maybe Hannity versus Colmes is nurture versus nature.

The names and faces change as years go by, but the basic issues don't. Americans are debating taxes, ways of dealing with poverty and medical care, family values, war and peace, just as we always have been. I would hope that regardless of the era in which God placed me, I would still stand for the values I believe in today. And I like to think I'm open to new views, and to reexamining my old ones on a regular basis. I don't take my ideologies for granted. And sometimes, to paraphrase Mark Twain, I question whether I want to be part of a political party that would have me as a member. As you read on, perhaps you'll reexamine some of your views, too, even if you already agree with what's being said.

I can't recall when I first thought of myself as a "liberal." Coming of age during the Vietnam era, I became interested in government and politics when I, and many other Americans, discovered our elected officials were lying to us. On August 6, 1964, in the Gulf of Tonkin, the destroyers *Maddox* and *C. Turner Joy* were on patrol. The captain of the *Maddox* determined that his ship was under attack, and both ships began firing, with airpower added for support. The trouble is, there was no attack, just a misreading of instruments by a captain whose ship actually had been attacked two days earlier, and who soon acknowledged that nothing had probably happened on August 6, after all. James Stockdale, who many years later ran for vice president as Ross Perot's running mate, was the pilot of a Crusader jet that did a reconnaissance flight over the Gulf of Tonkin that evening. When asked if there was an attack by the North Vietnamese, Stockdale said, "Not a one. No boats, no wakes, no ricochets off boats, no boat impacts, no torpedo wakes—nothing but black sea and American firepower."

The Johnson administration, however, used this nonevent to escalate the war. The Gulf of Tonkin Resolution passed the House

416 to 0 and the Senate 88 to 2, giving the president authority to "take all necessary measures to repel armed attack against the forces of the United States and to prevent further aggression." This led to a much larger commitment of troops and resources and an ultimate death toll of 58,212 American lives. The escalation and the resulting deaths were all based on a lie.

I became further disillusioned upon learning about the My Lai massacre, which took place on March 16, 1968. American soldiers systematically killed hundreds of innocent Vietnamese, including infants and the elderly. Americans later found out that leaders of the U.S. military lied to us about troop strength, casualties, how well the war was going, and how chemicals used affected our fighting forces (lies that were repeated during successive wars).

We will forever debate this unjust and immoral war, and in spite of our political differences forever be grateful to those who sacrificed life and limb. Unfortunately, it was the poorest of the poor and those with the fewest connections who were shipped off to the rice paddies of Southeast Asia. Those with the most connections either avoided the draft entirely or were able to secure cushy spots stateside. Say, for example, you were from a political family, and you knew people who knew people. And let's say those people, whom you knew, helped you get into the . . . oh, I don't know, let's just say, "National Guard." That way, if you ever ran for office, you could always say you served, even if you were AWOL for a year and they couldn't find you when it was medical exam time. Besides, when you're young and irresponsible, you're young and irresponsible, right?

Plus Ça Change, Plus C'est La Meme Chose

I stayed up nights worrying about being drafted, knowing I couldn't support the war. I attended a meeting of conscientious objectors to see if that was a path I could take. Shortly thereafter, my number came up in the lottery that determined who would be sent to war, and it was high enough to keep me out of the service. Had that not been the case, I can't say I wouldn't have tried for C.O. status. Sometimes, we like to think we would have acted courageously had circumstances been different. Had I been drafted and asked to serve in Vietnam, would I have gone? And would that have been the courageous thing to do? Conventional wisdom might say yes, risking your life for your country when it asks you to, even if you don't agree with what your country is trying to do, is heroic. During this time, some American boys made a very different and difficult decision and chose to flee to Canada. Odd as it sounds, I believe this might also be considered a heroic choice. In a way, it seems that leaving your homeland, going to a strange place with little money, no friends, and the condemnation of the majority of your fellow citizens because you strongly believe in a principle—that, to me, is heroic, too. This may anger conservatives who can't imagine this as a heroic—even patriotic—choice, but I can't deny that my romantic view of "what might have been" has me leaning this way. I have tremendous admiration for those who have defended and continue to defend this country, and for all in uniform who serve at the pleasure of our commander in chief. But I didn't believe that the war in Vietnam had anything to do with defending our country, just as I didn't believe that the war in Iraq had anything to do with defending our country. I trace my political roots to those days when we were warned that if we didn't take over Vietnam, the Commies would be on the shores of San Francisco when Khrushchev predicted that they would bury you, us, under Communism.

I suppose my Vietnam-era views made me, in the parlance of the day, "antiestablishment." I never consciously set out to be a liberal, but Vietnam opened my eyes to injustice. The men we sent to fight what I believed to be a political war were lied to. It took decades for our government to acknowledge the disfiguring and, in some cases, fatal effects of Agent Orange, just as we're now discovering that "Gulf War Syndrome" has afflicted almost two hundred thousand of America's finest. Gradually, I began to notice similar injustices and inequities elsewhere in our social structure. As I learned about history, I felt as though I was in sync with the great tradition of liberalism.

When your first impression of the powers that be is one of lying by both omission and commission, of promoting a caste system for the convenience of a politically motivated war, it really shapes how you view the world, and those who run it. And as I see history bizarrely replicating itself, it only reaffirms my pride in being a liberal. True, Bill Clinton lied. It was a white lie, something most of us do. And, yes, to repeat the mantra of the right, "He lied under oath." But rarely does a lie under oath about sex wind up being prosecuted. I'm not excusing this behavior, but don't tell me you've never told a white lie. In Clinton's case, the lie was an attempt to protect his dignity and to save his family from embarrassment. He lied about a personal relationship, not about troop movements and death tolls. And for that they wanted to run him out of town because they couldn't get him on anything else. Yet, we still have elected officials in the highest places telling us lies to promote political wars, hiding information that taxpayers should know, and advocating a society in which rich and poor are treated much differently by both the private sector and government policy. As the nineteenth-century French author Alphonse Karr said, "The more things change, the more things remain the same."

And Now, From the People Who Brought You Vietnam . . .

Patriotism seems too often tied up with war, as though supporting a war proves love of country. During Vietnam we saw how those who supported the war were defined as patriots and those who didn't were called anti-American. Now, it's happening again. Standing up for what you believe when you know you're not in the majority and when you know you will face likely ridicule for your views may be the *most* patriotic position. It's easy to ride with the herd, but it takes more fortitude to buck the tide. Unlike during Vietnam, though, today's government is marketing-savvy. White House chief of staff Andrew Card explained the timing of pushing for war with Iraq by saying, "From a marketing point of view, you don't introduce new products in August."

The Bush 43 administration has been effective in engineering a PR campaign to push its idea of patriotism. Literally. The Pentagon pays the Rendon Group, a worldwide PR firm, $100,000 a month to make us look good abroad. On March 12, 2002, the *Village Voice* reported, "During the Gulf War, Rendon furnished Kuwaiti citizens with American flags, and also boosted the CIA's effort to oust Saddam Hussein from power, producing videos, radio skits mocking Hussein, and a traveling photo exhibit. . . . Rendon also worked closely with the Iraqi National Congress—they even crafted the anti-Hussein group's name." The Pentagon hired Rendon without competitive bidding, which is how government contracts are usually awarded. Conservatives get bent out of shape about what they believe is misuse of taxpayer dollars going to help the poor. Here we have taxpayer dollars being used to sell war the way advertising dollars are spent on Madison Avenue. But why stop there? Why not use these time-tested techniques to sell whatever policy the government is trying to promote?

> *"The people of the Iraqi National Congress:*
>   *They're mmm . . . mmm good!"*

> *"There's ALWAYS room for missiles!"*

> *"You're in the Farsi generation."*

> *"A defense contract is a terrible thing to waste."*

> *"The death penalty: We take good things from life."*

> *"American bombs, good to the last drop."*

And what makes us think that terrorists won't take a licking but, in the long term, keep on ticking?

Before her March 2001 appointment as spokesperson for the Department of Defense, Victoria Clarke, the former assistant secretary of Defense for public affairs, was the head of the Washington office of PR giant Hill and Knowlton. Charlotte Beers, formerly of the advertising agencies J. Walter Thompson and Ogilvy and Mather, was named undersecretary of state for public diplomacy and public affairs. Maybe the woman who once sold us Uncle Ben's will be able to promote products like "the extra long-range missile." Did we need a PR guru to tell us how bad Saddam was, that he "kills Kurds dead"?

The Real Threat to Our Military

As for the military, I don't know that what I'm about to say here is a liberal position or a conservative position, but it is an *American* position. We ask men and women to put their lives on the line for our country; we send them into harm's way and they do so without blinking because they are America's finest. Having offered to make the ultimate sacrifice for their country, it is America's greatest shame that we don't take care of our veterans the way we should, and that we lie to them in the process.

By March 1996, eighty thousand veterans registered with the VA (Department of Veterans Affairs) as sufferers of Gulf War Syndrome. But in June 1997, the General Accounting Office issued a report that said, among other things, it was "unlikely that the health effects reported by many Gulf War veterans were the result of (1) biological warfare agents, (2) chemical warfare agents, (3) depleted uranium, (4) infectious diseases endemic to the region, (5) oil-well fire smoke, (6) pesticides, (7) petroleum products, (8) pyridostigmine bromide, or (9) vaccines."

The report did go on to advocate monitoring of Gulf veterans and research of these conditions. But this was said *after* they came to the preceding "conclusions." This is confusing at best, and certainly not comforting to those who were willing to and did serve our country, often making the ultimate sacrifice.

Paul Rodriguez of *Insight* magazine has done extensive investigative work on whether the Department of Defense (DOD) has been straight with veterans who became ill serving in the Persian Gulf War. Rodriguez reported, "After a year of stonewalling by the DOD, a new study at the prestigious Tulane University Medical School confirms that victims of a mysterious sickness may have been poisoned." It was long suspected that our troops had been exposed to something that caused autoimmune dysfunction; that antibodies injected to protect our troops from illness may, in fact, have been what made them ill. Rodriguez's investigative work was done without much cooperation from the government that sent these troops off to war. He says, "Veterans' fears are not being assuaged by DOD's refusal to release records involving its experiments with squalene (an antibody) nor is there comfort in its refusal to release details of what its various vaccines during the gulf war contained. The FDA, reportedly at the request of DOD, has declined to provide any information whatsoever related to those vaccines—even to the GAO [General Accounting Office]."

We already know that the government lied to us about how the Vietnam War was conducted. But it also lied to the soldiers who fought in Vietnam and got sick or died. For years, veterans complained about the ill effects of Agent Orange, the defoliant that was sprayed over a large part of South Vietnam so our troops could see the Viet Cong troops. Health concerns surfaced in 1970, and a 1984 class action suit resulted in chemical companies settling out of court for $180 million, while still denying any link between Agent Orange and cancer. It wasn't until 1990 that a formal link was made between Agent Orange and cancer. In March 2000, the air force found a "significant and potentially meaningful" connection between diabetes and bloodstream levels of dioxin, the harmful chemical contained in the herbicide. The VA concurred by August 2001 and announced it would begin to compensate veterans who experienced adult-onset diabetes, thanks largely to the efforts of Congressmen Chris Shays of Connecticut and Bernie Sanders of Vermont. Also in 2001, United States and Vietnam officials agreed, for the first time, to jointly study the effects of this poison. Today, more than ten thousand veterans receive Agent Orange–related disability pay, and the Supreme Court is considering allowing veterans whose illnesses surfaced after the 1984 settlement to take action against the chemical companies.

As recently as January 2003, almost thirty years to the day since the end of the Vietnam War, the VA agreed to pay benefits to veterans with chronic lymphocytic leukemia, or CLL. Not only did government officials finally agree there was a link between Agent Orange and this disease, but they also estimated that they'd discover five hundred new cases a year. And who knows how many other valiant warriors became ill and died without proper acknowledgment and benefits from the very government whose actions resulted in their conditions.

Sadly, the story of Agent Orange parallels an often-recurring relationship between our government and the men and women of the military who do its bidding. A staff report prepared for the Senate Committee on Foreign Affairs and released on December 8, 1994, had some chilling findings. Among them: "For at least 50 years, [the Department of Defense] has intentionally exposed military personnel to potentially dangerous substances, often in secret; DOD has repeatedly failed to comply with required ethical standards when using human subjects in military research during war or threat of war."

Shockingly, this Senate report reveals that the pattern of deception is more recent than many would have us believe and dates back decades:

As recently as 1993, the Institute of Medicine of the National Academy of Sciences reported that an atmosphere of secrecy still existed regarding World War II testing of mustard gas and lewisite. . . . During the years immediately following World War II, military personnel were intentionally exposed to radiation during the testing of atomic bombs and during radioactive release. . . . Similarly, military personnel were intentionally given hallucinogenic drugs to determine the effects of those drugs on humans. The service members were not told that they would be given experimental drugs, they had no choice of whether or not to take them, and even after the unusual effects of the drugs were obvious to researchers, the unwitting human subjects were given no information about the known effects of the drugs.

This astounding and outrageous mistreatment of our military by our own government continued at least through the 1991 Persian Gulf War. The report, chaired by West Virginia senator John D. Rockefeller, went on to state: "Persian Gulf veterans were also given investigational vaccines and ordered not to tell anyone." The treatment of those who are asked to fight and die for our country is our nation's greatest shame.

Furthermore, the Bush 43 administration continues the dishonorable longtime practice of failing to provide America's military heroes with proper benefits. Way back on May 27, 1944, Congress passed a law stating that retired soldiers would receive one dollar less in retirement benefits for every dollar spent on medical benefits. Those who were 100 percent disabled would forfeit their entire retirement pay. You would think an administration that talks so much about war would make it a priority to care for the souls who must fight those wars. But as the *Washington Post* reported in October 2002, "President Bush has threatened to veto the $355 billion defense authorization bill for the new fiscal year if House and Senate conferees do not eliminate new pension benefits for disabled military retirees that could cost from $18.5 billion to $58 billion over the next decade." According to Secretary of Defense Donald Rumsfeld, we just have to get our priorities right: "This would divert critical resources away from the war on terrorism, the transformation of our military capabilities and important personnel programs such as pay raises and facilities improvements." What he's saying is, how can we take care of those who have fought our wars when we have new wars to fight? Isn't this bass ackwards? How can we keep asking our finest to participate in wars, when we don't properly care for those who've sacrificed up until now?

The issue, which has become known as "concurrent receipt," has gained traction with both our active military and with veterans groups. Bob Manhan, assistant director of the Veterans of Foreign Wars legislative office, points out, "No other category of federal employee is required to relinquish a portion of their earned retirement pay simply because they are also receiving VA disability compensation." If you're a civil service employee and work in the Department of Defense, you're entitled to both retirement and disability pay, concurrently. Civil service is certainly noble but not as dangerous as serving in the military, unless, of course, your job involves using your hands in proximity to a paper shredder.

Liberty and Justice for All?

Given how many Americans have been injured and died to protect our flag, it's sad how politicized the love of our flag has become. Michael Newdow became Public Enemy Number One when a three-judge panel from the Ninth Circuit Court agreed with him that the recitation of the Pledge of Allegiance in public schools amounts to an establishment of religion because of the phrase "under God." I asked Newdow on the June 26, 2002, edition of *Hannity & Colmes* why he initiated this fight:

COLMES: What prompted you to do this? What brought this on?

NEWDOW: I'm an atheist, and the government's not supposed to impart its religion on society, and it does, and I tried to change that.

I mentioned that, contrary to the predictable charge from the right that the Ninth Circuit is a "liberal court," two of the three judges on that panel were Republican appointees. We also heard from the right that this "super liberal court" had "declared the Pledge unconstitutional." This is not accurate. What the court said was that it's unconstitutional to say the Pledge in a public school. If you want to get up in the morning and pledge allegiance along with your morning coffee, no one is going to come into your house and arrest you. Pandering came from both sides. After the ruling, members of the House rushed to the steps of the Capitol to recite the Pledge (can you say "Photo op?"). The next day, the Senate voted 99–0 against the ruling (when does the Senate ever vote on court rulings?); and members of the House recited the Pledge after the morning prayer, making sure to shout out "under God," before giving themselves a standing ovation.

The Pledge of Allegiance is now claimed as conservative property, and there is a fierce battle raging about two words it contains. The truth is that the original Pledge of Allegiance never included the words *under God*. In fact, it never contained the words *United States*. It was written in 1892 by Baptist minister Francis Bellamy to express the socialist utopian ideals he shared with his cousin Thomas Bellamy and to promote the idea of state control of the economy. So when all these tax-cutting, antigovernment conservatives scream the Pledge of Allegiance, they ought to know they're paying tribute to socialists.

The original pledge read, "I pledge allegiance to my flag and the Republic for which it stands—one nation indivisible—with liberty and justice for all." It appeared in the September 1892 issue of *Youth's Companion*, a family-oriented magazine run by a couple of liberals. The word *to* was then added before "the Republic." In 1924 the words *my flag* were changed to "the flag of the United States of America" by the American Legion and the Daughters of the American Revolution, against the wishes of Francis Bellamy. At the height of the McCarthy era, in 1953, the Knights of Columbus campaigned to add the words *under God* to the Pledge. This was approved by a joint resolution of Congress on June 8, 1954, and signed by President Eisenhower on Flag Day. According to John Baer, author of *The Pledge of Allegiance: A Centennial History 1892–1992*, Bellamy's granddaughter says he would have resented this change.

In a 1943 case, the Supreme Court ruled that requiring a pledge violates students' right to free expression, and that they don't give up their First Amendment rights when they go to school. Justice Robert Jackson, writing for the majority, said, "If there is a fixed star in our constitutional constellation, it is that no official, high or petty, can prescribe what shall be orthodox in politics, nationalism, religion or other matters of opinion or force citizens to confess by word or act their faith therein."

Isn't one of the things the flag stands for the right *not* to salute it? Isn't it ironic to force someone to say the words *liberty and justice for all?* Does recitation of a pledge make one more patriotic? David Kertzer, an anthropologist at Brown University whose specialty is political rituals, told me that pledges of allegiance are marks of totalitarian states, not democracies. "I can't think of a single democracy except the United States that has a pledge of allegiance," he said.

As for those two words inserted in the Pledge in 1954, Thomas Jefferson, in a letter to the Reverend Samuel Miller in 1808, wrote, "I consider the government of the United States as interdicted by the Constitution from intermeddling in religious institutions, their doctrines, discipline, or exercises."

I agree with both Kertzer and Jefferson. The idea of a mandated pledge defies the spirit of freedom upon which our country was founded. And if you need Washington to affirm for you that we are "under God," perhaps you're not that secure in your own sense of the Almighty.

The Great Divide

According to many on the political right, there are two kinds of people in this country: liberals and Americans. In fact, former Reagan Interior secretary James Watt immortalized that sentiment when he said, "I never use the words *Democrats* and *Republicans;* it's *liberals* and *Americans.*"

Secretary Watt, this exemplar of conservative decency, a man who once said in essence, "We don't have to protect the environment; the second coming is at hand," was indicted on twenty-five felony counts for perjury and obstruction of justice. He pleaded guilty to one misdemeanor charge of withholding documents from a grand jury and received five years probation, five hundred hours of community service and a $5,000 fine for influence peddling. So which of the "two kinds of people in this country" does he represent?

If you believe conservatives, they are the sole proprietors of the flag and the sole practitioners of love of country. They own God, patriotism, the military, national security, and family values. They believe that points of view other than their own don't belong in America. Conservatives still proclaim, "My country, love it or leave it," just as they did to protesters during the Vietnam era.

Amazingly, these are the same people who decried the former Soviet Union for having only one political party. Our forefathers, contrary to what today's right wing would have you believe, were not all Republicans. In fact, none of them were. Patriotism is not the province of the right. Why was it patriotic to speak out against Clinton, but unpatriotic to speak out against Bush? Why is supporting Bush's war ideas patriotic, but supporting Clinton's Kosovo plan enabling a lying adulterer? And why won't some conservatives respect points of view with which they don't agree? Why can't they acknowledge that those views are just as patriotic as their own? Is it unpatriotic to want peace? Isn't it possible that it's profoundly pro-American to hope that our armed forces aren't sent to fight what one believes is an immoral and unjust war?

Is *Peacenik* a Dirty Word?

David Horowitz, the son of Communist Party members, former Black Panther supporter, and former radical leftist, is now a radical rightist. About the left, Horowitz says, "Their goal remains the destruction of America's national identity and, in particular, of the moral, political, and economic institutions that form its social foundation."

When hundreds of thousands of demonstrators showed up in Washington to protest the United States going to war with Iraq,

Horowitz created an ad to solicit money to promote his "National Campaign to Combat the Anti-American Left." Charming. In this solicitation he claimed, "When your country is attacked, when the enemy has targeted every American regardless of race, gender or age for death, there can be no 'peace' movement. There can only be a movement that divides America and gives aid and comfort to our enemies." Horowitz went on to accuse the peace movement of being led by "the same hate-America radicals who supported American's totalitarian enemies during the Cold War."

First of all, this antiwar demonstration was against war with Iraq, not against "The 'War' on Terror." The "peace movement" was an effort to direct our energies toward the real threats facing America, not what many considered an immoral and unjust war.

This guilt by association is a McCarthyite game. It's easy to see why this former left-wing radical is such an angry right-wing radical now. Let me know, David, when you want to come home. I'm not quite as left as you once were, but I know people who know people, and I can get you back into "The Left-Wingers Club."

From: Frank W.
Sent: Wednesday, September 25, 2002 10:27 AM
To: Colmes
Subject: Supporting the President
Importance: High

Alan;
Heard the show last night, and you made a statement that "those who are not in lock step with the administration relative to the war on terror and plans concerning Iraq are somehow perceived as unpatriotic". I believe strongly that on those two issues you really are unpatriotic if you do not support the president 100% and that truth will be borne out at the polls in Nov. for Democrat and Republican alike.

By the way, in case you care, I am a registered Democrat.

Frank W.
Detroit, MI

From: Colmes
Sent: Wednesday, September 25, 2002 11:48 AM
To: Frank W.
Subject: RE: Supporting the President

Since when must you agree with a particular political party or president to be a patriotic American?

From: 'Frank W.'
Sent: Wednesday, September 25, 2002 12:36 PM
To: colmes
Subject: RE: Supporting the President

Alan;
By not supporting the President you give aid and comfort to our enemy who would destroy us . . . Alan, you have defined yourself, and you and like minded Democrats and Republicans are what you are i.e., unpatriotic. The president is right the Democratic controlled Senate does not care about the security of the nation and neither do you, Alan!

Frank W.
Detroit, MI

I don't think anything I could say would convince Frank W. that I'm as patriotic as he is. He, like many on the right, is convinced that because I didn't support the Bush policy in Iraq, I am an unpatriotic American. Were the Republicans who didn't support Bill Clinton's forays into Bosnia and Haiti unpatriotic? Of course not. Because they're Republicans.

But not every American agrees with Frank W., and it would be a stretch to accuse every dissenting American of giving aid and comfort to the enemy.

From: Jonathan
Sent: Saturday, February 15, 2003 12:56 PM
To: Colmes
Subject: You are a good man

Dear Mr. Alan Colmes,
Just to let you know, I think you are a good man. I believe in the things you are doing and saying regarding this whole Iraq deal. You speak as a man of peace would, and I personally thank you for that. When I listen to you, it is as if you are able to actually put into words that which I am thinking of. You are an asset to Fox news and people like myself who hope and pray for peace in this ever-changing world. May God bless you for being our spokesman.

Good day!
Jonathan, Arizona

Liberals Are Americans, Too

From: Debbie
Sent: Tuesday, February 18, 2003 2:04 AM
To: colmes
Subject: What are these protester true colors?

Just what are these protester true colors?

I see these protester but I can't believe what I'm seeing, just what do they stand for and what are there true colors? From my eyes it's not the RED, WHITE AND BLUE . . .

Proud to be an American
Debbie

From: Colmes
Sent: Tuesday, February 18, 2003 1:34 PM
To: 'Debbie'
Subject: RE: What are these protester true colors?

Red, White and Blue doesn't mean that every American must always agree with every other American or with American foreign policy. That there were hundreds of thousands protesting in America and millions world wide shows that there are many fine people on both sides of this issue who see it differently.

Color me Red, White and Liberal.

Alan

Frankly, I can't think of anything more patriotic than speaking out when I feel my country is doing something wrong. Conservatives favor "tough love" in personal relationships, so why can't that also apply in our relationship with our motherland? I know this is what my e-mailers are aiming for. They care so much that they want me to better myself.

From: Ralph
Sent: Wednesday, February 19, 2003 9:47 PM
To: colmes
Subject: Liberalism

Colmes
Liberalism is a mental disease and your are the virus, a traitor to American beliefs and a man with no common sense. An American Vet and Patriot.

God Bless America

Thanks for the tough love, Ralph. I know your goal is to make me a better American.

Being a good American isn't a matter of agreeing with government policy, supporting a war, or favoring a particular party. It isn't something that can be spread by Madison Avenue bottlers and packaged like deodorant. I do believe, however, that patriotism can be exemplified by a love and concern for our precious environment, empathy and action for our less fortunate countrymen, and by making sure that those who serve in our military never, ever have to fight their government to get the care they deserve. Love of country can be exhibited by showing tolerance, if not respect, for those who don't buy into politicized recitations, who disdain organized religion, and whose philosophies and positions on the issues are very different from our own. This is an ideal I strive for even when it's sorely tested by people like Ralph. But even he and I can find common ground, for I do agree with Ralph on one part of his e-mail: God Bless America.

TWO

"The 'War' on Terror"

Throughout this book you'll notice "The 'War' on Terror" with quotes around the phrase and around the word *war*. This is because I object to the use of "The 'War' on Terror" as a be-all and end-all catchphrase that has been used to justify everything from changes in our criminal justice system and national energy policy, to a war with Iraq. As for the inside quote around the word *war*, missions that begin with "The 'War' on . . ." generally fail, and the overuse of this phrase in our culture has rendered it trite. "The 'War' on Drugs" hasn't worked. "The 'War' on Crime" will never end, no matter how loud McGruff the Crime Dog barks. That's because there will always be crime. So since Bush 43 said he is not going to sleep until "The 'War' on Terror" is won, it is clear that his days of slumber are through. And let's face it, "The 'War' on Terror" is being used as a political tool. What Bush 43 really means is he's not going to rest until his next run for office is won, and that by hitching his presidency to "The 'War' on Terror," attention can be diverted from those pesky bread-and-butter issues like developing an economic plan that really benefits the middle and poorer classes, education, health care for the uninsured and, yes, "The 'War' on Crime."

I know this next statement is going to upset some Americans. And you know, I don't want to upset you. I want you to be relaxing with a nice, soft beverage and enjoying the soothing words in this book. But before you spill that nice drink all over yourself, hear me out.

September 11 was the best thing that could have happened to the Bush presidency. As former Bush 43 speechwriter David Frum writes in *The Right Man*, "George Bush was not on his way to a very successful presidency. . . . Bush's political vision was unclear. He was a politician of conservative instincts rather than conservative principles. . . . Above all, Bush lacked a big organizing idea." Well, September 11 gave him something around which to organize. This now became the basis of the Bush presidency: "It's 'The "War" on Terror', Stupid." And that morphed into the campaign against Iraq, and a push for a set of political objectives by this administration that couldn't have been accomplished without the help of Osama bin Laden and Saddam Hussein. Lost in all of this was what should have been our true objectives: stopping the very people who perpetrated the atrocity of September 11, and protecting the people of the United States of America. "The 'War' on Terror" became a sham.

It was a beautiful day, that autumn Tuesday in New York. It was primary day, and New Yorkers were getting ready to decide which Democratic candidate would be on the mayoral ballot eight weeks later. I woke up a few minutes before 9 a.m. and reached out to tap on the clock radio, relishing the idea of a few more minutes in bed while I listened just long enough to know that the world hadn't changed drastically overnight. Through my haze, however, I heard something about a plane going into the World Trade Center. What a horrible accident, I thought. Too troubled to stay in bed, I hastily made myself presentable enough to go out for the newspapers and a bagel. If you live in New York, bagels are mandatory. It's in the state constitution. As I returned home, I looked up, and saw the billowing smoke blocking the downtown Manhattan skyline. By the time I flipped on the television and logged online, there were reports of a second airplane, and then a third. I knew I had to get to the office as soon as possible, but the only way to get there was on foot, because mass transit had stopped operating, and large sections of New York City were blocked off to traffic. As I walked toward the midtown headquarters of Fox News, I was struck by an eerie sense of calm, as pedestrians stopped in their tracks and looked toward the smoke now blanketing the sky. Their faces were blank with disbelief, as though they were watching a distant movie. This couldn't be actually happening to us.

WMDs: Words of Mass Deception

On September 11, 2001, after being brutally attacked by a terror group that was based in Afghanistan, had cells in Iran and Pakistan, and consisted mostly of Saudi nationals, the Bush 43 administration did the only logical thing. It planned for a war against Iraq. You may think I'm being facetious, but on September 4, 2002, CBS News reported on its website that "barely five hours after American Airlines Flight 77 plowed into the Pentagon, Defense Secretary Donald H. Rumsfeld was telling his aides to come up with plans for striking Iraq—even though there was no evidence linking Saddam Hussein to the attacks."

Amazingly and outrageously, in the year-and-a-half period after the September 11 attacks, Bush 43 was able to convince much of the American public and a large number of nations that focusing on Saddam Hussein was a really good idea soon after we were attacked by forces with no proven operational links with Saddam Hussein. The reasons given for going to war were various, prolific, and, most sadly, not always true.

In his State of the Union address on January 28, 2003, Bush 43 averred: "The British government has learned that Saddam Hussein recently sought significant quantities of uranium from Africa." It was later discovered that the information came from a forged document bearing the signature of a Nigerian official who had been out of office for a decade.

It turns out that the CIA informed the White House ten months before the State of the Union address that one of their sources who went to Niger couldn't confirm that Iraq was trying to acquire uranium. "Three senior administration officials said Vice President Dick Cheney and some officials on the National Security Council staff and at the Pentagon ignored the CIA's reservations and argued that the president and others should include the allegation in their case against Saddam," reported Jonathan S. Landay of Knight Ridder Newspaper on June 13, 2003, concluding that this provided "the strongest evidence to date that pro-war administration officials manipulated, exaggerated or ignored intelligence information in their eagerness to make the case for invading Iraq."

A Sunday, July 6, 2003, op-ed piece in the *New York Times* by Ambassador Joseph Wilson suggested that he was that source. Wilson had been ambassador to Gabon from 1992 to 1995, and Bush 43's chargé d'affaires to Iraq, where he was the last diplomat to speak with Saddam Hussein before Gulf War I. In February 2002, Wilson was sent to Iraq by the CIA at the request of Vice President Cheney's office to investigate the intelligence report about Iraq attempting to purchase uranium from Niger.

"Based on my experience with the administration in the months leading up to the war," Wilson wrote, "I have little choice but to conclude that some of the intelligence related to Iraq's nuclear weapons program was twisted to exaggerate the Iraqi threat."

With questions swirling about the veracity of the president's State of the Union address, the White House issued a carefully worded statement on Monday, July 7, 2003: "Knowing all that we know now, the reference to Iraq's attempt to acquire uranium from Africa should not have been included in the State of the Union speech." Put another way: "Niger did not have commercial relations with that man, Mr. Hussein."

Donald Rumsfeld went on *Meet the Press* to claim that Bush's statement in the State of the Union address was "technically correct." He might as well have said, "It depends what the meaning of 'uranium' is."

Left out in all the official explanations was how our own CIA warned the administration to go with the British intelligence. But why believe our own sources, when another country stands by the story that supports your agenda?

Trotted out to accept blame for the uranium mess was CIA director George Tenet, who delivered the official mea culpa:

> First, CIA approved the president's State of the Union address before it was delivered. Second, I am responsible for the approval process in my agency. And third, the president had every reason to believe that the text presented to him was sound. These 16 words should never have been included in the text written for the president.

The problem here is that not only had the CIA already warned the administration not to go with the information nine months before the State of the Union speech, but on October 7, 2002, Bush 43 gave a major, nationally televised address at the Cincinnati Museum Center laying out the case for war, and Tenet told the administration to remove the uranium reference *then*. The top deputy to National Security Advisor Condoleeza Rice, Steven Hadley, was told by Tenet personally that the reference to Niger uranium story could not be supported.

It's inconceivable that Rice's top aide would get such information and not share it with his boss. Nevertheless, on the June 8, 2003, *Meet the Press*, Rice had this to say about the revelation that the uranium story was false: "We did not know at the time—no one knew at the time, in our circles—maybe someone knew down in the bowels of the agency, but no one in our circles knew that there were doubts and suspicions that this might be a forgery."

But wait a minute! One month later, this time after the Wilson piece had appeared in the *Times*, Rice offered a different story during a press briefing aboard *Air Force One* as she was accompanying Bush 43 on a trip to Africa. She was asked why just nine days after the State of the Union address, Secretary of State Colin Powell omitted the uranium reference when he gave a speech promoting the case for war to the United Nations Security Council: "I was with Secretary Powell when he was doing a lot of this. You will remember that it was the Secretary's own intelligence arm, the INR, that was the one that within the overall intelligence assessment had objected to that sentence, had said that they doubts about—not to that sentence, had doubts about the uranium yellow cake story."

It appears, then, that she *did* know there were doubts about the uranium story.

In a closed-door session with the Senate Intelligence Committee on Wednesday, July 16, a week and a half after Ambassador Wilson's mission became public, Tenet discussed negotiations between the CIA and the White House about the content of the State of the Union address. According to Senator Richard Durbin of Illinois, the White House was "hell-bent" on including the uranium story and they "had to go into bargaining mode with the CIA to skirt around the misleading nature of the statement." This jibes with a *New York Times* report on July 11, 2003, that said Robert G. Allen, a nuclear proliferation expert at the National Security Council had a negotiating session with Alan Foley, a CIA proliferation expert. The *Times* reported:

> There is still a dispute over what exactly was said in their conversations. Mr. Foley was said to recall that before the speech, Mr. Joseph called him to ask about putting into the speech a reference to reports that Iraq was trying to buy hundreds of tons of yellowcake from Niger. Mr. Foley replied that the C.I.A. was not sure that the information was right. Mr. Joseph then came back to Mr. Foley and pointed out that the British had already included the information in a report. Mr. Foley said yes, but noted that the C.I.A. had told the British that they were not sure that the information was correct. Mr. Joseph then asked whether it was accurate that the British reported the information. Mr. Foley said yes.

So the CIA warned the administration before both the Cincinnati speech and the State of the Union address not to go with the uranium story. And so what is that reason again to be blaming George Tenet?

Bush 43 defenders acted indignant that liberals would get all up in arms about "just sixteen words" in the president's speech. These are the same people who can't get over the fact that Bill Clinton used six fewer words when he said, "I did not have sex with that woman, Ms. Lewinsky." And it was more than just those sixteen words that were questionable. There appeared to be other examples of fudging in the State of Union address, the Cincinnati speech, and in various statements by top administration officials. For example, the president used his State of the Union speech to claim that Hussein had high-strength aluminum tubes suitable for nuclear weapons production. A month earlier, appearing on CNN's *Late Edition*, Rice said this about the aluminum tubing: "Saddam Hussein is actively pursuing a nuclear weapon. We do know that there have been shipments into Iraq of aluminum tubes that really are only suited to nuclear weapons programs."

But the National Intelligence Estimate, published in October 2002, and declassified on July 18, 2003, had a dissenting view from Powell's intelligence unit, stating it "considers it far more likely that the tubes are intended for another purpose, most likely the production of artillery rockets."

In September 2002, the Institute for Science and International Security (ISIS), the very group that Bush 43 used for information on past Iraqi weapons procurements, issued a report about Iraq's desire to procure these materials that said, "By themselves, these attempted procurements are not evidence that Iraq is in possession of or close to possessing nuclear weapons. They also do not provide evidence that Iraq has an operating centrifuge plant or when such a plant could be operational."

David Albright, the former UN nuclear scientist in charge of the ISIS, commented on the aluminum tubing issue in an in-depth analysis called "The Selling of the Iraq War," which appeared in the June 30, 2003, *New Republic:* "I became dismayed when a knowledgeable government scientist told me that the administration could say anything it wanted about the tubes while government scientists who disagreed were expected to remain quiet."

"The Selling of the Iraq War" concluded, "The administration ignored, and even suppressed, disagreement within the intelligence agencies and pressured the CIA to reaffirm its preferred version of the Iraqi threat. Similarly, it stonewalled, and sought to discredit, international weapons inspectors when their findings threatened to undermine the case for war."

Senior Editor John B. Judis and Assistant Editor Spencer Ackerman neatly summed up the various ways the Bush 43 administration tried to impress on the American public the imperative that we go to war with Iraq, and that we do so in a timely fashion:

> In Nashville on August 26, 2002, Vice President Dick Cheney warned of a Saddam "armed with an arsenal of these weapons of terror" who could "directly threaten America's friends throughout the region and subject the United States or any other nation to nuclear blackmail." In Washington on September 26, Secretary of Defense Donald Rumsfeld claimed he had "bulletproof" evidence of ties between Saddam and Al Qaeda. And, in Cincinnati President George W. Bush warned, "The Iraqi dictator must not be permitted to threaten America and the world with horrible poisons and diseases and gases and atomic weapons." Citing Saddam's association with Al Qaeda, the president added that this "alliance with terrorists could allow the Iraqi regime to attack America without leaving any fingerprints."

Would you agree that such dire warnings, if based on faulty intelligence, are a much more egregious offense than the words, "I did not have sex with that woman, Ms. Lewinsky"? Skewed statements that lead us to war have considerably more dire consequences for our nation than one person's belief about what just which activities should be rightfully called "sex."

In so many ways and on so many days the Bush 43 administration told the American public and the world it was convinced of Iraq's possession of weapons of mass destruction. On the September 8, 2002, *Meet the Press* Cheney said that Hussein was aggressively building his nuclear program, adding, "Increasingly, we believe that the United States may well become the target of those activities."

The president claimed in his Cincinnati speech, "It possesses and produces chemical and biological weapons." But a letter dated the very same day of this speech and sent to the Senate Intelligence Committee by John McLaughlin, the deputy CIA director, on behalf of Tenet said, "Baghdad for now appears to be drawing a line short of conducting terrorist attacks with conventional or CBW (chemical and biological weapons) against the United States."

On February 6, 2002, the *New York Times* reported, "The Central Intelligence Agency has no evidence that Iraq has engaged in terrorist operations against the United States in nearly a decade, and the agency is convinced that Saddam Hussein has not provided chemical or biological weapons to al-Qaeda or related terrorist groups."

In his February 8, 2003, weekly radio address Bush 43 said, "We have sources that tell us that Saddam Hussein recently authorized Iraqi field commanders to use chemical weapons—the very weapons the dictator tells us he does not have." As it turned out, no such weapons were used against our troops, thankfully. During his March 17 speech, when he gave the Iraqi dictator forty-eight hours to get out of town, Bush 43 said, "intelligence gathered by this and other governments leaves no doubt that the Iraq regime continues to possess and conceal some of the most lethal weapons ever devised. The regime has already used weapons of mass destruction. . . ." On the March 30 edition of ABC's *This Week* Donald Rumsfeld said that not only were there WMDs in Iraq, but "we know where they are, they are in the area around Tikrit and Baghdad and east, west, south and north of that."

It was reported in the June 7, 2003, *Los Anegles Times* that a Defense Intelligence Agency report entitled "Iraq: Key Weapons Facilities—An Operational Support Study" that was issued last September found "no reliable information on whether Iraq is producing and stockpiling chemical weapons, or whether Iraq has—or will—establish its chemical warfare agent production facilities." It was also revealed that a previously covert army group called "Task Force 20" had been in Iraq since before the war looking for weapons of mass destruction. Funny how when the UN inspection team couldn't find this stuff they were literally run out of town, but the inability of a secret army task force to do the same thing got scant attention.

Make that the "DN": The Divided Nations

How often did we hear that war with Iraq was proper because of Saddam's flagrant disregard for United Nations resolutions? Although it's true that Iraq has not been resolution-friendly, other countries have also ignored UN mandates. Indonesia disregarded mandates to withdraw from East Timor, which finally won its independence in 1999, after a twenty-four-year-long U.S.-backed occupation. Turkey ignored Resolutions 353 and 354 to get it to leave Cyprus,. Several countries have had even more violations than Iraq. Israel, for example, has thirty, Turkey more than twenty, and Morocco, more than fifteen. Morocco was asked in 1975 to withdraw its forces of occupation from the western Sahara, but it ignored that request. And Morocco has defied more recent resolutions calling for an internationally supervised referendum to be voted on by the western Saharan population. This defiance has been supported by Bush 43.

More important, since when can one country decide that a Security Council resolution has been breached without the consent of the other member nations? This is a basic Security Council guideline, which the United States accepted when it signed on as a member of the community of nations.

It was often argued that war was justified since Iraq violated Resolution 1441, which put it in "material breach." But 1441 didn't automatically allow the United States to start a war. Even our own ambassador to the United Nations, John Negroponte, offered this view: "There's no automaticity and this is a two-stage process, and in that regard we have met the principal concerns that have been expressed for the resolution. Whatever violation there is, or is judged to exist, will be dealt with in the [Security] Council, and the Council will have an opportunity to consider the matter before any other action is taken." But that consideration was not to be.

We were told by the president that the International Atomic Energy Agency had a report that the Iraqis were "six months away from developing a weapon." In fact, Mark Gwozdecky, the chief spokesman of the International Atomic Energy Agency said, "There's never been a report like that issued from this agency," and he added, "We've never put a time frame on how long it might take Iraq to construct a nuclear weapon in 1998."

Khidhir Hamza, a nuclear scientist who helped Saddam develop his nuclear program was trotted out to defend Bush's push for war. Hamza has appeared numerous times on *Hannity & Colmes*. During his February 13, 2003, appearance, I asked him how he could be such an authority on Iraq's capabilities when he hadn't been in the country in many years, and he admitted to me that his views were not based on firsthand knowledge:

COLMES: But you know, you have not been in Iraq . . . since— or at least not part of the weapons program since 1991. . . . You left the country in 1995. So why should we believe your information is current?

HAMZA: I didn't say it's current. I said—as I said in Congress in my testimony, that it is an assessment of what is going on right now from defectors, from various intelligence reports. The German intelligence report in 2000 was the most detailed of Iraqi reports, especially using corporations based in India and other places. . . .

COLMES: So you're not telling us firsthand information? You're basing this on other reports from Germany, for example, which is one of the most ardent antiwar countries going on right now. So when you speak, you say you're not talking from personal knowledge having been in Iraq ten years ago?

HAMZA: Yes. What I'm saying right now, I know the system very well. I worked in the Iraqi nuclear program more than twenty years. And I am in a better position probably to evaluate than many other people. And I am using this capability, the inside knowledge of the program, to analyze the data coming out of Iraq right now.

But that "inside knowledge" was of a program that was years old, and data coming out of Iraq at the time of that statement was questionable.

Other Questionable Arguments

We were told that there were links to al Qaeda when, in fact, al Qaeda was more sympathetic to the anti-Saddam forces in northeastern Iraq. During the president's ardent attempts to link al Qaeda and Iraq in the latter part of 2002, little evidence could be found that such a link existed. *The Wall Street Journal* reported on October 22, 2002: "Yet despite some intriguing leads, U.S. intelligence officials say they haven't found hard evidence of an active link between Iraq's secular regime and al-Qaeda's Islamic militants . . . there is little evidence that he has been willing so far to share his biological or chemical weapons with his partners in terror, even during the Gulf War."

Bush 43's Cincinnati speech, designed to galvanize the nation and the world to support an attack on Saddam, contained the claim that an al Qaeda leader was getting medical treatment in Iraq. Soon after that, our own intelligence officials acknowledged that the alleged terrorist, Abu Musab Zarqawi, was no longer in Iraq, and there was never any evidence that the Iraqi government knew he was there or had contact with him. The *Washington Post* reported that at a Senate hearing on February 11, 2003, Tenet said that "Zarqawi was not 'under the control' of President Saddam." The next day Tenet slightly altered his rhetoric, saying " 'it's inconceivable' that Zarqawi and two dozen Egyptian Islamic Jihad associates 'are sitting there without the Iraqi intelligence service's knowledge of the fact that there is a safe haven being provided." The *Post* pointed out another inconsistency: "The CIA director said Zarqawi took money from bin Laden, but later he said Zarqawi and his network were 'independent'."

In February 2003, as the engines were revving up to attack Saddam Hussein, and Secretary of State Colin Powell was about to address the United Nations, word was that the FBI and CIA were still at odds with the administration's attempt to tie Iraq to al Qaeda. The *New York Times* reported: "At the Federal Bureau of Investigation, some investigators said they were baffled by the Bush administration's insistence on a solid link between Iraq and Osama bin Laden's network. 'We've been looking at this hard for more than a year and you know what, we just don't think it's there,' a government official said."

Four months later, the *New York Times* also reported that Abu Zubaydah, the al Qaeda terror coordinator who was captured in March 2002, told the CIA, "Osama bin Laden vetoed the idea of working with Hussein's government because he did not want to be beholden to Hussein." A separate CIA interrogation of Khalid Sheikh Mohammed, a top al Qaeda leader who was captured in March 2003, revealed the same information. The *Times* reported that "spokesmen at the White House, State Department and Pentagon decline to comment on why Zubaydah's debriefing report was not publicly disclosed by the Bush administration last year." Could it be because it didn't fit their agenda?

Democratizing Iraq was another reason given for war. But the State Department issued a report just before the commencement of hostilities in Iraq stating that regime change would likely not lead to democratization. "Liberal democracy would be difficult to achieve," the *Los Angeles Times* reported. "Electoral democracy, were it to emerge, could well be subject to exploitation by anti-American elements." Funnily enough, the report was dated February 26, 2003, the same day that Bush 43, speaking to the conservative American Enterprise Institute, put forth his democratic domino theory.

Bush 43 also stirred fear by warning that Iraq had a growing fleet of unmanned aircraft that could be used "for missions targeting the United States." But intelligence and Pentagon sources knew that Iraqi aircraft lacked the range to reach the United States.

During Powell's United Nations address, he talked about trucks that were really mobile biological weapons laboratories, Iraqi scientists who had left the country to avoid being interviewed, leaks that allowed Iraq to know where inspections were going to be ahead of time, and ties to al Qaeda. But just five days earlier chief weapons inspector Hans Blix gave an interview to the *New York Times* that discounted much of what Powell laid out at the UN.

Blix disputed Powell's claims that inspectors discovered Iraqi officials hiding illicit materials, saying that the inspectors had reported no such incidents. Blix also took issue with Powell's statements that Iraq was sending scientists to Syria to prevent them from being interviewed and disagreed with the administration's contentions that his inspection agency had been infiltrated by Iraqi agents or that there were Iraqi ties to al Qaeda. "More broadly," the *Times* reported, "he challenged President Bush's argument that military action is needed to avoid the risk of a Sept. 11-style attack by terrorists wielding nuclear, biological or chemical weapons."

Most embarrassing to the administration was Powell's invocation of British intelligence, which turned out not to be intelligence at all: "I would call my colleagues' attention to the fine paper that the

United Kingdom distributed yesterday, which describes in exquisite detail Iraqi deception activities," Powell said. Britain claimed the report was based in part on "intelligence material" and that it gave "up-to-date details" of Saddam's security and intelligence network. It turns out that this "intelligence" was almost word for word the work of a research associate at the Center for Nonproliferation Studies in Monterey. The researcher, Ibrahim Al-Marashi, said he hadn't been approached by the British government: "It was a shock to me." It was embarrassing enough that this information had been published the previous September, but even more excruciating was that it was based on information from the 1991 Gulf War. Ouch!

We were also told that we had to go after Saddam because in the 1980s he gassed his own people, the Kurds. So let me get this straight. Saddam gassed the Kurds in 1988, and for that we must get him now, in spite of choosing not to get him then or during the Gulf War in 1991. Presidents Reagan and Bush were silent about that genocide. It was more important at the time to have Iraq as an ally against Iran than to speak up on a human rights issue. Only when it became useful as a political tool to argue against an evil regime did Republicans feign outrage about the fate of the Kurds, fourteen years after the fact. They've yet to find a way to blame Clinton for this one, although I know that there is a conservative laboratory somewhere, busily finding a way to do so retroactively. In fact, among conservative think tanks, there are the highly regarded "Heritage Foundation," the "Manhattan Institute," and the ever-expanding, "Institute for the Study of How Clinton Did It Worse."

All of these justifications paved the way for the war and its aftermath: nation-building, something candidate Bush said he *wouldn't* do: "If we don't stop extending our troops all around the world in nation-building missions," he said in October 2000, "then we're going to have a serious problem coming down the road. I'm going to prevent that." This promise was broken on the morning of March 20, 2003,

Iraqi time, when the first raid of Gulf War II commenced and became the first step in the remaking of Iraq. Or, to use the phrase from the October 3 debate, "nation-building."

Oh! What a Lovely War

Richard Attenborough made his directorial debut at the helm of a 1969 movie that satirized World War I. While poor British men were off fighting and dying for their country, the aristocracy limited its sacrifices to boycotting German wine. One nice touch in the film was a cricket scoreboard that kept track of the war's casualties. Sound familiar?

On the night of March 19, 2003, I debated former secretary of state Alexander Haig on *Hannity & Colmes* about the appropriateness of placing political blame on the eve of war.

> COLMES: . . . shouldn't we be rising above that now and stop pointing fingers at each other, whether it's left to right or right to left?

> HAIG: Well you know, Alan, you make a very good point. Our country does best when it has two viable vital political movements, one Democratic, one Republican. But . . . they—[the Democrats]—they are the ones that started this mess. In the first place, they participated wholly in the creation of the conditions that have made this war absolutely essential.

> COLMES: See, General, there you go, you're pointing fingers. You want to blame one political party for getting us where we are today. There's plenty of blame to go around on both sides, when you had a Reagan-Bush administration that tilted toward Iraq in the Iran-Iraq War. This is not a time for finger-pointing, is it?

> HAIG: Alan, . . . if you listened to the last three weeks, all of the criticism has come from the Democratic leadership. And

it's been outrageous, unconscionable, and totally wrong in terms of timing. And they're going to pay a heavy political price in my view.

Moments later news broke that Gulf War II had begun, and we broke away to Fox News anchor Shepard Smith and war coverage commenced. At that point I decided that it was no longer appropriate for me to debate the validity of the war while American men and women were in harm's way. Many on the left chose to continue their vocal and vociferous opposition. I felt that the beginning of hostilities rendered that debate obsolete. An unintended consequence was the suddenly positive responses I began to receive from conservatives.

From: Larry
Sent: Friday, April 04, 2003 10:18 AM
To: colmes
Subject: Liberals can be good Americans!

Dear Allen:
I watch the show solely for Seans point of view. However I must say the way you have conducted yourself since the war began has been exemplary. It is the first time I have ever thought of a liberal as patriotic. You have managed to communicate your obvious liberal views without shaming your country. Your comrades should take a lesson and they might survive to debate another day!

Respectfully,
Larry

We should never lose sight of the valor of those willing to make the ultimate sacrifice for their country. It's not the grunts in the field who make foreign policy; they're the foot soldiers carrying out the geopolitical objectives of others, usually selflessly and, in this case, brilliantly. The outcome, however, was never in doubt. Iraq had no nuclear capability, no long-range missiles, a debilitated air force, and a depleted army. The fear that the Iraqis would use chemical or biological weapons never materialized.

True, Iraq was proclaimed "free." But what did "free" mean; and, at what price, freedom? Even after Bush 43 proclaimed on May 1, 2003, "Major combat operations in Iraq have ended," the country was characterized by anarchy, looting, and guerrilla warfare that resulted in the regular killing and wounding of more Americans. Asked about the ravages of post-Saddam Iraq, Rumsfeld replied, "Freedom's untidy. And free people are free to make mistakes and commit crimes and do bad things." Or, as they used to say on *Saturday Night Live*, "No big whoop." It's so much more wonderful to commit crimes and do bad things in a free country than it is in a dictatorship. Listening to Rummy, you'd think newly freed Iraq was like Great Adventure; but instead of animals, it's criminals who "roam free."

Also untidy is acknowledging how many civilians died during Persian Gulf War II. Pentagon spokesman Lieutenant Colonel Jim Cassella said on June 10, 2003, that the U.S. military doesn't count civilian casualties, explaining, "Our efforts focus on destroying the enemy's capabilities, so we never target civilians and have no reason to try to count such unintended deaths." However, a five-week investigation by the Associated Press reveals that at least 3,240 civilians died in Iraq during the war. AP journalists looked at logs from 60 of Iraq's 124 hospitals between March 20, when the war began, and April 20, when the fighting eased. The AP included only those records that distinguished between civilian and military deaths. Furthermore, many of the dead never made it to hospitals; instead, they were buried by their families or lost in the rubble, so the actual count is likely much higher. The 1991 Gulf War, by comparison, saw an estimated 2,278 civilian casualties, according to Iraqi civil defense authorities.

Untidiness, it seems, is small price to pay for a lovely little war.

How We Wound Up Between Iraq and a Hard Place

This administration's Iraq obsession has its roots in something called the "Project for the New American Century." A group of neoconservatives, including Dick Cheney, his chief of staff Lewis Libby, Don Rumsfeld, Deputy Secretary of Defense Paul Wolfowitz, and Bush 43's brother Jeb got together in 1997 to formulate a plan to reshape the Middle East. In 1998, eighteen of them signed a letter to President Clinton urging unilateral action against Iraq, claiming, "we can no longer depend on our partners in the Gulf War coalition" to enforce UN resolutions. In 2000, they published a blueprint called "Rebuilding America's Defenses: Strategies, Forces and Resources for a New Century." Here is just one of its juicy tidbits: "Indeed, the United States has for decades sought to play a more permanent role in Gulf regional security. While the unresolved conflict with Iraq provides the immediate justification, the need for a substantial American force presence in the Gulf transcends the issue of the regime of Saddam Hussein."

Ten of the eighteen signers of that letter to President Clinton now serve in the Bush 43 administration, most in high-ranking positions.

Leave it to columnist Molly Ivins to put the situation succinctly: "We weren't attacked by Iraq—we were attacked by bin Laden's terrorist network. We weren't attacked with nuclear weapons—we were attacked with box cutters."

When it was clear that Osama bin Laden was the mastermind of the September 11 attacks, President Bush made his capture a priority, even if only for a few, brief moments: "I want justice," Bush 43 proclaimed. "There's an old poster out west, as I recall, that said, 'Wanted: Dead or Alive.' "

But as "The 'War' on Terror" morphed into the Saddam obsession, our priorities changed, even though the nature of the threats against the United States did not, and Bush 43 was soon singing a very different tune about bin Laden: "I truly am not that concerned about him. I was concerned about him when he had taken over a country. I was concerned about the fact that he was basically running Afghanistan and calling the shots for the Taliban. We shoved him out more and more on the margins."

Apparently, Bush thought he could get away with applying the first comment not to bin Laden, but to Saddam Hussein. As in a three-card-monte game, there was a bait and switch, and the hunt for bin Laden became the hunt for Saddam.

The Friendly Skies

While we're questioning this administration and "The 'War' on Terror," why have so few questions been raised about how and why our government, with the help of the Saudis, flew members of the bin Laden family out of the United States to Saudi Arabia in the wake of the September 11 attacks? Here's what the *New York Times* reported on September 30, 2001: "The young members of the bin Laden clan were driven or flown under F.B.I. supervision to a secret assembly point in Texas and then to Washington from where they left the country on a private charter plane when airports reopened three days after the attacks."

We never could get a straight story about the circumstances under which the bin Ladens left America. Conflicting press reports show that they either left voluntarily or were told to leave. The *Independent* of London reported on September 26, 2001: "A spokesman for the Saudi Arabian embassy in Washington denied claims yesterday that the bin Ladens had been told by the FBI and the Saudi government to return. He said: 'There was no official warning from the government that they should go but maybe they thought it would be better if they went home'."

But the *Boston Globe*, put it this way a few days later: "A Saudi diplomat said his government and the FBI advised the bin Ladens to leave for their own safety."

In all, twenty-four members of bin Laden family were escorted from the United States to Saudi Arabia. Did the FBI interview them?

Were questions asked about their relationship with their estranged relative Osama? Did investigations take place into any transfers of money between these rich relations and their prodigal wayfarer? So far, there have been no answers to these questions.

War Makes Good Politics

In late 2002, White House chief of staff Andrew Card chaired a meeting in which they discussed a document called "Possible '04 Signature Issues." The White House claimed that it was just an innocent list of issues that needed attention to ensure that 2003 issues and 2004 issues didn't conflict, although it refused to reveal who wrote the list. The meeting in question was conducted by Karl Rove's strategic planning unit. And just what might they be planning for in 2004? Oh, I don't know, could it be an . . . election? And why deny the obvious? Rove's job is not to set policy; he's not a member of the cabinet. Rove's job is to position the president politically.

So should we be surprised that General Rove would politicize a war? "We can go to the country confidently on this issue because Americans trust the Republican Party to do a better job of keeping our communities and families safe. We can also go to the country on this issue because they trust the Republican Party to do a better job of protecting and strengthening America's military might and thereby protecting America," he said in early 2002 to the party faithful.

It's unseemly at best and detestable at worst that this administration would conflate the push for votes with a policy that could result in a tremendous loss of American life. This is not proceeding with "moral clarity" as the Bushies love to claim; it's an amoral and crass exercise in retaining power.

This is the same Republican Party that sold pictures of Bush 43 aboard *Air Force One* as a remembrance of September 11 for $150 dollars. I'm not sure this is illegal, although the use of White House photographers for this kind of thing is questionable, but it certainly is tasteless. It's unseemly to use even the hint of anything having to do with an attack on Americans as a political tool; using it for both political and monetary gain is revolting.

And then there was The Great American Duct Tape Fiasco of 2003. When the terror alert was raised to Code Orange, America's fire administrator, David Paulison, listed duct tape as an essential product to help keep homes safe in the event of an attack. Even after that particular alert subsided, Homeland Security czar Tom Ridge told Jim Lehrer on PBS that "You may want to have a safe shelter for four or six hours," and "you may need that duct tape." As it happens, 46 percent of the duct tape sold in America is manufactured in Avon, Ohio, by Henkel Consumer Adhesives, whose CEO, John Kahl, gave $100,000 to Republicans in the 2000 election cycle. Far be it for me to take a cynical view of this, but I'd be comforted by the belief that our government gave equal promotion to left-wing companies if, during the next heat wave, someone high up in the Bush 43 administration urges Americans to go out and buy Ben and Jerry's New York Super Fudge Chunk.

In *Bush At War*, Bob Woodward quoted Bush 43 trying to explain why he could only handle one conflict at a time: "If we tried to do too many things—two things, for example, or three things—militarily, then . . . the lack of focus would have been a huge risk." And Paul Wolfowitz is quoted as saying "war against Iraq might be easier than war against Afghanistan." Was that yet *another* rationale for war with Iraq, because it was "easier"?

I'm so glad that George "You're either with us or again us" Bush came out against the evildoers. As former Libertarian presidential candidate Harry Browne has pointed out, does "You're either with us or agin us" mean we have to bomb neutral Switzerland?

Capitalism at Its Finest

Just who or what enabled Iraq to be a fighting power in the first place? The answer: us. We supplied Iraq with some of the ingredients to concoct weapons of mass destruction. The mere mention of the desire to understand what we did and why we did it is enough to send conservatives rushing to their keyboards. Here's an e-mail I received after I suggested we look at what we have wrought in Iraq:

From: BrainGuy
Sent: Friday, September 20, 2002 9:20 PM
To: Colmes
Subject: no mo

clones,
u disgust me to the point I am bout to puke. we dont need traitorous anti American liberals like you in this country. we are at war. if you spoke like this during WWII you would have been jailed or at least humiliated beyond reproach. I hope you die in an airplane crash. If you do i will laugh.

BrainGuy
Montpelier, VT

As for that self-examination, it isn't pretty.

In 1994, then Michigan senator Donald Riegle acknowledged that we exported dangerous bacteria, such as *E. coli*, to Iraq between 1985 and 1989: "I am deeply troubled that the United States permitted the sale of deadly biological agents to a country with a known biological warfare program." Back then, we disliked Iran more than we disliked Iraq and our goal was to help fight the country that took American hostages. What a shame that we conveniently ignored that a pendulum can come right back and whack you in the solar plexus.

Michael Dobbs, writing in the *Washington Post* on December 30, 2002, focused on the key role the United States played in the building of Iraq's nuclear arsenal. A key player in this enterprise was Donald Rumsfeld. Dobbs wrote: "Among the people instrumental in tilting U.S. policy toward Baghdad during the 1980–88 Iran-Iraq war was Donald H. Rumsfeld, now Defense Secretary, whose

December 1983 meeting with Hussein paved the way for normalization of U.S.-Iraqi relations. . . . Declassified documents show that Rumsfeld traveled to Baghdad at a time when Iraq was using chemical weapons on an 'almost daily' basis in defiance of international conventions."

The fog of time has changed the spin on this trip, it seems. Dobbs reports, "In a September interview with CNN, Rumsfeld said he 'cautioned' Hussein about the use of chemical weapons, a claim at odds with declassified State Department notes of his 90-minute meeting with the Iraqi leader. A Pentagon spokesman, Bryan Whitman, now says that Rumsfeld raised the issue not with Hussein, but with Iraqi Foreign Minister Tariq Aziz. The State Department notes show that he mentioned it largely in passing as one of several matters that 'inhibited' U.S. efforts to assist Iraq." But those silly "inhibitions," like chemical and biological weapons, didn't actually "inhibit" our relationship with Iraq.

On February 25, 2003, the National Security Archive and George Washington University published previously declassified information about the U.S. embrace of Saddam Hussein in the 1980s and the specific role played by Donald Rumsfeld. During the time we reached out to Saddam he had invaded Iran, had long-range nuclear aspirations, harbored known terrorists in Baghdad, was guilty of human rights violations against his own citizens, and possessed and used chemical weapons on Iranians and his own people. Our response was to renew ties with Iraq, provide high level intelligence and aid, and to send a high-level presidential envoy named Donald Rumsfeld to shake hands with Saddam, which he did on December 20, 1983.

These documents also suggested something many conservatives have tried to deny: the administration's real objectives for war in Iraq. They mentioned two Rumsfeld trips to Baghdad, reports on Iraq's use of chemical weapons while the Reagan administration supported Iraq, and directives signed by President Reagan that reveal that our specific priorities for the region included preserving access to oil, expanding our ability to project military power in there, and ensuring the security of our allies. One telling document from senior State Department official Jonathan T. Howe to Secretary of State George Shultz, dated November 1, 1983, states "We have recently received additional information confirming Iraqi use of chemical weapons. We also know that Iraq has received CW production capability, primarily from Western firms, including possibly a U.S. foreign subsidiary." While this memo acknowledged our desire to get Iraq to halt its use of chemical weapons and our policy of stopping their use wherever they appear, it went on to state: "As you are aware, presently Iraq is at a disadvantage in its war of attrition with Iran. After a recent SIG meeting on the war, a discussion paper was sent to the White House for an NSC meeting . . . a section of which outlines a number of measures we might take to assist Iraq." So in spite of this desire to persuade Iraq to stop using chemical weapons, the fact remains that the State Department proceeded with plans to help a country they knew to be using chemical weapons "almost daily."

60 Minutes and the *St. Louis Post-Dispatch* reported in 1998 that we sold cell cultures and equipment for biological warfare to Iraq in the late 1980s. The *Baltimore Sun* reported on February 13, 1998, that Britain's Channel 4 discovered U.S. intelligence documents that showed "14 consignments of biological materials were exported from the United States to Iraq between 1985 and 1989. These included 19 batches of anthrax bacteria and 15 batches of botulinum, the organism that causes botulism." These shipments were licensed by the Commerce Department and backed by the State Department. Furthermore, the report stated, "At least 29 batches of material were sent after Iraq had used gas in an attack on the Kurdish town of Halabja in 1988, killing 5,000 people." One of the reasons given for attacking Iraq in 2003 was that Saddam had attacked his own people in the past. This argument seems disingenuous since we continued to help him build weapons of mass destruction even after these attacks.

In 1986, the Commerce Department overrode an objection to the grant of an export license to a New Jersey computer manufacturer. The Pentagon was concerned that the equipment would be used for secret military research, but the deal went through. In fact, the Commerce Department allowed $1.5 billion worth of goods to go to Iraq between 1985 and 1990. According to the *Los Angeles Times* of February 13, 1991, among the items we sent to Iraq were "advanced computers, electronic instruments and high-grade graphics terminals for rocket testing and analysis; flight simulators and test equipment; microwave communications gear; radar maintenance equipment, and computer mapping systems."

Iraq also bought sixty Hughes helicopters, ten Bell Huey helicopters, and twenty-four Bell 214ST helicopters. Even though Congressman Howard Berman of California begged Secretary of State Shultz to reconsider these sales and pointed out how ludicrous it was to sell this equipment to Iraq, the Reagan administration's argument that it was good business prevailed. W. Tapley Bennett Jr., then assistant secretary of state for legislative affairs, replied to Berman: "We believe that increased American penetration of the extremely competitive civilian aircraft market would serve the United States' interests by improving our balance of trade and lessen unemployment in the aircraft industry." Nice of the Republicans to think about the low-wage laborer for once.

A February 13, 1991, *Los Angeles Times* piece reported: "In 1988, Kurdish civilians were attacked with poisonous gas from Iraqi helicopters and planes. U.S. intelligence sources say they believe that the American-built helicopters were among those dropping the deadly bombs." *Newsweek*, on September 23, 2002, reported similar findings: "The (American) helicopters, some American officials later surmised, were used to spray poison gas on the Kurds."

And let's not forget some long-standing personal and corporate ties to Iraq. Vice President Dick Cheney's former company, Halliburton, held major stakes in Dresser-Rand and Ingersoll-Dresser, two companies that helped rebuild Iraq's oil industry. Dick

Cheney's responses to questions about his company's involvement with Iraq were not consistent. The *Washington Post* reported on June 23, 2001: "During last year's presidential campaign, Richard B. Cheney acknowledged that the oil-field supply corporation he headed, Halliburton Co., did business with Libya and Iran through foreign subsidiaries. But he insinuated that he had imposed a 'firm policy' against trading with Iraq."

On the July 30, 2000, edition of *This Week*, Cheney denied that his company or any of its subsidiaries did business with Iraq and repeated the "firm policy" line. When Sam Donaldson asked if Halliburton, through subsidiaries, was trying to do business with Iraq, Cheney said, "No, no, I had a firm policy that we wouldn't do anything in Iraq, even—even arrangements that were supposedly legal . . . we've not done any business in Iraq, since the sanctions are imposed, and I had a standing policy that I wouldn't do that."

But a few weeks later, on August 27, 2000, this statement was played back to the Republican vice presidential nominee by Donaldson, who added that Halliburton's spokesman, Guy Marcus, had confirmed that the two Halliburton subsidiaries, Dresser-Rand and Ingersoll-Dresser, did business with Iraq. Donaldson reminded Cheney that he knew Halliburton had those subsidiaries three weeks earlier when the "firm policy" statement was made. Cheney replied, "No. No. I made the statement, Sam. I made the statement, and—and I meant the statement. I was, from time to time, while I was at Halliburton, importuned to go do business with Iraq, in some cases in perfectly legal and proper fashion, in the oil-for-food program, and I said we would not do that." Cheney said he didn't know that at the time Halliburton took over those companies, they were doing business with Iraq. Furthermore, he said, Halliburton sold off those divisions of the company. But the June 23, 2001, *Washington Post* reported that Halliburton's two subsidiary firms "signed contracts to sell more than $73 million in oil production equipment and spare parts to Iraq while Cheney was chairman and chief executive officer of the Dallas-based company." The *Post* went on to report, "The divestiture, however, was not immediate. The firms traded with Baghdad for more than a year under Cheney, signing nearly $30 million in contracts before he sold Halliburton's 49 percent stake in Ingersoll Dresser Pump Co. in December 1999 and its 51 percent interest in Dresser Rand to Ingersoll-Rand in February 2000, according to U.N. records."

At the time, reporters who called Cheney's spokesperson were referred to Halliburton. Halliburton referred all calls to Cheney's office. Bouts of dizziness broke out among the fifth estate.

Partisanship Uber Alles

The democratization of Iraq is going to take awhile. In the meantime, "The 'War' on Terror" and its subsidiary, "Gulf War II," can be used to justify a host of Bush 43 initiatives. When convenient, Bush 43 gets to be a "wartime president," since that gives greater heft and push to his agenda. During a daily press briefing in late March 2003, White House press secretary Ari Fleischer justified tax cuts at a time of huge war expenditures as a way of creating jobs for returning troops:

> FLEISCHER: Let me cite to you some of the reasons that guide the President when he seeks to make sure that the economy can grow and that jobs can be created, so that when our men and women in the military return home, they'll have jobs to come home to.

You mean all these troops were unemployed until March 20, 2003?

Throughout "The 'War' on Terror," various interest groups played laughable games of connect-the-dots to advance their own agendas. The gun lobby claimed that gun control would make citizens less safe from terrorists; the religious right argued that we needed to get back to our roots as a Christian nation. I could even imagine the antichoicers saying that abortion would reduce the population at a time when we're going to need young men to fight the decades-long " 'War' on Terror." Next thing you know, the antienvironmentalists will argue that "The 'War' on Terror" requires that we just *have* to drill at the Arctic National Wildlife Reserve.

Wait a minute ... that ANWR argument *was* used. Interior Secretary Ann Norton said in April 2002 that we had to increase our level of oil production because Iraq was threatening an embargo. And coincidentally, ANWR had just the right amount of oil to make up such a shortfall. This is a decidedly short-range view. The United States consumes a quarter of the world's oil but possesses less than 4 percent of global reserves. Instead of fighting for a questionable amount of oil to be gleaned from the Alaskan wilderness, a better way would be to finance research into fuel efficiency and renewable clean energy resources. Ninety-five percent of Alaska's north slope is open to oil and gas exploration, but the big oil companies *must* have that extra 5 percent. Hey, if Alaskan oil is so important to us, why do we sell sixty thousand barrels a day of it to Asia? But it sounded good to proclaim we need that oil because Iraq was making threats. And why was Iraq making threats? Because *we* were making threats against Iraq.

Bush 41 versus Bush 43

It was the height of irony that something called the Bush administration was using tortured logic to accomplish something that was so rationally rejected by something called—albeit at an earlier time—the Bush administration. There was a reason we never did go all the way to Baghdad in 1991, when the troops and the international coalition were already assembled during the first Persian Gulf War. And no one explained it better than Bush 41 and his national security advisor, Brent Scowcroft:

> Trying to eliminate Saddam, extending the ground war into an occupation of Iraq, would have violated our guideline about not changing objectives in midstream, engaging in "mission creep," and

would have incurred incalculable human and political costs. Apprehending him was probably impossible.

Why would this option be any more appealing or realistic during the Bush 43 administration? Could it be that it helped the Bushies push the rest of their agenda to have the backdrop of a war?

Here's something else Bush 41 said: "We should not march into Baghdad. . . . To occupy Iraq would instantly shatter our coalition, turning the whole Arab world against us, and make a broken tyrant into a latter-day Arab hero."

And see if you can guess the author of *these* words: "The Gulf War was a limited-objective war. If it had not been, we would be ruling Baghdad today—at unpardonable expense in terms of money, lives lost and ruined regional relationships."

Was it some left-wing liberal? An antiwar protester? A Democratic presidential candidate? No, it was Bush 43's secretary of state and get-Saddam advocate, Colin Powell.

Another definition of "mission creep" involves being attacked by one group of terrorists and retaliating against another. The obsession with Saddam Hussein for more than a year after the September 11 attacks took our eyes off the ball.

But was it on the ball in the first place?

On January 31, 2001, "The U.S. Commission on National Security/21st Century" issued a report that should have been heeded by our government. This fourteen-member bipartisan panel, created by Congress and headed by former Colorado senator Gary Hart and former New Hampshire senator Warren Rudman, had no political axe to grind. Among its findings:

America will become increasingly vulnerable to hostile attack on our homeland, and our military superiority will not entirely protect us. . . . The combination of unconventional weapons proliferation with the persistence of international terrorism will end the relative invulnerability of the U.S. homeland to catastrophic attack. A direct attack against American citizens *on American soil* is likely over the next quarter century. . . . We therefore recommend the creation of an independent National Homeland Security Agency (NHSA) with responsibility for planning, coordinating, and integrating various U.S. government activities involved in homeland security. States, terrorists, and other disaffected groups will acquire weapons of mass destruction and mass disruption, and some of them will use them. Americans will likely die on American soil, possibly in large numbers.

The Bush administration decided it didn't want anything to do with this report, opting instead to ask Dick Cheney to study the issue four months after the report was issued and to give FEMA, the Federal Emergency Management Agency, responsibility for coordinating an effort. FEMA was headed by Joseph Albaugh, who just happened to be Bush 43's former campaign manager.

Hmmm . . . how do you like that? A Homeland Security Department! Proposed even *before* "The 'War' on Terror" by a bipartisan group. And yet Republicans had no trouble shamelessly taking credit for it during the 2002 midterm elections.

As blasé as the Bush 43 administration was about homeland security prior to September 11, it was actively disinterested in having a commission figure out what happened after the attacks. Were there some things they didn't want us to know? After 9/11, victims' families wanted information about what led to the deaths of their loved ones. Instead of a proactive commission to investigate what happened, they got a homeland security bill that sought to give the Eli Lilly company relief from lawsuits by parents of autistic children. These lawsuits involved Lilly's alleged use of a mercury-based vaccine preservative. Lilly, by the way, contributed $1.6 million during the 2002 campaign cycle, with 75 percent of that money going to Republicans. Mitch Daniels, then Bush's budget director, worked for Lilly for a decade before joining the president's team in 2001, and Lilly chairman and CEO Sidney Taurel was appointed to the president's Homeland Security Advisory Council. Senate majority leader

Bill Frist, long before his post-Lott ascent to Republican stardom, was another beneficiary of Lilly's largess, and was instrumental in pushing relief for Lilly in the Homeland Security Bill.

The political trail of the Homeland Security Bill is a beauty. This idea was initially put forth by Senator Joe Lieberman, Democrat of Connecticut. The administration rejected the bill repeatedly. But when they realized that various departments were not working well together, Republicans gutted the bill of collective bargaining protections for government employees and presented it as their own. But that wasn't enough. During the 2002 election, this bill was wielded as a club against Senator Max Cleland of Georgia who, partially as a result of this is, unfortunately, now ex-Senator Cleland. His opponent, now Senator Saxby Chambliss, ran an ad impugning Cleland's commitment to homeland security, saying, "Since July, Max Cleland has voted against the president's homeland security efforts 11 times."

Chambliss's campaign team conveniently left out that Senator Cleland supported a Department of Homeland Security before Bush 43 did. And he voted for legislation to establish the new agency when it cleared committee earlier that year. When the administration eliminated labor protections, he opposed the bill. As a result, he was accused of being unconcerned about national security. I suppose national security means reducing workers' rights.

Once there was agreement on the Homeland Security Bill, the Republicans slipped in seven provisions in the dead of night that hadn't been there at the twilight's previous gleaming. One stealth provision, for example, gave immunity to companies that make faulty antiterrorism equipment. Another, thankfully removed because of the resulting furor, gave protection from lawsuits to pharmaceutical companies like Lilly. Can someone please explain to me how protecting pharmaceutical companies helps us find bin Laden? Maybe they're afraid if we find him and drug him, he'll sue. I challenged Oliver North on this issue on *Hannity & Colmes* in November 2002 and asked him how he could defend this sneaky maneuver. He offered the "they all do it" defense:

COLMES: Do you support it?

NORTH: Well, first of all, there's nothing sneaky about it. Second of all, I'm shocked, absolutely shocked, that a member of a Congress in any party would put pork . . .

COLMES: Oh, so your argument is they do it, too. That's your argument.

NORTH: No, I'm telling you this is the way this town works. This is the Capitol Building that's right behind me here. That's the way this town works . . .

According to the good colonel, this was just "business as usual" in a government town, and that made it okay. I'm waiting for the next time he defends a Democratic Congress doing the same thing.

The Republicans played a linguistic game. They name something "The Patriot Act." If you have the temerity to oppose it, how dare you call yourself a "Patriot"? If Max Cleland doesn't like the revised "Homeland Security Bill," that must *prove* that he doesn't care about the protection of America. I'm surprised the Republicans didn't also get behind the "Conservatives Love America and Liberals Don't Act," the "George Bush Is the Commander in Chief and If You Criticize Him You're Going to Hell Act," and the "Tom Daschle Is Satan Act." Liberals might consider "Liberals Know Better Than Conservatives What's Good for the Country Act," and the "We Don't Need a Word to Prove We Have Compassion Act."

Bush 43 balked for more than a year at creating a commission to investigate the intelligence failures leading to September 11. When the joint House-Senate intelligence committee asked for information about the Saudi money flow, Bush 43, FBI director Robert Mueller, and Attorney General John Ashcroft refused to declassify the information. Perhaps they didn't want too close a look at the financial links between the Saudis and terrorism, because it could have hampered the flow of oil and their effort to utilize Saudi land for staging areas in the upcoming war against Iraq.

Protecting industry seemed to be a priority of the Bush 43 administration, at the expense of the truth and of holding big business accountable. There was much fear that the September 11 attacks would destroy the airline industry. Bush 43's press secretary, Ari Fleischer, informed the American public that the hijackers purposely used box cutters and plastic knives because regulations allowed those instruments through security. But the truth is that box cutters were not allowed by the airlines, which were in charge of security on September 11. "Airlines failed to enforce existing security guidelines on Sept. 11 that required airport screeners to confiscate box cutters from passengers," reported the Associated Press on November 11, 2002. The AP went on to report, "The manual for security screeners was issued by the airlines' trade groups to comply with FAA regulations and was in effect at the time of the terror attacks. The document lists box cutters and pepper spray as items not allowed past security checkpoints. Screeners were told to call supervisors if either item were to be found."

So why were we led to believe that box cutters were permitted? It would have cost airlines billions of dollars and certain bankruptcy if the story were otherwise. As the *New York Times* pointed out:

> Most prominent, the measure includes a section inserted by House Republican leaders that will limit the liability of airport screening companies for any negligence they may have committed in allowing box cutters aboard the planes that day. . . . "Why would the House Republicans give the screening companies a get-out-of-jail free card at the last minute?" asked Kristen Breitweiser [who lost her husband in the September 11 attacks] . . . who has been considering a lawsuit against the screeners.

When the administration was finally dragged kicking and screaming to appoint the commission sought by Breitweiser and other aggrieved families, it chose former secretary of state Henry Kissinger as its chairman. His calling card was secrecy, and yet he was chosen to lead a commission that was to unearth secrets. Frank Rich of the *New York Times* pointed out that Kissinger's first act as head of this commission was to keep secret the name of his firm's client list, which might have posed a conflict of interest. Columnist Molly Ivins wrote that he offered up "a two-lie answer" when he said that law firms aren't required to reveal the names of their clients. The problems with that answer are (1) Kissinger Associates isn't a law firm; and (2) law firms do have to legally disclose clients if lobbying is involved. But this is consistent behavior for the man who was complicit in prolonging the Vietnam War by secretly expanding it to Cambodia and Laos; who secretly helped to arrange a coup to overthrow the Chilean government in 1973 to replace a democratically elected leader with a brutal dictator, and who, along with President Gerald Ford, secretly gave President Suharto of Indonesia the go-ahead to invade East Timor in 1975, resulting in the death of two hundred thousand people.

This was the man who was going to shed openness and sunlight on what our government knew and didn't know concerning September 11, 2001. At the time of his appointment, Kissinger's ability to travel the world had been compromised, as he feared some countries would call for his arrest. Chilean courts, for example, wanted him to testify about his role in the 1973 coup, as did French authorities, who were concerned about the disappearance of French citizens in Chile. When the Shah of Iran asked our country to give secret aid to the Kurds in northern Iraq, Kissinger agreed, but when the Shah made a deal with Saddam Hussein, all bets were off, and thirty-five thousand abandoned Kurds were slaughtered while two hundred thousand became refugees.

What's next, appointing Winona Ryder as national security advisor?

Kissinger did agree to sever ties with any clients deemed conflicts of interest, and he claimed he represented no Middle Eastern governments. But as it turned out, push met shove, and Kissinger resigned from the commission because he didn't want to disclose the names of his clients. Correct me if I'm wrong, but shouldn't this have been discussed and agreed to *before* the appointment and attendant controversy? But then, nothing like a little delay in a commission the administration didn't want in the first place. Kissinger's resignation followed on the heels of the departure of the commission's deputy chairman, former Maine senator George Mitchell. Mitchell didn't want to sever ties with his law firm and realized he could not make the time commitment necessary to do an effective job.

A fair, honest, and nonpolitical commission would force the United States to examine its own policies, actions, and internal failures. A truly great nation is strong enough to withstand a candid assessment and should be able to admit when it's wrong.

A year after September 11, 2001, former senators Hart and Rudman issued another report, compiled by a bipartisan group that included two former secretaries of state, two former chairmen of the Joint Chiefs of Staff, and former directors of the CIA and FBI, among other leading authorities. It said, in part:

> A year after September 11, America remains dangerously unprepared to prevent and respond to a catastrophic terrorist attack on U.S. soil . . . a war with Iraq could consume virtually all the nation's attention and command the bulk of the available resources. While 50,000 federal screeners are being hired at the nation's airports to check passengers, only the tiniest percentage of containers, ships, trucks, and trains that enter the United States each day are subject to examination—and a weapon of mass destruction could well be hidden among this cargo.

Using history as a guide, you'd think that another Hart-Rudman report would have gained a bit more credence with the Bush administration. But the talk about airport, border, and port security was overshadowed by talk of Iraq, as if the death of Saddam Hussein would make us all sleep better at night.

In a March 16, 2003, editorial, just days before our invasion of Iraq, the New York *Newsday* pointed out that while 95 percent of our foreign trade arrives by sea, just 2 percent of the 6 million shipping containers that arrive at our ports annually are inspected.

The *News* went on to report that the Coast Guard says it will take $1.4 billion to secure our ports immediately, but that Congress, the same august body run by a party claiming to have the market cornered on understanding our national security needs, has allocated only $318 million to this effort.

Instead of heeding well-thought-out warnings, we had an administration living up to its cowboy image. It issued a policy alternately known as National Security Presidential Directive (NSPD) 17 and Homeland Security Presidential Directive 4, calling for the possible first use of nuclear weapons and for preemptive strikes on countries we considered threats, even if they had not yet done anything overtly threatening. This was a radical change in our way of doing business—the idea that we'd go after countries we *thought* were developing nuclear weapons and *might* want to harm us. If I thought you might want to hurt me, and decided to preemptively slap you upside the head, you *might* want to get an attorney and *would* win in court.

And why is it acceptable for some countries to dream of a nuclear future, and not others? Pakistan, for example, never signed the Nuclear Non-Proliferation Treaty and is believed to have provided nuclear assistance to North Korea. But our shotgun marriage with Pakistan, consummated after September 11, renders its nuclear program of little import to us. For that matter, why should the United States be allowed to have nuclear weapons and be the arbiter of which other nations are permitted such a luxury? If the answer is that we are the world's policeman, does that mean our philosophy is might makes right?

When North Korea announced that it was restarting a nuclear reactor that was capable of producing weapons-grade plutonium, it underscored some disturbing questions and contradictions: why we did we rev up the guns of war against Iraq because it *wanted* nuclear capability, but go out of our way to state that we didn't want war with North Korea, which already *has* the capability and, like Iraq, is guilty of years-long agreement violations? North Korea also expelled inspectors from the International Atomic Energy Agency, moved fresh fuel rods to the power plant storing the reactor, removed UN monitoring seals and cameras from nuclear facilities, and refused to heed warnings from Japan, China, Russia, South Korea, and the European Union. And guess whom conservatives blamed for North Korea's actions? That's right, Bill Clinton. After all, Clinton *is* responsible for every world crisis.

When Bush 41's last secretary of state, Lawrence Eagleburger, appeared on *Hannity & Colmes* in early 2003, I challenged him on Bush 43's actions and how they might have contributed to North Korea's behavior, and on the notion that Iraq was a diversion from a more imminent danger:

> COLMES: I would argue that George W. Bush has pushed North Korea to the brink, that the 1994 agreement worked, that indeed, as Colin Powell stated on *This Week*, Clinton had a declaratory policy toward North Korea. He began to—he actually was poised to attack, if necessary, at the same time he was conducting negotiations. Yet, President Bush comes in now, refers to them as an "axis of evil," says "I hate Kim Jong-Il." He cuts off oil shipments that were agreed to under the 1994 agreement. And he pulls out of the ABM Treaty, forcing North Korea into a situation, which is where we are today. Didn't any of President Bush's actions that I just suggested have anything to do with what North Korea's doing?

> EAGLEBURGER: You could make that argument if you want, but I'm afraid I don't buy much of it. Look, the fact of the matter is, you know, if you want to cast this in terms of, you know, looking for ways in which we have contributed to the problem, instead of looking at the base of the problem, be my guest. . . .

Do you know why they're doing what they're doing now?

Because they see us tied up with the Iraqi situation. . . . And they see this as a great time to flex their muscles.

COLMES: Well, then wouldn't that be an argument that Iraq is a diversion, that we are misdirected at Iraq, that instead of looking at Iraq, we should really take seriously what's going on in North Korea? And you've just made the argument that this obsession that President Bush has with Iraq could be causing us damage in other parts of the world, Korea being Exhibit A.

EAGLEBURGER: Nice try.

COLMES: I'm just reflecting what you said.

EAGLEBURGER: . . . if you're saying we can't walk and chew gum at the same time, again, the fact of the matter is we've had a problem with Iraq. Now all of a sudden, you're saying that well, we can't do two things at once. Maybe we, in fact, can't. I will have to see.

A few minutes later I quoted Warren Christopher, another former secretary of state, which seemed to cause Mr. Eagleburger to back off the "walk and chew gum at the same time" position:

COLMES: Here's what he said. He said, "My experience tells me that we cannot mount a war against Iraq and still maintain the necessary policy focus on North Korea and international terrorism."

You know, is he—does he not know whereof he speaks?

EAGLEBURGER: No, I think he's got a good point.

First Eagleburger argued in favor of Bush policies, but then he agreed with Christopher. Do you want to agree with your party, or what makes sense?

"The 'War' on Terror": Failure

Many Democrats have been shy about confronting this administration on its conduct of "The 'War' on Terror." They think the debate is untouchable. Here we had Iraq and North Korea center stage, reports of al Qaeda cells still in the United States, and plenty of evidence, in addition to the Hart-Rudman report, that "The 'War' on Terror" has been a failure. As *Time* magazine reported in July 2003, almost two years after the September 11 attacks, the United States was spending $1 billion a month to keep ten thousand troops in Afghanistan to prop up Afghanistan's new president, Hamid Karzai, who additionally required a retinue of U.S. taxpayer-financed bodyguards to protect him from his own people. The *San Diego Tribune* reported on December 12, 2002, "In November, the Afghan police killed two students who were part of a demonstration protesting the lack of electricity and running water in their dorms." The United Nations relief agency UNICEF reported in October 2001 that half of Afghani children were malnourished and a quarter died before the age of five.

Eric Margolis in the *Toronto Sun* on December 19, 2002, argued that Afghanistan was far from stable; that U.S. troops there were being fired upon almost daily; that our buddies in the Northern Alliance had revived opium, morphine, and heroin production; and that some of the dollars the United States was pouring into Afghanistan were going to bribe warlords.

In spite of these continual reports about problems in Afghanistan, glowing, self-congratulatory comments from the administration proclaiming Afghanistan a success went largely unchallenged. Rumsfeld, during one of those news conferences that had women likening him to a matinee idol, said our success in Afghanistan should be a blueprint for what we could do in Iraq: "Afghanistan is a model of what can happen if people are liberated and begin to try to elect their own people and people are allowed to vote who weren't allowed to vote and people are allowed to work who weren't allowed to work. It is a breathtaking accomplishment."

"Breathtaking accomplishment"? Does that apply to the war-lords, the al Qaeda cells that are reforming, the firing upon U.S. troops, and the drug dealing?

In December 2002, Barton Gellman wrote a *Washington Post* piece entitled, "In U.S., Terrorism's Peril Undiminished: Nation Struggles on Offense and Defense, and Officials Still Expect New Attacks." Kind of says it all, doesn't it? The key sentence in this article should have been a wake-up call about what our priorities *should* have been: "But there is nothing in al Qaeda's former arsenal—nothing it was capable of doing on Sept. 11, 2001—that the president's advisers are prepared to say is now beyond the enemy's reach."

Gellman went on report that we lost our best chances to kill our choicest targets during the first month of the Afghanistan war. Our troops were embroiled in disputes over rules of engagement and lines of command, which detracted from the mission itself.

If we're so interested in exporting our kind of government to the rest of the world, why not use that money to put them all on planes, fly them out of there, and have them settle in a sparsely populated state, like Wyoming, for example? If we can't bring democracy to the mountain, how about bringing the mountain to democracy? Better yet, why not strive to be the best example of democracy we can be, that "shining city on a hill" as Ronald Reagan imaged us. We can start by acknowledging that nation-building should begin at home.

America: "I Vant to Be Alone"

We were hell-bent to go into Iraq, and a case was made to promote that effort. Proponents of the war sometimes worked to prevent facts from getting in the way of the agenda. Most hypocritical was our claim that Iraq's UN violations could no longer be tolerated. But then we were willing to violate the UN ourselves to accomplish our goals! Our blatant disregard for what other countries think creates an image problem for the United States. While the go-it-alone cowboy image sounds romantic, it doesn't serve us well in the long run.

Besides not wanting any part of the Kyoto treaty that has been glob-
ally accepted, Bush 43 wanted no part of the START agreement to
reduce nuclear warheads because, he said, he and Russian president
Vladimir Putin had "a new relationship based on trust." After all,
after their first summit in Slovenia in June 2001, Bush 43 proclaimed
that Vladimir was someone in whom he could place his trust
because, "I looked into his eyes and saw his soul." That's all well and
good when you're dating or marrying your high school sweetheart,
but what if our next president and their next president are less *Love
Boat* and more *ElimiDate?* I'll take the Reaganesque maxim "trust
but verify" over this questionable approach any day.

America should not be the Greta Garbo of nations. It needs to
act as though it welcomes being a part of the international community. I bet if they did a survey they'd find that children who grew up
to be liberal scored well in the grammar school category "works well
with others." Rather than fight the UN, we should embrace it as a
true opportunity for dialogue with those who are not our allies.

Embracing true liberal values will move us toward a better world.
Just as in any personal relationship, our relationship with other
countries should be based on decency and mutual respect. Harry
Truman's 1949 inaugural speech could be a valuable blueprint for us
more than half a century later. Truman's four courses of action
involved support for the UN and related agencies, devotion to world
economic recovery by reducing barriers to world trade, collective
defense arrangements under the charter of the UN, and making our
scientific advances and industrial progress available for the growth
and improvement of underdeveloped nations. Generating goodwill
won't, by itself, guarantee a more secure America, but it's a start.

Bush 43's isolationism isn't limited to the way he shuns interaction across the sea; it also extends to the way he shuns interaction
across the aisle. We need domestic leadership that will tear down the
walls of partisanship in the interest of protecting our country.
Failure to do this has been one of the most egregious errors in "The
'War' on Terror." Congress approved $1.5 billion in antiterrorism

assistance to local police departments and emergency agencies for fiscal year 2003 and the administration sat on it for months. Money that should have gone to first responders: emergency teams, local police, fire departments, and emergency agencies was not distributed. The White House claimed that the holdup was because Congress hadn't acted on appropriations bills it wanted. In the meantime, local authorities were left without needed resources. In fact, just when the drive to protect our country was revving up, these agencies were facing budget cuts and layoffs.

Speaking at the Brookings Institution in late 2002, Democratic presidential hopeful John Edwards, the North Carolina senator, offered some positive steps America could take to be safer. He pointed out that many old buildings lack fire retardants; security at rail stations could be beefed up (hazardous materials are carried every day over our thirty-three thousand miles of track); food and water supplies could be better protected. Additionally, he noted that while chemical sensors were being installed in the Washington, D.C., subway system, other cities didn't have such systems and could be better guarded. According to the U.S. Customs Service, 5.7 million containers arrive on our shores each year, on 214,000 vessels. This is a lot for our Coast Guard to keep track of without financial assistance and advanced technology.

The real threat to America on September 11, 2001, was not a long-range missile, a nuclear weapon, or an organized government. And yet, our focus shifted to going after governments we didn't like because they might one day get weapons they shouldn't have. Two years later, many of us still don't feel safer flying; our homeland doesn't feel more secure, in spite of a Homeland Security Department; our ports and water systems remain vulnerable; and there are regular reports of U.S.-based sleeper cells. And no matter how many color-coded threat levels the Homeland Security Department comes up with to identify threat levels, we're a more anxious society.

We've seen that politics can get ugly when played against a backdrop of fear and how agendas don't always change just because the world does. It's time to take politics out of the equation, examine our priorities, and focus on actions that are going to protect our homeland. A warning issued by the Department of Homeland Security at the end of July 2003 stated that al Qaeda was interested in using the commercial aviation system to initiate more attacks and that terrorists would use common items carried by travelers as weapons. When we talk of the cost of war abroad, the sky is the limit. If we don't invest more in airport security, the result will be limited skies. Every bag left at curbside should be checked; everyday objects should be reassessed as possible weapons; personnel who have access to aircraft should be given complete background checks. I hope that one day the irony will be gone and we can unwrap the quotes around "The 'War' on Terror."

THREE

Uncivil Liberties: America's War on Americans

From: Gavin and Joanne
Sent: Tuesday, December 10, 2002 10:23 PM
To: colmes
Subject: better off

If all the liberals in the U.S. had been in the twin towers we would be better off ! ! ! ! ! ! ! ! ! ! ! ! ! . . .

I consider you and your kind My ENEMY! ! ! ! ! ! ! ! ! ! ! ! !

Gavin
Juniper, FL.

P.S. I dont get riled up or mad when the conservative talk show host speaks, just when you and Daschhole and the other Liberal's speak !

From: Colmes
Sent: Tuesday, December 10, 2002 10:43 PM
To: Gavin and Joanne
Subject: RE: better off

Let me get this straight . . . you wish I and every liberal in America were dead, killed by terrorists, right?

From: Gavin and Joanne
Sent: Thursday, December 12, 2002 9:31 PM
To: Colmes
Subject: RE: better off

Yes it would not hurt my feelings.

Gavin
Juniper, FL

Be careful, Gavin. There might be liberals in your own family you don't know about. Of course, they're not going to come out to *you*. Can you imagine *that* dinner table conversation?

SON: Dad, Mom, there's something I feel I must tell you.

DAD: What!

SON: I don't quite know how to say this; and I hope it doesn't make you love me any less. For a long time now I've had these feelings, and I know you won't think they're normal, but this is what I am. Dad, I'm liberal.

MOM: (breaks into uncontrollable tears)

DAD: I never thought I'd ever see this day when my own son, my own flesh and blood, would tell me he's a lib. You can pack your bags and go live with one of your liberal friends. I don't want anyone else in the family around this.

MOM: (still sobbing) Where did I go wrong?

"The 'War' on Terror" became a new backdrop for a left-right debate that has been raging in America for some time. The September 11 atrocity ratcheted up the hostility of an increasingly aggressive right wing in vilifying liberals as un-American. Now, they had a "war" they could use to underscore their own patriotism while impugning the patriotism of their political adversaries, as though there were a left-right patriotic tug-of-war based on a zero-sum game. Bush 43 used the "war" as an argument not only for consolidating power in the executive branch, but also for grabbing more presidential powers. As John Ashcroft used his more-than-bully pulpit to argue for changes that seemed extraconstitutional, the power grab ultimately became a war on our criminal justice system and our civil liberties. "The 'War' on Terror" also provided our president with a vehicle to buttress his penchant for secrecy. Secrecy is not quite the spirit I believe our forefathers had in mind.

Sadly, "The 'War' on Terror" fed another, already-raging war, an American war . . . against America.

POP QUIZ: The knee-jerk right-wing reaction to the atrocities of September 11, 2001, was to:

(a) Get angry at the terrorists and band together as Americans to go after those who would do us harm.

(b) Blame the liberals.

If you answered (b) then you have a good memory.

From: R.W.
Sent: Tuesday, October 01, 2002 9:33 PM
To: colmes
Subject: democtrats

colmes
It's dumb ass liberal democrats like you . . . that brought 9-11-01
up on us!! You liberal bastards ought to move to iraq, then ya all
can feel at home!! You bastards would never fight for the United
States of America!!

R.W.
Lexington, KY

Right, R.W. No liberal ever served or gave his or her life for this
country. Tell that to U.S. senators Max Cleland, Bob Kerrey, and
John Kerry. Come to think of it, the last time I was at the Vietnam
War Memorial in Washington I noticed that every name had an (R)
after it.

Conservatives love to brag about how *they* are the true guardians
of our freedoms and the real warriors against totalitarianism. Let's
have a look at the political scale:

LEFT   RIGHT
Communism Socialism Liberalism Conservatism Fascism Totalitarianism

Hmm . . . which American ideology is closer to the form of government offered by the evil dictators we all detest? I'll give you a
hint . . . the word "right" doesn't always mean "correct."

I wish I could convince those who hate the guts of liberals in general and me in particular that we care very deeply about this country,
that we share the same goals of liberty, freedom, and justice for all,

and that although we prefer different policies for the country, our visions aren't all that different. Those who have raised significant questions about the government's handling of "The 'War' on Terror" have been shouted down by loud voices on the right, conservatives who feel they need to protect us from self-criticism.

Americans who've said we need to look at our own history in order to understand September 11 have been all but silenced by loud cheerleaders for the status quo. MIT Professor Noam Chomsky is considered an authority on global politics and gets far more media attention outside of the United States than he does in his own country. That's because his critical views of America are extremely controversial. In his book *9-11*, he writes, "We should not forget that the U.S. itself is a leading terrorist state." He lists places where our actions have caused undue destruction: Vietnam, Laos, Cambodia, Nicaragua, El Salvador, Guatemala, East Timor, Sudan, Iraq, Yugoslavia, and Afghanistan. Should we ignore this in discussing those who would do us harm?

And if we swing over to the other side of the political spectrum, it was conservative Patrick J. Buchanan who titled his book *A Republic, Not an Empire*. Let history be our guide to remembering the disastrous results that happen to empires that use war to spread their philosophies to foreign lands, exporting their version of culture and government because they believe they know what's best.

The refusal on the part of hawks to examine our own consciences goes against the very Christian teachings they often profess to believe. New York's Cardinal Edward Egan has said, "we have to examine our consciences," and that doing so "is one of the things you do in the pursuit of holiness. You say: 'What have I been doing wrong?' even in times when there's not a tragedy, but how do we account for what has happened?" At a press conference in Rome on October 1, 2001, with the pope in attendance, Egan said, "words like vengeance, retaliation and so forth are not the words of civilized people." This would mean Americans and, of course, Christians.

Vietnam Redux

Sadly, government secrecy has not been limited to recent times. I mentioned in the opening of this book how I opposed the Vietnam War because, among other reasons, I felt the government lied to us about the necessity for such a war. Seeing "The 'War' on Terror" so focused on Iraq reminds me of the famous quote of philosopher George Santayana: "Those who do not remember the past are condemned to repeat it." This has never been so apropos.

This point was driven home to me when Daniel Ellsberg agreed to appear on *Hannity & Colmes*. In 1971, Ellsberg risked his job, his career, and his freedom by giving a historical study of the Vietnam War known as the "Pentagon Papers" to the *New York Times*. This former marine, Vietnam veteran, and staunch anti-Communist, decided he could no longer withstand the lies of the government, which was heralding the success of a war that was, at the time, killing American youth by the thousands. He came on *Hannity & Colmes* to discuss his book, *Secrets*, which came out just in time to point out the sickening parallels between the lies we were told in the '70s to promote an illicit war and the ones being promulgated about Iraq. Ellsberg revealed how during this period his phones were tapped, thugs were recruited to break his legs, and the presiding judge in his case was looking for political favoritism to become head of the FBI. G. Gordon Liddy and E. Howard Hunt, of Watergate infamy, masterminded a break-in to his psychiatrist's office to try to get some damning information on him. And the party that accuses the Democrats of playing the "politics of personal destruction" is seen scheming to destroy Ellsberg for being the country's most prominent and effective whistle-blower. *Secrets* also reprints a chilling conversation among President Richard Nixon, National Security Advisor Henry Kissinger, and Attorney General John Mitchell:

NIXON: Let's get the son of a bitch.

KISSINGER: We've got to get him.

NIXON: . . . Don't worry about his trial . . . try him in the press . . . We want to destroy him in the press . . . Is that clear?

KISSINGER AND (ATTORNEY GENERAL) JOHN MITCHELL: Yes.

Boy, those Nixon tapes! More pornographic than anything the Messe Commission on Pornography ever had to listen to.

As for the parallels between Ellsberg's time and now, the issue of secrecy rarely serves an administration well. On November 1, 2001, Bush 43 signed Executive Order 13233, part of a post-9/11 executive branch power grab. This order allows a president to prevent a previous president's papers from becoming public, even if that previous president has provided for such publication. It just so happens that sixty-eight thousand pages of former presidents' records were to be released under the Presidential Records Act in January 2002, just two months after the order was signed stopping the release. In the interest of disclosure, the Public Citizen group filed suit, and when it did, the Reagan Presidential Library suddenly released eight thousand pages. As Public Citizen Litigation Group attorney Scott Nelson said, "It looks as if they're nervous about whether the executive order will hold up in court and are trying to avoid the issue by not claiming executive privilege."

Information is power, and by controlling the flow of information available about the doings of former presidents, Bush 43 was grabbing executive branch power. And by setting a precedent about what could or could not be revealed about former presidents, he was trying to control what could eventually be withheld about his days holding the reins.

By the way, I wonder which previous president Bush 43 was looking to protect. Someone with a similar name, maybe? And while we're at it, Bush 43 sent his gubernatorial papers to his father's library rather than to the archives at Texas A&M where they were slated to go; this way, they would be on federal, rather than state, property, and not subject to Texas's more open freedom of information laws. It turns out that Texas attorney general John Cornyn ruled these papers would be subject to the state laws anyway.

A penchant for secrecy is not inconsistent with executive branch politics, but the Bush 43 administration has taken it to new heights. The media made much of Bill Clinton's attempt to claim executive privilege when he didn't want his aides to testify before Congress in the Monica Lewinsky case. When Dick Cheney invoked executive privilege with regard to his meeting with Enron officials, I didn't hear a peep out of those who had been furious with Clinton for trying to keep his counsel private. I guess it's more fun knowing about a president's sex life than which officials a vice president meets with to help determine policy.

Unlike Clinton, Cheney was not the president (contrary to what many may have thought). And the people to whom he spoke were not advisers or cabinet members; they were corporate people outside of government. Bill Clinton wanted to keep personal conversations about a personal relationship—having nothing to do with running the country—personal. Dick Cheney wanted to keep secret conversations with big donors that helped to steer policies that affected every American. But the supposed "liberal media" only made a big deal about it when Clinton invoked executive privilege.

When the General Accounting Office, the investigative arm of Congress, sued to get access to information about Cheney's secret meeting with energy lobbyists, Judge John D. Bates of Federal District Court ruled for Cheney that no injury was caused to the GAO by keeping the information private. But don't the American people have a right to know with whom its elected officials meet to create policy? And if those officials are campaign contributors, isn't that a significant factor in policy creation?

Adam Clymer had a featured piece in the *New York Times* on January 3, 2003, about the lack of government openness in the Bush 43 administration. You remember Adam Clymer. This is the man to whom then candidate Bush referred as a "major league" orifice at a Labor Day event in Illinois in 2000. That's when Cheney earned the nickname, "Big Time." In the twelve months ending on September 30, 2001, Clymer points out, 18 percent more documents were classified than in the previous year, and three new agencies—the Environmental Protection Agency, the Department of Agriculture, and the Department of Health and Human Services—were given permission to classify documents as "secret."

A tour of the subterranean landscape wouldn't be complete without a look at the Carlyle Group. This relatively privately held organization manages billions of dollars in assets, with huge investments in defense companies that do business with the government. Reagan's defense secretary, Frank Carlucci, former secretary of state James Baker, and former president George Bush 41 all advise Carlyle. The former president gives speeches around the globe on their behalf. Other investors have included a family named bin Laden. Heavy defense spending is good for business. When the March 5, 2001, *New York Times* featured Bush 41 on its front page posing next to next to Saudi King Fahd on a Carlyle-sponsored trip, Charles Lewis, executive director of the Center for Public Integrity, was quoted saying, "George Bush is getting money from private interests that have business before the government, while his son is president. And, in a really peculiar way, George W. Bush could, some day, benefit financially from his own administration's decisions, through his father's investments. The average American doesn't know that. To me, that's a jaw-dropper." Lewis and his Center for Public Integrity are equally scathing to Democrats who fall off the ethics wagon, and his conclusions aren't tainted by partisanship. The Carlyle connection has been underreported. It's a shame that the complexity of these interconnected relationships make our eyes glaze over. The sting of potential for duplicity should pry them wide open.

Should War Diminish Justice?

If a tree falls in a forest and no one is around, does it matter whether it is felled illegally? It should. As signatories to the Geneva Convention of 1949 and the Hague Convention of 1907, we pledge to abide by certain humanitarian principles. In spite of our claims to be a country that has a high moral imperative, we too often seek revenge over justice. This has especially been true since September 11, 2001.

Seymour Hersh had a stunning piece in the December 23, 2002, issue of the *New Yorker* called "The Bush Administration's New Strategy in the War on Terrorism." It addressed the U.S. policy of denying judicial recourse to individuals we believe to be terrorists. Hersh asked Rummy's office about a secret directive issued on July 22, 2002, that detailed how to approach alleged terrorists. The directive said, in part, "The objective is to capture terrorists for interrogation or, if necessary, to kill them, not simply to arrest them in a law-enforcement exercise." Hersh was pointed toward a December 3 press briefing during which the defense secretary was asked about the use of the Predator reconnaissance plane "to assassinate or to kill an Al Qaeda." Rumsfeld replied by saying, "They are not trained to do the word you used [assassinate] which I won't even repeat. That is not what they're trained to do. They are trained to serve the country and to contribute to peace and stability in the world."

But Qaed Salim Sinan al-Harethi, an al Qaeda leader, had been driven with five other men to a remote desert area in Yemen where they were fired upon by a Predator, leaving all the men dead. Even when it was possible to find suspected al Qaeda members and bring them to justice, the United States had a secret policy to have them murdered far away from the prying eyes of civilization. The United States, presenting itself to the world as a beacon of morality, was nonetheless practicing selective assassination, contrary to our country's stated policy. Hersh quoted a former top-level intelligence officer, "They want to turn these guys into assassins. They want to go on rumors—not facts—and go for political effect, and that's what the Special Forces Command is really afraid of. Rummy is saying that politics is bigger than war, and we need to take guys out for political effect: 'You have to kill Goebbels to get to Hitler'."

Essentially, "The 'War' on Terror" became a pretext for war on the American criminal justice system. Detainees were held without being charged with offenses and denied access to attorneys, and the Bush 43 administration invented a system of "justice" never before seen in this country. On November 14, 2001, the *Washington Post* offered these chilling words about self-declared presidential powers: "President Bush declared an 'extraordinary emergency' yesterday that empowers him to order military trials for suspected international terrorists and their collaborators, bypassing the American criminal justice system, its rules of evidence and its constitutional guarantees."

Similarly chilling, and eerily consistent, was Attorney General Ashcroft's statement before the Senate Judiciary Committee on December 6, 2001, which he directed to critics of the Justice Department's handling of "The 'War' on Terror": ". . . to those who scare peace-loving people with phantoms of lost liberty, my message is this: Your tactics only aid terrorists, for they erode our national unity and diminish our resolve."

Did John Ashcroft forget a seminal statement of one of our founding fathers? As Ben Franklin said to the Pennsylvania state legislature in 1755, "They that can give up essential liberty to purchase a little temporary safety, deserve neither liberty nor safety."

In one area, however, Ashcroft was a staunch defender of rights: gun rights. At that same December 6 Senate Judiciary hearing, Ashcroft stated that gun data from the National Instant Criminal Background Check System could not be shared with the FBI and other agencies looking into terrorism. "I don't want to hear two messages from this committee . . . that you want me to enforce some laws and not other laws . . . or respect some rights and not other rights," Ashcroft declared. What happened to that "extraordinary emergency" declared less than a month earlier? Suddenly, here was Ashcroft talking about "rights." Senator John McCain, not exactly an NRA enemy, came out in favor of eliminating this loophole, and said that as this stood, "suspected terrorists were able to acquire guns, hide their immigrant status, and shield their criminal records."

But thanks to the powerful NRA lobby, gun shows remain open territory for anyone wanting a nice, warm gun.

For many conservatives, gun rights clearly trump gay rights in fighting "The 'War' on Terror." In this fight, if you have special skills you're an asset to your country. Unless you're gay. In November of 2002, right after the Republicans ensured their hold on all branches of government, nine army linguists were dismissed for the offense of being gay. Six of these language experts were Arabic experts. Bear in mind that we had and have a critical shortage of personnel fluent in Arabic. On November 15, 2002, the *Associated Press* said: " 'We face a drastic shortage of linguists, and the direct impact of Arabic speakers is a particular problem,' said Donald R. Hamilton, who documented the need for more linguists in a report to Congress as part of the National Commission on Terrorism." And *USA Today* reported shortly after the 2001 World Trade Center attacks how the 1993 attacks there might have been prevented: "In 1993, after the first World Trade Center bombing, the FBI learned that it had evidence of the plot before the attack but that the vital documents had never been translated from Arabic."

So let me get this straight (no pun intended). You have a unique specialty that few others possess and your area of expertise can help us fight "The 'War' on Terror." However, because the government doesn't like your choice of sleeping partner(s), this great, inclusive country will refuse your services.

"Sorry, Mr. Michelangelo, we'd love to hang that beautiful piece of art in the Sistine Chapel, but we can't because you're gay." Margaret Mead did some wonderful work in Samoa, but sorry, Maggie, your groundbreaking anthropological finds are meaningless. You're a lesbian. And tell Will Shakespeare that we'd love to put his play on at the next meeting of the Garden Club, but his lifestyle was, well, you know a little "different." And while we're at it, let's go through those names on the wall at the Vietnam Memorial in Washington. Let's make sure that none of those names was ever sexually linked with another name of the same gender.

According to the administration, other rights are similarly fungible in arbitrary ways. Jose Padilla, a onetime Chicago street thug, was arrested in May 2002 for allegedly hatching a plot to set off radioactive bombs. He was labeled an "enemy combatant," which, under the Bush/Ashcroft justice system, entitled him to sit indefinitely in a military brig with no charges cited against him and no access to counsel. From the term "enemy combatant" you wouldn't know that Padilla was actually an American citizen. I wonder if the American public would have been more outraged about this if, instead of "Jose Padilla," his name had been "Bucky Smith." Defenders of this egregious misreading of the Constitution cite a 1942 move by FDR who, they claim, applied similar standards of justice; but those actions were taken against German saboteurs who arrived here by submarine after war had already been declared against Germany. Not quite the same thing. And FDR gave them a speedy trial, something the Bush 43 administration did not intend to give Padilla.

The injustice of Jose Padilla's plight was underscored by Judge Jack Coughenour. "Mr. Padilla is an American citizen," Coughenour said. "He is before a military tribunal. This is unprecedented." Coughenour, by the way, is a U.S. district judge in Seattle who owes his job to Ronald Reagan, lest you think he's some wild-eyed liberal appointee.

Here we have another example of an executive branch power grab: our president said he would decide which defendants would be tried by military tribunals, while our secretary of defense would appoint panels and sets rules and procedures with no judicial review. There is a little problem here called the United States Constitution. We're *supposed* to have a separation of powers that does not imbue the executive branch with totalitarian control.

If the Padilla case is any guide, we risk having an executive branch that interprets rulings and laws as it sees fit, without regard to the constitutional rights of American citizens. On January 8, 2003, a three-judge panel from the Fourth U.S. Circuit Court of Appeals in Richmond, Virginia, agreed, in an unprecedented decision, that our government has the right to detain U.S. citizens indefinitely if they participate in foreign battles or if they take part in terrorist activity against U.S. interests. But this ruling did not include actions that take place on U.S. soil. This means our own citizens have more to fear from our own government if they're outside the United States. This was the case of Yasar Esam Hamdi, twenty-two-year-old native of Louisiana, who was arrested in Afghanistan in November 2001, accused of fighting with the Taliban and al Qaeda. Last I heard, the American justice system exists to protect all Americans, regardless of where they are in the world. Jose Padilla was also accused of conspiring with al Qaeda, but he was arrested at O'Hare Airport in Chicago, not in the wilds of Afghanistan. Both Padilla and Hamdi are American citizens and, as such, should be subject to the American system of justice or declared prisoners of war, in which case they'd be covered by the Geneva Convention.

The Geneva Convention gives protections to those in custody such as the right to choose their own lawyers, protections the Bush 43 administration has allowed the attorney general the right to remove. The Convention also guaranteed the right to trials in independent courts not subject to the whims of a president and the right to appeal unanimous verdicts. Conservatives love to cite "the rule of law." But how about applying it consistently?

Amazingly, even military justice is less severe than what this administration wanted to do. According to military law, defendants have a right to review cases against them, death sentences have to be unanimous, and they can file appeals to higher military courts and the Supreme Court.

Even Nazi murderers were given a trial at Nuremberg because of a bold decision by President Harry Truman: "Undiscriminating executions or punishments," he said, "without definite findings of guilt fairly arrived at, would not fit easily on the American conscience or be remembered by our children with pride."

In California, immigrants from Iran and other Middle Eastern countries were asked to register with the state by December 16, 2002, and some of those who came forward were detained and mistreated. On December 19, the *Los Angeles Times* told of hundreds of detainees who had been living, working, and paying taxes in America who were handcuffed, hosed down with cold water, and forced to sleep on concrete floors. They were denied access to community lawyers who wanted to help them. Men with no known criminal history were shackled and kept in freezing conditions. The INS refused to make the number of arrests public. In fact, it was the INS that was responsible for many of these immigrants not having their paperwork in order because of that agency's inability to process applications in a timely manner. If it had been Americans abroad who'd been treated this way, you'd hope the State Department would use strong measures to protect them. But these citizens of other countries, motivated to begin life anew in a strange land, must have wondered what it was they had bargained for.

Constitutional rights, it should be noted, apply not only to "citizens" but to "persons." This shows that the humanity of our forefathers was not limited to only Americans.

The Patriot Act was another illicit exercise in toying with our rights. Nat Hentoff, one of the leading beacon-carriers for our civil liberties, wrote in the *Washington Times* about this heinous piece of legislation:

> With a warrant, FBI agents may now enter homes and offices of citizens and noncitizens when they're not there. The agents may look around, examine what's on a computer's hard drive and take other records of interest to them. These surreptitious visits are not limited to investigations of terrorism, but can also be used in regular criminal investigations. . . . While in the office or home, the FBI can plant a "Magic Lantern" in your computer. It's also called the "sniffer keystroke logger." The device creates a record of every time you press a key on the computer.

In a six-month period that ended July 15, 2003, an internal Justice Department report said that the inspector general's office had received thirty-four credible complaints of civil rights and civil liberties violations by department employees, directly related to enforcement of the Patriot Act. These accusations ranged from verbal abuse of immigrants to allegations that Muslims and Arabs in federal detention centers had been beaten. Among the substantiated charges were those against a prison doctor who, as the *New York Times* reported on July 21, 2003, told an inmate he was examining that "if I was in charge, I would execute every one of you" because of "the crimes you all did."

And from the friendly folks who brought you the Patriot Act comes the Patriot Act II. They've yet to snooker us into this one that would, among other things, set up a national DNA database and give the attorney general the power to strip citizenship from individuals who are members of groups the government doesn't like.

One big government initiative, as in sync for a freedom-loving nation as David Duke at a Kwanzaa celebration (and thankfully, it disappeared as fast as he would, were he ever to find himself in such a situation), is the TIPS Program. TIPS stands for the "Terrorism Information and Prevention System." What it *should* stand for is "Tattletales In Private Spying." This was a program whereby the government was going to recruit approximately one in twenty-four citizens to spy on fellow citizens. If the cable guy saw a magazine on your coffee table he didn't like, he would report it to the government. Okay, maybe the cable guy isn't such a threat, since he rarely shows up. But let's say your mail carrier had been recruited for this program and noticed you were getting mailings in what she thought were suspicious brown wrappers. In the name of "national security" she might think she was doing her patriotic duty by turning you in to the "authorities."

And from the people who brought us TIPS came the "Information Awareness Office." Doesn't this sound like a section of the Politburo? Did you even know that your supposedly "conservative" government, with your taxpayer dollars, was considering funding an

"Information Awareness Project"? The plan was to gather information about your personal life and make it available to the federal government, a conservative one that claims it wants government out of our lives.

In his important November 14, 2002, column in the *New York Times*, titled "You Are a Suspect," William Safire had this to say about yet another Republican movement toward bigger, more intrusive government:

> Every purchase you make with a credit card, every magazine subscription you buy and medical prescription you fill, every Web site you visit and e-mail you send or receive, every academic grade you receive, every bank deposit you make, every trip you book and every event you attend—all these transactions and communications will go into what the Defense Department describes as "a virtual, centralized grand database."

Irony of ironies, the head of the Information Awareness Office was John Poindexter, the man who helped bring us Iran-Contra, whose idea it was to secretly sell arms to Iran to free American hostages and give the proceeds to the Contras in Nicaragua, and who thought it wise not to tell the person who was elected to make such decisions. Yes, the very same John Poindexter who lied to the United States Congress that barred aid to the Contras, and who defended his actions by saying he "made a very deliberate decision not to ask the president so that I could insulate him from the decision and provide some future deniability if it ever leaked out." Poindexter ignominiously resigned from the Bush 43 administration when it was revealed that he had planned an online futures market where wagers could be made on when terrorist attacks were likely to happen. Why did this man have a position of responsibility in the first place? Maybe, in government, no punishable deed goes unrewarded.

Is This What Our Forefathers Had in Mind?

If we're fighting for the values embodied in our Constitution, why throw them away? Why should we become more like the people we're fighting? As a country that considers itself a beacon of freedom, we should be judged by how we treat civil liberties when it's difficult to uphold them, not when it's easy to do so. My good friend and Fox News colleague, the brilliant Judge Andrew Napolitano, put it beautifully in his October 15, 2001, article, "Don't Tread on Freedom," in the *New Jersey Law Journal*: "Without due process, of which probable cause is one step, the government becomes a monster: Whom will it incarcerate or deport? Mexican busboys who look like Arabs, Middle Eastern chemical engineering students who don't wear American flags, political radicals who hate all war?" He went on to pose some crucial questions: "What is the value of security if the freedoms within it are subject to the government's unchecked will? What freedoms are we defending if, in the name of freedom, the government can take them away because of a person's appearance or nationality? Who will decide—and under what standards—whose freedom stays and whose freedom goes?"

One night, after I expressed similar sentiments on *Hannity & Colmes*, here's what was in my e-mail inbox:

From: bigdog
Sent: Monday, January 21, 2002 9:49PM
To: colmes
Subject: YOU NEED

YOU NEED A TRAGEDY TO HAPPEN TO YOUR FAMILY LIKE THE 4,000 IN NEW YORK BEFORE YOU CAN EVER SEE THE LIGHT SORRY TO SAY.

P.S. IN CASE YOU ALREADY FORGOT THE 4,000 AMERICANS DIED BY TERRORISTS THAT YOU WOULD SAY HAD MORE RIGHTS THAN THE INNOCENT VICTIMS.

From: colmes
Sent: Monday, January 21, 2002 10:05 PM
To: bigdog
Subject: RE: YOU NEED

Thank you for wishing a tragedy on my family. You're a true American.

Since, if you had your way, bigdog, I would already be dead by the time you read this, I'll let Judge Napolitano respond on my behalf: "In a democracy, personal liberties are rarely diminished overnight. Rather, they are lost gradually, by the acts of well-meaning people, with good intentions, amid public approval. But the subtle loss of freedom is never recognized until the crisis is over and we look back in horror. And then it is too late."

From: Dave P.
Sent: Friday, November 15, 2002 2:03 PM
To: colmes
Subject: RE: Homeland Security measures

I have no problem with the government looking into any aspect of my life. I have nothing to hide. Believe me, if you live a lawful, honorable lifestyle, you have nothing to worry about . . . Only those with something to hide holler about ABSOLUTE privacy. What are you afraid of? I would be looking very hard at you and yours.

Sincerely,
Dave P
Denver, CO

Some conservatives claim that we shouldn't be concerned if we truly have nothing to hide. This argument, which I've heard often from non–civil libertarians, goes against the grain of our Bill of

Rights. Our forefathers were prescient enough to realize that we American citizens should always be protected from an overreaching government, and they made such protections a bedrock of our Constitution. How many times must one endure a 3 a.m. knock on the door from a governmental "authority" lacking a search warrant before realizing that our lives should not be open to government inspection on demand?

Unfortunately, we have a government that shrouds its own actions in secrecy while caring less about privacy rights for its citizens. It restricts the availability of presidential records that would inform us about its past actions, while invoking executive privilege to curtail our ability to know its present ones. Just as our government tries to ensure that we know less about them, it is constantly seeking ways to know more about us. And good Americans who cry out for self-examination are vilified by the louder voices of those who try to shame them into silence.

But *not* to speak up would mean not to exercise our American rights. A German pastor, the Reverend Martin Niemoller, crystallized this concept in 1945 in a now-famous passage:

> In Germany they first came for the Communists, and I didn't speak up because I wasn't a Communist. Then they came for the Jews, and I didn't speak up because I wasn't a Jew. Then they came for the trade unionists, and I didn't speak up because I wasn't a trade unionist. Then they came for the Catholics, and I didn't speak up because I was a Protestant. Then they came for me, and by that time there was nobody left to speak up.

FOUR

The Myth of the Liberal Media

Any dictator would admire the uniformity and
obedience of the [U.S.] media.

—NOAM CHOMSKY

The media is conservative. Not liberal. Conservatives have said
the phrase "liberal media" so often, they've convinced people
that the media has a liberal bent. They're wrong, although it's a useful technique to repeat something so often that it becomes part of
the zeitgeist. Worked beautifully for Joseph Goebbels, Hitler's information minister. Consider who owns the media: is it a bunch of rav-
ing lefties? Or is it a bunch of corporations more concerned with
corporate welfare than national health care? In a January 2002 piece
in the liberal magazine *The Nation*, Mark Crispan Miller wrote that
in 1996 "the national TV news appeared to be a tidy tetrarchy: two
network news divisions owned by large appliance makers/weapons
manufacturers (CBS by Westinghouse, NBC by General Electric),
and the other two bought lately by the nation's top purveyors of Big
Fun (ABC by Disney, CNN by Time Warner)."

Miller went on to chronicle the rise of Fox News and the unsuccessful attempts by other channels to clone what Fox has accomplished. On what basis do conservatives rant and rave about the liberal bias of the three network nightly newscasts? You'd think, listening to them, that it's the "NBC Liberal News" or ABC's "Liberal News Tonight." Is it the way Peter Jennings raises his eyebrow that proves his leanings?

The fact is, conservatives try to preserve the status quo, and liberals are more comfortable with progress. When news reporting tells us that things are not staying the same, this disturbs the conversative sense of stasis. Conservatives love to pine about the way things used to be. Liberals love to dream about the way things *can* be.

Listening to the right, you'd think they have only a small piece of the media pie, the piece the liberals don't want; you'd believe that only liberals (the ones who supposedly control the media) lie; you'd discount any piece of information believed to come from what is perceived as a "liberal source," and you'd believe that their side is far more victimized by the press than liberals are. But a look at talk radio, talk television, syndicated columnists, and the national best-seller lists would indicate a very different picture from the ones conservatives portray. Even if you believe that liberals did control the media until conservatives staked their claim, you have to consider what Stanley Kurtz says in the January 11, 2002, *National Review Online*, when he writes of the left, "its stranglehold on the cultural life of the country now appears to have been definitively broken. The Internet and cable are at last enabling conservatives to do an end run around the media elite. The system will never be the same."

Conservatives have done a wonderful job of using the media for positioning purposes by playing the aggrieved group that is victimized by the "liberal press." But it was Jeff Gerth in the purportedly "liberal" *New York Times* that broke the Whitewater scandal on March 8, 1992, and it was the supposedly "liberal" *Washington Post* that, on March 14, 1992, first questioned the relationship between the Rose Law firm that employed Hillary Clinton, and the State of Arkansas, whose governor was Bill Clinton.

Conservatives know they're just positioning when they use the phrase "liberal media." William Kristol, editor of the *Weekly Standard* and former chief of staff to Vice President Dan Quayle, famously said, "I admit it: the liberal media were never that powerful, and the whole thing was often used as an excuse by conservatives for conservative failures." And Pat Buchanan, during his 1996 run for president, acknowledged: "The truth is, I've gotten fairer, more comprehensive coverage of my ideas than I ever imagined I would receive. I've gotten balanced coverage and broad coverage—all we could have asked. For heaven sakes, we kid about the liberal media, but every Republican on earth does that."

When a liberal does appear on prime-time television, it doesn't sit well with some people:

From: Veronica101
Sent: Wednesday, June 26, 2002 9:31 PM
To: colmes
Subject: YOU MAKE MY HEAD EXPLODE! ! ! ! ! !

TONIGHT I HAD TO LEAVE THE ROOM. (USUALLY I JUST WANT TO RIP OUT THAT EYEBROW) YOU ARE THE DEVIL, WHY DON'T YOU JUST GET A JOB WITH THE A.C.L.U.? BETTER YET- WHY DON'T YOU JUST GO TO A SOCIALIST FREAKIN COUNTRY? I REALLY WANT TO PROJECTILE VOMIT, YOU SUCUBUS.

SINCERELY.
Veronica101
Anniston, AL

From: colmes
Sent: Wednesday, June 27, 2002 8:02 AM
To: Veronica101
Subject: RE: YOU MAKE MY HEAD EXPLODE

Thanks for the kind e-mail.
I love you, too.

Alan

Mouth versus Ear

Certain media platforms lean right and others lean left. Control and ownership leans right, even if many journalists in newsrooms tend to be on the left. The real question is whether those making editorial decisions do so on the basis of their own personal biases. How a particular media brand is perceived depends, to large extent, on where the perceiver is coming from ideologically. The great radio personality Dick Summer used to play "Mouth versus Ear" on his show. This most entertaining feature proved that what is said is often not what is heard.

When conservatives refer to "the liberal media," what they're really saying is, "Everything this media outlet says is a lie." To them, the word *liberal* might as well not contain the "b", "r", "a", or "l." Here are some other buzzwords and phrases:

When a Liberal Says	What the Conservative Hears
Democrat	Communist
Liberal	Anti-American
Left Wing	Wants to overthrow the country
Homosexual	Pedophile
Rockefeller Republican	See "Democrat"
Environmentalist	Tree-hugger
Pro-Choice	Baby killer
Union member	Socialist
Antiwar	Traitor
Liberal publication	Lying Communist rag

Conservatives have been very good at playing the poor little, ignored souls, hardly able to get their message out in the "mainstream media." How is it, then, that all branches of government are now conservative? Is it because conservatives aren't being heard? It may be true that at one time conservatives were marginalized and their views not well represented, but now they *are* the mainstream media, and their strong voices are being heard, as evidenced by the rightward swing of the federal government over the last decade or so. Truth is, they've played the media as skillfully as Yehudi Menuhin plays the violin.

Breaking It Down

The media world today consists of talk radio, cable television, and the more traditional news sources like newspapers, magazines, and the broadcast television network. E. J. Dionne nicely laid this out in the *Washington Post* in his December 6, 2002, column: "Two of these three major institutions tilt well to the right, and the third is under constant pressure to avoid even the pale hint of liberalism," wrote Dionne. And Dionne was correct to point out that the media has shown "a preference for the values of the educated, professional class—which, surprise, surprise, is roughly the class position of most journalists." And, so, the media has slanted left socially and culturally, but right economically, cheerleading free trade and balanced budgets—not exactly the underpinnings of Marxism.

Maybe many of those who work in newsrooms *are* liberal. And maybe it's for the same reason teachers tend to be liberal: they're educated. Conservatives love to whine about how Tim Russert once worked for a Democrat, Senator Pat Moynihan. But can they honestly claim that he shows bias one way or the other on *Meet the Press?* And why aren't the liberals bellyaching about Diane Sawyer because she used to work for Richard Nixon? That's right, you don't have an answer. That's because liberals don't complain about Diane Sawyer. They support people having jobs, even if those jobs are for Republicans.

Conservatives love to cite the fact that liberals in newsrooms out-number conservatives in newsrooms, as proof of media bias. But all those liberals running around newsrooms don't make the *Wall Street Journal*, the *New York Post*, or the *Washington Times* liberal newspapers. That's because all those horrible liberals on the loose in news-rooms don't set the newspapers' policies. It's usually a newspaper's executives who decide what editorial positions to take on key issues.

Just before the 2000 election, the industry's trade publication, *Editor and Publisher* magazine, found a strong pro-Bush bias in its sur-vey of two hundred editors and publishers. In its November 6, 2000, issue, *E&P* reported "the survey revealed that the nation's newspapers have endorsed Bush over Gore by a better than 2–1 margin." *E&P*'s partner, the TechnoMetrica Institute of Policy and Politics, which con-ducted the poll, added: "The *Editor & Publisher/* TIPP poll also asked who the editors and publishers plan to vote for themselves next week. In another surprise, those willing to reveal their vote named Bush by a 2–1 margin. Publishers will vote for Bush at a 3–1 ratio, with editors favoring the Texas Governor by a narrow margin."

Henry Waxman, the Democratic congressman from California, claimed that on election night 2000, the chief executive of General Electric, NBC's parent company, showed his political bias in full view of his news organization. Waxman alleged that Jack Welch came into the newsroom that night and asked the man running the show, Sheldon Gawiser, "how much would I have to pay you to call the race for Bush?" Although it was said in jest, NBC had an interesting response to the charge. The network's spokesperson, Cory Shields, issued a statement saying, "Congressman Waxman comes up with the shocking revelation that Jack Welch was interested in the results of what was perhaps the most riveting night in the history of presiden-tial elections and that he supported George W. Bush. Not exactly a news flash." So NBC basically admitted it happened. But can you imagine what would have resulted if a network chief went into the newsroom and revealed how much he wanted Gore to win? Do you think conservatives would have stayed quiet about it? I think not.

Talking Right

Conservatives do better in the talk media. Talk radio has become a conservative bastion. Opinion shows almost always favor the conservative. That's because they often see things in black and white, and that is more palatable to a mass audience. Further, many conservatives are great moralists who like to tell others how to live (as long as they don't have to live by those rules themselves). Some of the conservatives who spent the '90s trying to run Bill Clinton out of office, such as former Louisiana congressman Bob Livingston, have had their own personal misdeeds exposed. How is it we heard so much about the Clinton scandal? Could it be because stories about it appeared day after day, month after month, year after year in the "liberal media"?

Radio programmers, with a few exceptions, don't particularly like to take chances. There's an old show-biz joke that your career goes like this: "Who is Alan Colmes?" followed by "Get me Alan Colmes." Then Alan Colmes becomes so successful that you can't get him (reminder: this is only a joke), so it's "Get me someone like Alan Colmes." And the last phase is, once again, "Who is Alan Colmes?" For years, the talk radio industry has been in the "Get me someone like Rush Limbaugh" phase. When I was nationally syndicated during the '90s, the program director of one of my stations told me that my show was tremendously entertaining, was doing well, and was personally one of his favorites, and that he was canceling my show, but would have kept it on his station if only I were a conservative.

What this (now former, I hope) program director didn't seem to get was that it's not just about whether you're left or right, but rather whether can you entertain an audience. Too many radio professionals (and too many Americans in general) get caught up in labeling. Michael Harrison, the editor and publisher of *Talkers* magazine, has featured in his pages the adventures of "The Lone Liberal." With mask, cape, and the flashlight of truth clipped to his belt, "The Lone

Liberal" has racked up hundreds of media appearances where he has brought logic, reason, and sanity to what has become a right-leaning medium. "The Lone Liberal" believes in non-race-based solutions, basic human decency, and a strong moral code. "The Lone Liberal" voted for George W. Bush for president. But conservative hosts and listeners vilify "The Lone Liberal" simply because of his name: "The Lone Liberal"; so much so that he has to fight the good fight anonymously.

As for talk radio, the numbers speak for themselves. Rush Limbaugh, according to *Talkers* magazine, has 14.5 million plus listeners a week, and is the most listened-to talk-show host in America. Following Rush is my television partner Sean Hannity with 105 million plus listeners, then Dr. Laura, with 8 million plus, and Michael Savage with 6 million plus. And the single most listened-to radio personality is Paul Harvey, also a conservative, who attracts 23 million listeners a week.

Among syndicated columnists, the ones with the most newspapers under their belts are conservative. Cal Thomas comes in first with 537 newspapers, followed by George Will with 450. Arthur E. Rowse in his book *Drive-By Journalism: The Assault on Your Need to Know* shows that conservative columnists outreach liberal columnists 3–1 based on the number of newspapers in which writers of each political persuasion appear.

If you look at the best-seller lists, you'll see that books by liberal authors are far less popular than those by their conservative counterparts. (Of course, I aim to be totally wrong on this one, should what you're holding in your hand rocket into that piece of the conservative media firmament.) Ann Coulter's book, *Slander*, debuted on the *New York Times* best-seller list at number one, on July 14, 2002, and her book *Treason* was another immediate best seller a year later, entering the *Times* chart on July 13, 2003, at number two (albeit this time behind Hillary Clinton's best seller). My friend Sean Hannity's book debuted at number three on the *New York Times* best-seller list on September 8, 2002. As Stanley Kurtz pointed out in the *National*

Review Online, "The January 6 [2002] list was chock full of conservative books. Bill O'Reilly's *No Spin Zone* has been holding down number one for weeks. Bernard Goldberg's *Bias* comes in at number six, followed at seven by Barbara Olson's *The Final Days*. At number twelve there's Peggy Noonan's Reagan biography, *When Character Was King*. Next week, Pat Buchanan's *Death of the West* will make its debut on the list. And those are only the most obviously conservative entries."

By March 17, Bernie Goldberg's *Bias* made it to number one, and is now doing wonderfully in paperback.

GOP-TV?

I've often had to fend off critics on my own side of the political fence who have accused me of working for "GOP-TV," as some like to call the Fox News Channel. Most disappointing was Al Gore, who suggested during an interview I'd agree with his assessment of Fox News as a conservative outlet if we were talking off camera. But we were talking on camera, and here's what was said:

COLMES: . . . You singled out Fox News, among other conservative media outlets, and said that they were kind of a fifth column in American journalism. You know, conservatives for years have complained about CNN and said it was too liberal. Is this just the flip side of that coin?

GORE: No, I don't think it is. I think it's a different phenomenon. I think that your network finds it profitable to orient the news in opinion format toward the expectations of a core audience . . . that forms a profitable part of your base. I think that cable television news changed the economics of the news business. And once again made it profitable to try to deliver a more predictable point of view. Now you're one of the Democrats . . .

COLMES: Well, I'm a liberal. I'm on every night prime time on the Fox News Channel.

GORE: Absolutely.

COLMES: My views . . .

GORE: I understand.

COLMES: . . . and my support of you has been prominent.

GORE: I appreciate that very much.

COLMES: So clearly . . .

GORE: But you probably wouldn't—well, maybe you would—but maybe if we got off camera, you might not dispute the proposition that overall, Fox is pretty well tilted toward the conservative Republican.

COLMES: Well, we got Geraldo. We've got Greta Van Susteren. We've got me. O'Reilly, I think, is pretty unpredictable.

GORE: But overall, wouldn't you say that it's more sort of . . .

COLMES: I would say that we give vent to conservative voices . . .

GORE: Yes.

COLMES: . . . that previously have not been heard necessarily as loudly on cable news.

GORE: Well, I'm not going to urge you to bite the hand that feeds you.

During my interview with Gore, I wasn't shilling for my network because I had a Fox News camera aimed at my head. The network isn't successful because it's a Republican mouthpiece. And research bears out that, contrary to conventional wisdom, the audience is not all that different ideologically than that for CNN, a network perceived as more liberal in its appeal. Indeed, in its August 13, 2003, edition, the *Hollywood Reporter* wrote that the ad agency Carat USA found that in any given week, CNN reaches more viewers who term themselves "very conservative"—37 percent compared to 32 percent for Fox News. A Pew Research Center poll of 3,002 adults, conducted between April 26 and May 12, 2002, showed that 46 percent of Fox News viewers considered themselves conservative, 32 percent moderate, and 18 percent liberal. Among CNN viewers, 40 percent claimed to be conservative, 38 percent moderate, and 16 percent liberal. Maybe all the liberals are watching QVC because of their patriotic desire to turn around a failing economy. And for a network that has been unfairly characterized as a cheerleader for the Bush 43 administration, Fox News devoted plenty of time to debating accusations that Persian Gulf II was based on trumped-up intelligence and outright lies.

No media outlet that was truly a mouthpiece for one party or the other would be successful. The public is too smart for that. When news came out that well-heeled financiers wanted to put together a liberal radio network to combat all the conservative talk on radio, I had my doubts. Although they never asked my opinion and never approached me to participate, I don't want to be the mouthpiece for a political party or a rich political operative. If I'm beholden to someone with an agenda, then I don't have the independence I need to state my views honestly. And if the audience knows that I'm a paid operative, my credibility is damaged. A broadcasting company, not an agenda-driven patron, gives me the best opportunity to compete in the free marketplace of ideas.

On February 24, 2003, Fox News debuted *Fox News Live with Alan Colmes*, the initial offering of Fox News Radio. Talk radio is known as a conservative bastion, and Fox News is regularly criticized as having a right-wing agenda. Interesting, isn't it, that their first radio host is a liberal? So, either Fox doesn't have a political agenda or I'm not a real liberal.

People tune in to the Fox News Channel because it was founded on the premise that all sides should be presented fairly. This has upset the "media establishment" but has made Fox the most powerful name in news. I'm proud that *Hannity & Colmes* has contributed to this success, an achievement that has been often dissected by liberal media pundits who argue that Sean is more aggressive than I am and therefore dominates the show. In fact, some of my harshest critics have been liberals who regret that my style on the left doesn't exactly mirror what Sean does on the right:

From: Damian
Sent: Thursday, February 20, 2003 6:14 AM
To: colmes
Subject: The worst

Alan,
You are the worst liberal I have ever seen. You lack the strength, fire and guts that Hannity displays on the show, and you seem (at the core) shameful for being a liberal. Do us a favor and leave Fox.

Disgusted Liberal

Most of our viewers, however, are too smart to try to equate Sean and me stylistically. They understand that our show works *because* our styles are different, not in spite of it. And, as you've seen from some of the e-mails in this book, I get under conservative skin as effectively as Sean causes rashes in liberals. But sometimes they like me in spite of themselves:

From: Martin R.
Sent: Saturday, February 08, 2003 2:28 AM
To: colmes
Subject: my favorite liberal

Hello Alan,

Just wanted to let you know there are at least 2 Texas
conservatives who are big fans of yours. My wife and I are very
conservative in our political views, but enjoy hearing your
passionate and articulate opposing views. It's obvious, to us, that
you genuinely love your country and are truly sincere in your
beliefs. You haven't coverted us yet, but you have made us realize
that not all liberals are crazy.

Sincerily,
Martin R.
Lafayette, LA

Martin, I'm not looking to convert you or your wife, but I'm glad I
have your attention.

And by the way, so what if my boss is a Republican? Larry Tisch
is a Republican, and he used to own something called CBS. Richard
Parsons and his predecessor Steve Case of CNN/TimeWarner/AOL
are Republicans. And Michael Eisner of Disney, which owns ABC,
gave more to Bush 43 and Senator John McCain than he did to Gore
and Bradley, and supported Rick Lazio over Hillary Clinton in the
2000 New York Senate race.

Bias, Schmias

Bernie Goldberg, the former CBS newsman, wrote a best-selling
book called *Bias*, in which he tried to make the case that the media is
biased to the left. But Goldberg is often selective in his criticism and
guilty of the same offenses he tags on others. It disturbs him, for
example, that a staffer at CBS referred to then presidential candidate
Gary Bauer as "the little nut from the Christian group" in 1999. And
it should. But he then refers to gonzo journalist Hunter Thompson
as "an acid-popping weirdo."

The Media Research Center, an admittedly right-leaning group headed by Brent Bozell, backs up Goldberg, of course, and claims, based on a Nexis search, that ABC, NBC, and CBS are four times as likely to label someone "conservative" as they are to label someone "liberal." But Geoffrey Nunberg, a Standford University researcher, challenges this claim, saying it can be made only if the names of liberal and conservative groups appear with equal frequency. Only then can you see if they are being labeled to the same extent. What Goldberg and the Media Research Center really discovered, says Nunberg, is that conservatives get mentioned more than liberals:

> But in my own data, I found, for example, that the Heritage Foundation was mentioned in press stories five times as much as the [Americans for Democratic Action], and that Jesse Helms was mentioned five times as often as Barney Frank. By choosing not to report the use of labels as proportions of the frequencies of the names of groups, or to report those frequencies at all, the MRC loaded the results—in fact, it implies that the fact that the networks generally talk about conservatives more than about liberals is evidence for their liberal bias!

As a matter of fact, Nunberg, who combed newspapers, looked at references on ten well-known politicos in thirty newspapers. He came up with one hundred thousand references and discovered that liberal lawmakers had a much greater chance of getting tagged politically than conservatives. Nunberg reported this on the March 19, 2002, broadcast of NPR's *Fresh Air*: "I did find a big disparity in the way the press labels liberals and conservatives, but not in the direction that Goldberg claims. On the contrary: the average liberal legislator has a thirty percent *greater* likelihood of being identified with a partisan label than the average conservative does."

Bob Somerby, who was Al Gore's roommate in college and runs a nifty website called "The Daily Howler," studied Goldberg's book and refutes some of his claims. For example, Somerby points out,

Goldberg tries to convince us that two networks went out of their way to imply that the homeless problem got worse because Bush 43 was president.

> I also choose not to believe that when the Sunday edition of *ABC World News Tonight* rediscovered the homeless story just three weeks after George W. Bush was sworn in as president it was nothing more than coincidence. That when reporter Bob Jamieson said, "In New York City, the number of homeless in the shelter system has risen above 25,000 a night *for the first time since the late 1980s*," it was not an attempt to say, "*Here we go again—a Republican is in the White House and the homeless are back.*" And on August 4, 2001, when CNN also rediscovered homelessness and quoted sources saying, "The number of homeless people is on the rise this summer," I choose to believe it was not CNN's way of suggesting that now that a conservative Republican is president, Reagan-era misery will soon be back with us in full force.

You're right, Bernie, it was *not* either ABC's or CNN's way of suggesting that homelessness was attributable to the Bush 43 White House. What ABC reported on February 11, 2001, the date in question, was: "The 175-bed shelter in this city of 130,000 has recorded a steady increase in homeless for the last year, particularly families with children." And CNN's John Palmer said on August 4 of the same year, "It's not just New York City. Many cities across the country report sharp increases in the number of people searching for places to live. Demand for emergency shelter in 25 surveyed cities increased an average of 15 percent in 1999, according to the U.S. Conference of Mayors." So you see, they were blaming *Clinton*, not Bush. Is this anti-liberal bias, then?

Bernie is much closer to the mark when he points out that there may be a *cultural* bias, and that the media would go tough on your liberal grandmother if it would help them get an audience. But if we agree that our system is based on supply and demand, are we also to believe that the media is much more liberal than the people who watch it? Is the media really controlled by a bunch of left-leaning media monoliths? And if there is such a bias in the media, why was *Bias* treated so favorably? One of its major targets, the *New York Times*, gave it a positive review, saying, "*Bias* should be taken seriously." Even Goldberg himself acknowledged the favorable treatment he received during his book tour while appearing on Fox News: "I would say ninety percent of what I've heard and read about the book has been positive."

Not bad for such a "biased" media.

Gored

The media is not the liberal's best friend. The "liberal" media really did a number on Al Gore. It tried to paint him as a liar in the same way it did Clinton. The most often-repeated lie about Gore is that he claimed to invent the Internet. What he *really* said to CNN's Wolf Blitzer on March 9, 1999, was, "During my service in the United States Congress, I took the initiative in creating the Internet." Gore spokesman Chris Lehane explained the context here, stating that Gore "was the leader in Congress on the connections between data transmission and computing power, what we call information technology. And those efforts helped to create the Internet that we know today." He did take the initiative, which helped to pave the information superhighway, but he never used the word *invented*.

Trouble began when the magazine *Wired* took issue with Gore's comment and said he couldn't possibly have invented the Arpanet, since Gore was much too young at the time it was created. But Gore never mentioned the Arpanet, which was developed by the Defense Department and was the forerunner of the Internet. Congressman Dick Armey jumped on the anti-Gore bandwagon and released a statement that said, "If the Vice President created the Internet, then I created the Interstate highway system." "Created" morphed to "invented" in a March 15, 1999, *USA Today* article called "Inventing the Internet," and the rest, as they say, is history.

The "liberal media" also continued to repeat a falsehood that had Gore taking credit for investigations into toxic waste in the "Love Canal." Gore addressed a group of students at Concord High School in Concord, New Hampshire, on November 30, 1999, about a letter he received from a girl in Toone, Tennessee, about toxic waste in her town. Gore said, "I called for a congressional investigation and a hearing. I looked around the country for other sites like that. I found a little place in upstate New York called Love Canal. Had the first hearing on that issue, and Toone, Tennessee—that was the one that you didn't hear of. But that was the one that started it all."

But the next day the *Washington Post* reported that "Gore boasted about his efforts in Congress 20 years ago to publicize the dangers of toxic waste." The piece then went on to misquote Gore: " 'I found a little place in upstate New York called Love Canal,' he said, referring to the Niagara homes evacuated in August 1978 because of chemical contamination. 'I had the first hearing on this issue.' . . . Gore said his efforts made a lasting impact. 'I was the one that started it all,' he said."

"*It* was the one that started it all," became "*I* was the one that started it all." This misquote was repeated until it became generally accepted that Gore took credit where none was warranted.

Another Gore lie the "liberal media" loved to repeat was that he attended a fund-raiser at a Buddhist Temple on April 29, 1996. So what if he did? The truth is there were to be two events that day— the temple event and a fund-raiser at another location. At the last minute, the two events were combined into one at the temple, but Gore wasn't aware of that decision.

One of the most insidious charges leveled at Gore was that he race-baited by being the first to bring up Willie Horton during his first run for president in 1988. What Gore did was to highlight the furlough program that his opponent for the Democratic nomination, Massachusetts governor Michael Dukakis, had initiated, a program that resulted in Horton being freed to commit more crimes.

Willie Horton was no saint. He was a convicted murderer who killed Joey Fournier on October 17, 1974, and stuffed him in a trash can near the gas station where Fournier was working in Lawrence, Massachusetts. And all for a payday of $276.37. He was released by Governor Michael Dukakis as part of the furlough release program, and while he was loose in Maryland he pistol-whipped, bound, and gagged Clifford Barnes and knifed and raped Barnes's fiancée, Angela. Conservative columnist Jeff Jacoby, writing in the *Boston Globe* on January 20, 2000, set the record straight: "But to be fair, it is not true that Gore 'used Willie Horton' in 1988. In a debate with that year's Democratic presidential hopefuls, Gore noted that the Massachusetts practice of letting first-degree murderers take weekend 'furloughs' from prison had freed some killers to commit new crimes. He asked whether Governor Michael Dukakis intended to grant similar furloughs to federal prisoners. That was it." Gore never heard of Willie Horton until he was dredged up by Dukakis's Republican opponents.

I spoke with Willie Horton in the mid-nineties, trying to convince him to come on the radio with me. He declined. But he did tell me that he was always known as "William Horton," that the Republicans purposely diminished him by changing the form of his name, and that they took the most menacing picture of him they could find to use on campaign literature. Now, keep in mind, I had no sympathy for him, and his actions were far more heinous than what the Republicans did here, but I also have no sympathy for dirty, racially motivated political tricks in order to smear a candidate.

My Country: Breathe It or Leave It

The "liberal media" spent much more time spreading lies about Al Gore during the 2000 campaign than it did highlighting his environmental ideas, which should have been the strong suit of his candidacy. Gore offered an energy efficiency plan with a goal of solar-powered homes, gasoline-free cars, and independence from foreign oil. Energy plants would be fueled by methane from landfills or other renewable sources. Tax breaks would encourage businesses to develop energy alternatives that don't pollute. If Gore had spoken more often on his energy plans, as he did on June 27, 2000, he might have added the electoral vote to his popular vote victory: "We can clean up pollution, make our power systems more efficient and more reliable, and move away from dependence on others—all with no new taxes, no new bureaucracies, and no onerous regulations. In fact we will cut taxes to help families and businesses buy the clean technology of our time."

And Gore should have made more of Bush 43's spotty environmental record as governor of Texas. The Environmental Laboratory Washington Report of June 10, 1999, stated that Texas released more than 260 million pounds of toxic pollution in 1997, and that every year since 1995 Texas has had the greatest number of toxic releases into the environment of any state in the country.

Bush 43's environmental record as a private businessman also left much to be desired. The Associated Press reported on October 6, 2000, "During Bush's tenure with Harken, between 1986 and 1992, environmentally hazardous gasoline and petroleum leaked from at least six E-Z Serve storage tanks in Florida, according to state DEP records." Harken had purchased E-Z Serve, which ran retail gas stations. The story went on to report, "Records show Harken did nothing to clean up the mess. The tanks were removed two years later only after the gas station changed hands and the state ordered an emergency review of the site. . . . In June, the state agreed to clean up the spill, charging the cost to taxpayers." That there was taxpayer responsibility to clean up after a company of which Bush 43 was a director should have been driven home by Democrats; driven home using a gasoline-free car, preferably.

All of this would be less significant today were the Bush 43 presidency focused on improving the environment and moving our country toward low-cost renewable energy sources. Instead, we have an administration that meets with campaign contributors to help decide energy policy, and does so in private, without the taxpayer knowing who, what, when, and where. Public interest groups seeking information about these meetings faced eleven months of resistance. The Energy Department grudgingly came forth with information just hours before a court-ordered deadline. As the *Washington Post* reported on March 31, 2002; "Energy Secretary Spencer Abraham met with 36 representatives of business interests while helping to write President Bush's energy policy, and he held no meetings with conservation or consumer groups, the Energy Department disclosed Monday night." Enron's CEO Ken Lay and CFO Jeffrey Skilling met with members of the task force six times. According to the report, "The Bush administration relied almost exclusively on the advice of executives from utilities and producers of oil, gas, coal and nuclear energy." Environmental groups, meanwhile, had no such luck gaining access to those determining energy policy. Of course, these citizens weren't big donors to the Republican cause, either.

Bush and Vice President Richard Cheney weren't the only hugely successful oilmen in the administration. Don Evans, the Commerce secretary, had spent twenty-five years at Tom Brown, a Denver-based oil and gas company, and White House chief of staff Andrew Card had been a lobbyist for GM, fighting against stricter fuel-emission standards. Their influence was palpable: Bush's energy plan called for $27.6 billion in subsidies to the oil, coal, nuclear, and auto industries, and just $5 billion for renewable energy or conservation. A *Boston Globe* story on August 3, 2001, highlighted how the Bush 43 energy plan not only offered to open the Arctic National Wildlife Refuge (ANWR) in Alaska to invasive oil drilling, but also allowed "federal agents to seize private lands by eminent domain for transmission lines, and offers small rebates for conservation unlikely to affect the behavior of anyone not inclined to conserve anyway."

Among other goodies in the Bush plan, large vehicles would be classified as light trucks. This gift to SUV owners would mean they wouldn't be subject to the 27.5 mile-per-gallon standard required of ordinary cars. Reducing vehicle fuel consumption would save more than a million barrels a day by 2015, more than ANWR would produce. The whole ANWR debate was neatly summed up by a *Boston Globe* editorial on February 21, 2001, quoting the U.S. Geological Survey which found that "any potential benefit" to drilling in ANWR was "far outweighed by the risks," and that there was only a 50 percent chance of finding a six-month supply of oil that, even if found, would take ten years to extract.

Many Republicans who voted in 1985 to export Alaskan oil to the Far East now say we have to drill in ANWR to have more oil for domestic use. Alaska already produces a million barrels of crude oil a day, much of it sold overseas, including 26 million barrels a year to Japan and China. So why upset a pristine part of America for oil that will make us more self-sufficient, while we're busy selling domestic product overseas—oil that's being produced in the very state whose wilderness some wish to destroy?

Besides all this, Bush 43 wants no part of the Kyoto Protocol, negotiated by a hundred countries to restrict gas emissions, even though we produce a quarter of the gases associated with global warming. He acted to overturn requirements that contractors conform to environmental laws, opposed requirements for more efficient air conditioners, cut the EPA budget by $500 million, and favored "voluntary compliance" for corporations that may pollute. Would Republicans support "voluntary compliance" for laws they support? I'll take "voluntary compliance" for the Patriot Act, please.

And the administration's argument to reduce carbon dioxide emissions? "If you want to do something about carbon dioxide emissions," said Dick "Secret Meetings" Cheney, on *Hardball* on March 21, 2001, "then you ought to build nuclear power plants." Right, nuclear power plants sound like a great idea, save for that pesky nuclear waste problem.

Bush versus Gore: The Media Version

If the media is so biased to the left, why didn't we hear more during the last presidential campaign about Bush 43's environmental record in Texas and his failed business dealings? And why wasn't more made of allegations of alcohol and drug use by Bush in his younger days? Bill Clinton was mocked for *not* inhaling. Furthermore, where was the "liberal media" on charges that Bush 43 was AWOL for a year of his National Guard duty? The *Times* of London reported on November 5, 2000, "Bill Burkett, a former lieutenant-colonel, said Bush aides had been 'scrubbing the files' to bury disparities between his record while serving as a reserve pilot during the Vietnam war and an account of the period in his official biography." This, of course, was reported by the foreign press, and not by the American press, which is what the people voting in American elections generally read.

In a little-noted story on May 23, 2000, the *Boston Globe* pointed out the contradictions between Bush 43's official autobiography and his official military record: "Bush himself, in his 1999 autobiography, *A Charge to Keep*, recounts the thrills of his pilot training, which he completed in June 1970. 'I continued flying with my unit for the next several years,' the governor wrote." Shortly after he became governor of Texas in 1995, a Houston National Guard unit decided to honor Bush 43 for his work as a pilot, which it claimed continued until 43's discharge from the army in October 1973. The *Globe* story, however, goes on to state that Bush 43's military records, or lack thereof, contradict these claims: ". . . both accounts are contradicted by copies of Bush's military records, obtained by the *Globe*. In his final 18 months of military service in 1972 and 1973, Bush did not fly at all. And for much of that time, Bush was all but unaccounted for: For a full year, there is no record that he showed up for the periodic drills required of part-time guardsmen." Bush had asked to be transferred to Alabama in 1972 to work on the Senate campaign of Winton Blount, a friend of Bush 41. But the commander of the Alabama unit, retired Colonel William Turnipseed, says Bush 43 never showed up. After the election, Bush returned to Houston, but his commanders at Ellington Air Force Base, Lieutenant Colonel William D. Harris Jr. and Lieutenant Colonel Jerry B. Killian, wrote in his annual efficiency report, "Lt. Bush has not been observed at this unit during the period of this report." So his Texas commanders thought he was in Alabama; his Alabama commander never saw him; and other than scant coverage in the *Boston Globe*, this was barely an issue during the 2000 presidential campaign. And the "liberal media" didn't question whether a sitting commander in chief shirked his own military obligations as he sent other Americans off to war.

Paul Begala, who served as an adviser in the Clinton White House, offered up some hard facts with regard to media coverage of Clinton and Bush 43's respective military records. Speaking at a UAW legislative conference on February 6, 2001, Begala said, "I worked for Bill Clinton in 1992 and . . . in anticipation of this very question, I looked this up on Nexis. There were 13,641 stories about Bill Clinton 'dodging the draft' . . . and there were 49 stories about Bush and the National Guard."

I take heart in knowing that a man who used family connections to get into the National Guard, who was then nowhere to be found for the last year of his alleged service, and who didn't show up for mandatory physicals is now leading our young fighting men and women in war. And his handlers revel in referring to him as a "wartime president." His media-designed swoop-down to the deck of the USS *Abraham Lincoln* on May 1, 2003, where he swaggered in his flight suit, helmet under arm, while proclaiming, "Yes, I flew it," was very becoming for a commander in chief. It would have been nice if he wore that flight suit a little more often during the actual time he was supposed to be serving his country in the National Guard.

Clinton Scandal? What Clinton Scandal?

Every time I hear conservatives complain about how poorly they're treated in the media, I just hearken back to the Clinton era. It wasn't long into the Clinton presidency before the media began to mention allegations of scandal. The right-wing *American Spectator* put out an eleven-thousand-word piece called "His Cheatin' Heart" for the cover story of its January 1994 issue. Two days later the *Los Angeles*

Times ran with the story, as did the three major evening network newscasts. In fact, the *Los Angeles Times* had been preparing a major investigative piece on the issue, which it then rushed into print. It was *Newsweek*, not exactly a minor media outlet, to whom Lucianne Goldberg brought the allegations of Clinton's affair with Monica Lewinsky. Matt Drudge got wind of this and mentioned Lewinsky by name in his *Drudge Report* on January 19, 1998, and it became a *Washington Post* story five days later. When Juanita Broaddrick came forward with the charge that she was raped by Bill Clinton, the media was not shy about reporting these allegations: according to the *Washington Times* on December 21, 1999, "Juanita Broaddrick's story became widely known publicly in February when newspapers printed detailed accounts of her story. NBC News then aired an interview with Mrs. Broaddrick." The idea that Clinton got favorable treatment by "the liberal media" is just preposterous.

Paula Jones was referred to by her then spokesperson, Susan Carpenter McMillan, as "a modern-day Joan of Arc." McMillan became a staple of the "liberal media" as did women like Gennifer Flowers, Kathleen Willey, Dolly Kyle Browning, and their defenders, and just about every conservative group with an anti-Clinton grudge.

The media furiously covered "Travelgate," painting Hillary Clinton as a harridan who mercilessly fired workers in the White House travel office. But Independent Counsel Robert Ray's final report on the matter acknowledged that she could not have known that her statements to aides would have resulted in firings. Clinton was also cleared of charges in "Filegate," where she has been accused of seeking confidential background reports of former White House staffers. In this case, Ray said there was "no substantial and credible evidence" of this. Similarly, Ray's office found there was insufficient evidence to pursue charges against the Clintons in Whitewater, the land deal that was the jumping-off point for various charges against the Clintons. Coverage of Travelgate, Filegate, and Whitewater went on for years, but word of the dismissal of these charges had a very short life span in the "liberal media."

Look for the Liberal Label

It's very easy to immediately brand something "liberal" or "conservative" and decide, based on that branding, that a particular piece of information is invalid. Some conservatives try to invalidate something just by using the word *liberal*. Sometimes the word *liberal* isn't enough. It wasn't enough, for example, to call Nancy Pelosi a "liberal" when she became the Democratic House leader. She had to be called a "San Francisco liberal."

You'd think the "liberal media" would have celebrated a woman's ascension to political heights previously unknown. The allegedly liberal *New Republic* celebrated her new position by saying, "Even if she does stake out sensible positions on the issues, her background will make it hard for her to frame them effectively." *The Economist*, a British publication, and not exactly a right-wing rag, referred to Pelosi's election to a leadership position as "a disaster for the Democrats." So it didn't matter to many of those writing about her what her actual positions were. They had already begun to frame her with modifiers and buzzwords as something unacceptable to mainstream America.

I love being paid to give my opinions, but I work hard to substantiate them with facts, using the best research available. I sift through dozens of newspapers, magazines, and Internet articles every day, and carefully develop arguments based on the information I consume. During a November 26, 2002, debate on the economy with former attorney general Ed Meese, I quoted figures from the Center on Budget and Policy Priorities. I argued that instead of proposing tax cuts that favored the wealthy, the president should be proposing a reduction in payroll taxes that would benefit far more Americans than the cut the Republicans had been pushing.

I pointed out that payroll taxes take a much bigger share from low- and middle-income Americans, 6.2 percent on incomes up to $84,900. I added that if you make more than that, the percentage of these taxes of your total income decreases. Republicans love to talk about cutting income taxes while totally ignoring the many other taxes that hit middle- and lower-income Americans the hardest, like payroll taxes, excise taxes, and sales taxes.

Bush's initial tax-cut plan would have resulted in after-tax income for the top 1 percent rising 6.2 percent, compared with growth of 1.9 percent and 0.6 percent for the middle and lowest-income fifths of families. Here's what Ed Meese said on our show when I quoted these numbers and attributed them to the Center on Budget and Policy Priorities.

MEESE: But Alan, you know that that outfit is nothing but a mouthpiece for the liberals anyway.

COLMES: I stand by it, and so do they.

MEESE: You may stand by it, but I wouldn't waste the paper to read that.

HANNITY: I agree with Attorney General Meese.

And while we're at it, let me further add that the Center reported that "between 1979 and 1997 . . . the average after-tax income of the top 1 percent of households adjusted for inflation, rose by $414,000, a 157% gain. The middle fifth of households gained 10% and the bottom fifth was stagnant. The highest percentage of tax relief at 6.6% goes to those earning $297,350 and above." Take that, liberal-bashers!

Sean Hannity and Ed Meese immediately discounted my statements because they were based on research done by the Center on Budget and Policy Priorities, known to be a "liberal" think tank. Should I then automatically discount every piece of information that comes out of the conservative Heritage Foundation or the libertarian CATO Institute? What's more, should I automatically disbelieve everything in the conservative *Washington Times?* It's easy to wave off information you don't agree with by proclaiming, "Oh, it was said by a 'conservative'," or "Horrors, a 'liberal' spewed this." The only question I ask is, is the information true?

The Myth Continues

Those parts of the media that truly do have a liberal agenda have done a lousy job of conveying a strong message. False ideas about the Clintons linger, as the real skinny on some of Al Gore's statements and some of the truth about Bush 43 have barely seen the light of day. Conservatives have done a much better job promoting their ideas on talk radio and cable news and have been at the forefront of commandeering the Internet as a tool to spread their views.

I admire the success of those who have said "liberal media" so many times that it is accepted as fact in some quarters. But ultimately, it doesn't matter whether there are more liberals or more conservatives in the media; what matters is that there are enough choices for the media consumer, a true concern in the age of consolidation. Unfortunately, in June 2003, the FCC voted to allow media companies to own more television, radio, and print outlets in the same market, which works against the idea of diversity. Since it is the government that controls the broadcast airwaves by awarding licenses, it has an obligation to see to it that the wealth is spread fairly. Policies should favor platforms for more voices, not fewer.

With the advent of broadband, DSL, and cable Internet access, one would think that diversity has arrived. But small DSL and cable providers are being pushed aside by the big boys; companies like Time Warner control not only access, but also content. And our regulatory agencies aren't exactly greeting newcomers with candy and flowers.

Diversity, options, and opportunity are hallmarks of a truly democratic society. As Hugo Black said in the majority opinion in the 1945 *Associated Press v. United States* case, "The First Amendment . . . rests on the assumption that the widest possible dissemination of information from diverse and antagonistic sources is essential to the welfare of the public."

FIVE

Straw Men, Hypocrisy, and Conservative Lies

Conservatives are more likely to go to church; liberals are more likely to worship trees and snail darters in their natural habitat.

—SUZANNE FIELDS

Here is what conservatives do so well. They construct liberal straw men by trying to define what a liberal is, they lie about liberals in the process, and then they recoil in horror at what they've just invented. Often, they don't live up to the high moral standards to which they hold others. It would be nice if on little issues like sex, war, and government, they'd practice what they preach.

From President Bush's insinuation that the Democrat-led Senate was not interested in the security of the American people to the more generic and egregious claim that "Liberals don't care about this country," conservatives have talked trash about liberals to advance their own agendas. Some liberals become perennial targets. Do you think some people will *ever* let go of their hatred for the

Clintons? Conversely, won't Ronald Reagan only become *more* of an icon as time goes on, regardless of the true record of his presidency? Listening to the mythmakers, you'd think Reagan presided over budget surpluses and got us out of debt. Sure, conservatives have wonderful things to say about some liberals. They praise JFK and Martin Luther King Jr. Seems as though they believe the only good liberal is a dead one.

According to some conservatives, liberals are a bunch of flag-burning, dope-smoking, welfare-collecting (yes, all welfare recipients are liberal), Jesus-hating sexaholics hell-bent on the destruction of America. I hope I'm able to bring more perspective to these inane perceptions.

I see the left/right dichotomy a bit different than the columnist Suzanne Fields does. For example, if we want to do a little stereotyping, and with apologies to comedian Jeff Foxworthy, the creator of "You might be a redneck if . . ."

You Might Be a Conservative If . . .

> *You believe Clinton gutted the military, and yet you're forced to acknowledge that that same military performed magnificently in both Afghanistan and Iraq.*

> *You believe government should be off the backs of business but in the uteruses of women.*

> *You think it's okay to overspend if the money goes to a defense contractor, but not if it goes to a single mother with no husband and no job.*

> *You can't stand Democrats if they're named Ted Kennedy, but you love them if they're named James Traficant or Zell Miller.*

> *You despise the fact that Bill Clinton tried to bring peace to the Middle East, but you love that George Bush brought war there.*

You believe the government doesn't know how to run schools, but it does know how to run school prayers.

When a Democrat agrees with you he or she has an agenda, but when you agree with him or her, you're bipartisan.

You believe in family values, unless the head of that family happens to be gay.

You believe that when Democrats control the Congress and they stop you from doing things, it's proper to blame them for obstruction, but when you control the Congress and they try to stop what you're doing, it's proper to shut down the government.

You don't think this is very funny, but it would be hilarious if it were mocking Democrats.

It's much more difficult for a liberal to be hypocritical than it is for a conservative. Conservatives are more likely to take absolutist positions because they see the world in stark, good versus evil terms. Because the world isn't just black and white, conservatives back themselves into ideological corners from which they cannot be easily extracted. For example, Larry King asked then vice president Dan Quayle what he'd do if his thirteen-year-old daughter told him she was having an abortion. Quayle gave a very real, human answer, not the answer of a politician with an agenda: "I hope I never have to deal with it. But obviously I would counsel her and talk to her and support her on whatever decision she made."

As though guns were going off at the beginning of a horse race, you could practically hear the judges saying, "Let the backpedaling begin." The next day the vice president said he'd support her decision only if she were an adult. Marilyn Quayle, the vice president's wife, said that if her daughter became pregnant "she'll take the child to term."

Dr. William Bennett became an easy target for critics when it was reported that he lost $8 million playing the slots in various casinos. I like Bill Bennett and if it's true, as he avers, that he "didn't bet the milk money," then this is really an issue between himself, his family, and his God. Nevertheless, because of his image as the country's "morality czar," the author of *The Book of Virtues* had to endure jokes like, "Did you hear about Bill Bennett's new book? It's called *The Virtue of Bookies.*" I'm sure that even Dr. Bennett would agree that when you have a carefully cultivated public image, being teased in this manner comes with the territory.

Maintaining a strong moral code while allowing for the vicissitudes of life can be a tough balancing act. Before you conservatives start yelling "moral relativism," I would argue that relativism is a fact of life, not just a theory. It's easy to say that abortion should be outlawed, that teenagers should practice abstinence, and that people who need public assistance should be thrown off the rolls after eighteen months. But if it's your daughter who is pregnant, your son who is indulging in adult behavior, or your brother who is jobless or homeless, you face a problem that won't be solved by absolutist positions.

If They Just Say It Often Enough . . .

When lies are repeated often enough, using the Goebbels model, they become part of common parlance and are challenged less and less as time goes by. Conservative political operatives have used this technique to support their own ideas and invalidate liberal ones. Let's examine some of the oft-repeated sentiments and statements injected by the right into America's bloodstream.

Republicans have been quite successful in feeding the perception that Democrats are soft on defense and national security. We have a president who didn't know the leaders of Pakistan, India, and Chechnya when asked to name them by a Boston television reporter during the 2000 presidential campaign, but that didn't seem to hurt him. It may be that Bush 43's most significant multicultural experience prior to moving to Washington was dining at the International House of Pancakes. As we've found out, it's good for a potential president to know about those other countries out there. Might come in handy one day. But it's the Democrats who get blasted for being out of the loop on issues of national security and foreign affairs.

Did Tom Daschle Gas the Kurds?

Speaking in Trenton, New Jersey, on September 23, 2002, Bush 43, the man who claimed to be "a uniter not a divider," made this uniting comment on the Homeland Security Bill: "The House responded, but the Senate is more interested in special interests in Washington and not interested in the security of the American people."

Tom Daschle, in an emotional speech on the Senate floor, rightly took Bush 43 to task for the insinuation that Democrats are less interested in protecting America: "You tell those who fought in Vietnam and World War II they are not interested in the security of the American people because they are Democrats. . . . That is outrageous. Outrageous." Daschle was criticized for using the Senate floor to make a political speech. Where was he supposed to make his impassioned plea, the floor of the New York Stock Exchange? Perhaps only Republican views should be offered on the Senate floor. On that same Senate floor were Democrats Daniel Inouye of Hawaii, a highly decorated World War II veteran, and Max Cleland of Georgia, who sacrificed the use of his limbs while fighting for our country in Vietnam. I suspect these two American heroes care very much about national security.

Although Republicans have positioned themselves as having the market cornered on foreign affairs, it was the Democrats who argued successfully for the creation of NATO, a move staunchly opposed by Republicans from the Midwest, especially Senator Robert Taft of Ohio. Democrats engineered the Marshall Plan, navigated the success of the Cuban missile crisis, the enduring peace between Israel and Egypt, the halting of genocide in Bosnia and Kosovo, and have been at the forefront in negotiating various treaties that have reduced nuclear threats.

Even before his emotional reaction to Bush 43's attempt to brand him, Tom Daschle has been a target. Literally. During the anthrax attacks Daschle's office was hit. The minute he became majority leader he was branded an "obstructionist." When Republican John Thune ran against Democrat Tim Johnson for Senate in Daschle's home state of South Dakota, a conservative group ran ads comparing Daschle to Saddam Hussein. In 2001, Richard Lessner, head of "American Renewal," part of the right-wing Family Research Council, ran a newspaper ad in South Dakota that asked, "What do Saddam Hussein and Senate Majority Leader Tom Daschle have in common?" And the oh-so-logical answer: "Neither man wants America to drill for oil in Alaska's Arctic National Wildlife Refuge." This piece of advertising loveliness then juxtaposed pictures of the two men. Gee, I wonder which one is more dangerous to America?

Jimmy, Billy, and Hilly

Jimmy Carter and Bill and Hillary Clinton are three of the most demonized Americans these days. In a September 5, 2002, op-ed piece in the *Washington Post*, former president Carter had some harsh words in his analysis of America: "Formerly admired almost universally as the preeminent champion of human rights, our country has become the foremost target of respected international organizations concerned about these basic principles of democratic life. We have ignored or condoned abuses in nations that support our antiterrorism effort, while detaining American citizens as 'enemy combatants,' incarcerating them secretly and indefinitely without their being charged with any crime or having the right to legal counsel."

Predictably, this led to a great outcry. Former Reagan defense secretary Caspar Weinberger, appearing on *Hannity & Colmes* on November 20, 2002, responded to one of Sean's questions by accusing liberals of believing that America deserved to be attacked, and then reduced that, upon further questioning, to an accusation against Carter.

WEINBERGER: . . . you'll hear more and more people of a broad liberal stripe taking this position that makes them apparently feel good because then they're not praising the country. And you can't praise the United States if you want to be a good liberal . . .

When it was my turn, I asked Mr. Weinberger to elaborate on that:

COLMES: . . . Do you honestly believe that's the liberal view in America?

WEINBERGER: Some of the liberals have taken that position.

COLMES: Who?

WEINBERGER: It's the blame America first.

COLMES: Who?

WEINBERGER: Well, you've heard Mr. Carter. You've heard a number of other people . . .

COLMES: Jimmy Carter thinks we deserve to be attacked?

HANNITY: He said we ought to look at the reasons why.

COLMES: Well, he didn't say we deserved to be attacked. He never made that statement.

HANNITY: He suggested it.

COLMES: No, he did not. Let me ask Mr. Weinberger.

WEINBERGER: Well, he came close to it. And the basic doctrine is that it's America's fault. The first thing you look for with any trouble is to find out what America has done wrong. And that's the philosophy that I hoped that we reversed by President Reagan and I hope . . .

COLMES: I would take great umbrage with your contention that Jimmy Carter believes that America deserves to be attacked; as a former president of the United States, you think he really hates this country and would welcome an attack from bin Laden?

WEINBERGER: No, but I think he takes positions that gives substantial comfort to people who do attack the United States. I think he's in great sympathy with many of the European criticisms of the United States. And that, I think, is a very unfortunate place to be.

When Jimmy Carter won the Nobel Peace Prize, his detractors unceremoniously and cruelly demeaned him. Even the chairman of the awards committee took a shot at Carter at the ceremony, saying that although Carter is the best ex-president America ever had, "Jimmy Carter will probably not go down in American history as the most effective president." Bill Bennett came on our show on October 15, 2002, and, in response to a question from Sean, had this charming comment about President Carter's achievement:

BENNETT: It's now the Nobel Peanut Prize, you know.

When it was my turn I questioned his choice of words:

COLMES: Dr. Bennett, I want to get back to what you said about Jimmy Carter. I'm outraged that you would diminish the Nobel Prize and Jimmy Carter, what he's done to earn it by calling it the Nobel Peanut Prize. . . .

HANNITY: It's a great line.

COLMES: . . . as I said, it may sound poetic and funny, but I think it's inappropriate.

BENNETT: . . . I mean, I think his record, trotting around the world coddling dictators is not particularly impressive. . . . We can disagree on that. But I did not diminish the significance of the prize. They diminished the significance of the prize. And they did it long before this happened. Remember, the Nobel Peace Prize, I think, also went to Yasser Arafat, which makes you question the judgment of these folks.

COLMES: I think Jimmy Carter has been a beacon of peace. And certainly, this was wrapped pretty much [up at] the Camp David Accords. He's brought—helped bring—democracy to lots of places in the world, overseen elections, risked a lot of personal time and personal capital to do it.

BENNETT: Look, I think what he's done with Habitat for Humanity is fine. I think some other things he's done are fine. As a president he was a failure.

Okay, Dr. Bennett. In the interest of being fair and balanced, we'll give you the last word and let the readers decide.

As you can see, the man who brokered an Israeli-Egyptian peace deal in 1978, but was denied the prize at the time in favor of Menachem Begin and Anwar Sadat, was viciously attacked by the right for his "coddling of dictators." Funny how that phrase was never used by right-wingers to describe Richard Nixon, who received only praise for his 1972 trip to Red China. While Donald Rumsfeld was traveling to Iraq to visit Saddam Hussein in 1983 and American corporations were getting licenses to do business with Iraq, Carter was doing globe-trotting of a different nature. He oversaw elections in third world countries, helped produce a cease-fire in the former Yugoslavia in 1993, and negotiated a peaceful transition of power from Raoul Cedras to the democratically elected Jean-Bertrand Aristide in Haiti.

When Carter traveled to Cuba in May 2002, he had the approval of the State Department. Before he left, he asked to be briefed about Cuba's involvement with biological weapons and whether they were aiding terrorists. Satisfied that there was no such involvement, Carter was on his way. Six days before the former president left for Havana, Undersecretary of State John Bolton spoke at the conservative

Heritage Foundation and claimed that Cuba had provided rogue states with information about biological research and development. It's interesting timing to suddenly bring up Cuba and bioweapons, just as a Democratic former president is to become the first sitting or former chief executive to visit Havana since Calvin Coolidge in 1928. Subsequently, Carter's trip became a subject of great controversy. While there Carter gave a nationally televised speech, urging Cuba to become part of the "democratic hemisphere," and pressing for more freedoms of speech and assembly. You'd think the ardently antisocialist American government would want our Cuban neighbors to hear just such a message. But apparently the Bush 43 administration wants to have that message delivered only by Republican messengers.

Bill and Hillary Clinton are, of course, America's most prominent straw couple. One conservative canard is the oft-repeated line that the Clintons' health care plan would have hijacked one-third of the economy. When resources are used for essential services for needy Americans, it is not a hijacking. Using this logic, how much of the economy is "hijacked" by Social Security, corporate welfare, and the Pentagon?

Perhaps the most egregious attack on Bill Clinton's legacy is the conservative charge that he is to blame for what happened on September 11. One of the biggest misstatements is the contention that Clinton was offered Osama bin Laden on a silver platter and forfeited a chance to get him. This is patently false. There was never a credible offer for Osama bin Laden, according to Clinton's national security advisor Sandy Berger, then secretary of state Madeleine Albright, and other key officials.

Here is what President Clinton said about bin Laden:

> We knew he (bin Laden) wanted to commit crimes against America. . . . At the time, 1996, he had committed no crime against America so I did not bring him here because we had no basis on which to hold him, though we knew he wanted to commit crimes

against America. So I pleaded with the Saudis to take him, 'cause they could have. But they thought it was a hot potato and they didn't and that's how he wound up in Afghanistan.

Conservatives have repeatedly claimed that Clinton could have had bin Laden just for the asking. They use his words in the preceding statement, "so I did not bring him here," to imply that Clinton purposely turned down an opportunity to get bin Laden off the street. But it was the Saudis to whom bin Laden was offered, not the United States, and the Saudis wouldn't take him. Many conservatives leap over this fact to blame Clinton for not doing enough to fight terrorism.

Here's what really happened according to those involved:

> U.S. government representatives met with Sudanese officials on terrorism issues on multiple occasions from 1996–2001 in venues ranging from Addis Ababa, to Virginia, Washington to New York and Khartoum. In none of those meetings, despite repeated U.S. requests for detailed information on bin Laden's network, finances and operatives and other terrorist organizations, did the Government of Sudan hand over its alleged files or provide detailed information deemed of significant operational value by U.S. Government counter-terrorism, law enforcement or CIA officials.

The website *Jane's Intelligence Review* reported on October 1, 1998, that President Clinton spent ten weeks trying to get the Saudis to accept Sudan's offer of bin Laden.

Frankly, it's shameful that the Clinton administration had to defend itself from charges that it didn't do enough to combat terrorism. Do the promoters of anti-Clinton propaganda really believe that the president didn't care about the safety of our country and was indifferent to terrorist threats? Do they honestly think President Clinton, his cabinet, and his advisers were cavalier about our vulnerabilities? And did the Republican-controlled Congress bear any responsibility as the legislative powers that were?

As part of a report in the *Washington Post* about how terrorism was handled leading up to the Bush 43 administration, Barton Gellman pointed out how much the Clinton administration accomplished. He said, "By any measure available, Clinton left office having given greater priority to terrorism than any president before him. His government doubled counterterrorist spending across 40 departments and agencies."

In the spring of 1996, President Clinton authorized the CIA to go after bin Laden's network using any means necessary. A multinational mercenary force was put together to hunt down bin Laden. In early 1998, we had trained commandos in Pakistan to be ready to go into Afghanistan and capture bin Laden. But the Pakistani government was overthrown before this plan could be executed. And who was the new sheriff in town? Our newly minted good friend General Pervez Musharraf. Also in 1998, the United States signed a secret agreement with Uzbekistan to initiate joint covert action against bin Laden. When there was credible evidence of bin Laden's terrorist activities, the United States took action, including launching a number of CIA operations.

Nevertheless, after September 11, conservatives viciously attacked Clinton for not doing enough during his presidency to fight "The 'War' on Terror." And when he did take action, as when he bombed what was believed to be a weapons facility in Sudan and another target in Afghanistan, was there appreciation from our security-conscious friends on the right? Not at all. They immediately accused the president of manufacturing a diversion from the effort to impeach him and downplayed the argument that his actions had to do with any terrorist threat. And the words *aspirin factory* were repeated so many times in reference to the Sudanese weapons facility that the mere thought of it relieves headaches. But it was more than an aspirin factory. I asked Sandy Berger, who was national security advisor at the time, if he would comment on conservative charges that this was nothing more than a commercial plant that we bombed based on poor intelligence. Here's what he told me:

The Sudan factory we bombed was a part of the Sudanese Military Industrial Corporation, which operated their chemical weapons program. We knew bin Laden had cooperated with the Sudanese on chemical weapons and had invested millions in its Military Industrial Corporation. Soil samples taken close to the plant tested positively for a chemical whose only known use is to make VX, a deadly poisonous chemical weapon. We bombed the plant at night when only one person was present. Had we not bombed that plant under these circumstances and chemical weapons had shown up subsequently in, say, the New York City subway system, such a failure would have been inexcusable. Since the bombing, the Sudanese have spent vast sums of money on lobbying firms and PR firms in the United States to try to confuse the facts, but they can't be erased.

The cruise missile strike in Afghanistan was launched in retaliation for the August 1998 bombing of the U.S. embassies in Africa. But the right wing would have us believe that Clinton cared only about taking attention away from his affair with Monica Lewinsky. So Clinton got accused of doing nothing, except for those times he did something, in which case he did it in the wrong places and for the wrong reason.

POP QUIZ: Who said: "We need to keep this country together right now. We need to focus on this terrorism issue"?

(a) George W. Bush in 2002

(b) Bill Clinton in 1996

The answer is (b), much to the chagrin of those who would like to argue that the word *terrorism* was not in the Clinton vocabulary.

At a news conference on July 30, 1996, Clinton urged Congress to pass antiterrorism legislation before it left for the August recess. Among the things he wanted were taggants, or markers in explosives, something Senator Orrin Hatch of Utah called a "phony issue." Clinton also wanted expanded wiretapping powers, which was also opposed by many Republicans. John Ashcroft, who opposed this initiative as a senator, was more than happy to endorse those powers once he became Bush's attorney general. Clinton also wanted to prevent foreign banks from having access to our financial markets if they didn't cooperate with U.S.-led investigations into terrorist financing. That one was killed by Republican Phil Gramm, who was then chairman of the Senate Banking Committee. Attempts to ban foreigners from entering the United States if they were suspected of having terrorist ties and plans to deport foreign nationals thought to have terrorist links were rejected by conservative groups. One of the groups most opposed to some of these ideas was the National Rifle Association, which was concerned about expanding government power. But that kind of governmental authority didn't bother them so much when Bush 43 did the very same things.

Another Clinton initiative involved asking all laboratories to list all dangerous biological agents, including anthrax, with the federal government. This didn't gain traction because the threat of bioterror wasn't considered much of an issue.

There's plenty of blame to go around if we want to point fingers for our lack of preparedness and for the misplaced priorities that left our country vulnerable. I point a finger directly at those conservatives who were hell-bent on destroying Clinton and could think of nothing else. The brazen attempt to disable the president took up the time of Congress, the courts, and the media and hobbled the executive branch's ability to focus its full energies on the well-being of the nation. The visceral contempt many conservatives had for one man, Bill Clinton, blinded them to what was best for our country as a whole and undermined and diverted our attention from the real issues of the day. I hope the lens of history enables those who were more obsessed with the president's sex life than the country's real needs to see how wrong they were for their irresponsible and, unfortunately, successful misdirection of our focus during the last part of the Clinton presidency.

One would think, given the behavior of the Bush 43 White House, that if Clinton initiated it, it must not have been worth pursuing. During most of 2000, submarines carrying sea-based missiles were ready to attack bin Laden if his location could be determined. The CIA tried to recruit tribal leaders in Afghanistan to take bin Laden out.

A report presented in December 2000 by Clinton terrorism expert Richard Clarke to senior administration officials called for the breakup of al Qaeda cells, the arrest of their personnel, action against financial support of their activities, reduced aid for nations supporting these cells, and an increase in covert activities in Afghanistan. Outgoing national security advisor Sandy Berger set up a series of briefings with Bush officials such as Dick Cheney and Condoleezza Rice. The Clinton administration didn't want to start a war or to begin initiatives that would largely fall on the Bush administration to carry out. Clinton had been on the receiving end of such a mess, having inherited the Somalia debacle from Bush 41. There was an attempt to coordinate policy, but there was hostility between the outgoing administration and the new one. According to Daniel Benjamin, a counterterrorism official who served in the Clinton administration: "A number of initiatives that were underway either lost speed or were sidetracked, and valuable time was lost."

Time magazine reported, for example, that a Predator Drone, one of the best instruments to gather information on terror camps, sat idle from October 2000 through September 11, 2001. According to a senior CIA official, "Once we were going to arm the thing, we didn't want to expose the capability by just having it fly overhead and spot a bunch of guys we couldn't do anything about."

I see: Bill Clinton was pro-terror because he didn't capture bin Laden, even with no basis on which to hold him, but the Bush 43 administration gets a pass when they "couldn't do anything about" known terrorists.

It seemed acceptable for Republicans to blame Clinton for not getting bin Laden, even though Bush 43 did little to try to achieve the same goal until September 11, 2001, in spite of being told by outgoing Clinton officials that terror should be a top priority and that bin Laden was the one to watch. But wasn't it the Republicans who controlled both houses of Congress, and who controlled the agenda? Oh, that's right, the agenda consisted of trying to run Clinton out of office because he had a dalliance in the Oval Office. Terrorism could wait. And it did. Until September 11, 2001.

Meanwhile, the Bush administration gave $43 million to the Taliban in May of 2001 as a reward for its ban on growing opium poppies. Can you show me a conservative who has made this point? Meanwhile, Bill Clinton, who is still accused of doing nothing to fight terrorism, signed an executive order that froze $254 million in Taliban assets in the United States. And let's not forget that the United States supported the Taliban's forerunner, the Mujahedin, in its fight against the Soviets in Afghanistan.

The accusation that President Clinton failed to adequately fight terrorism diverts attention from the failures of previous administrations. On the Reagan/Bush 41 watch, there was the April 18, 1983, destruction of the U.S. embassy in Beirut, which killed 17 Marines. Six months later, on October 23, Shiite suicide bombers hit a marine barracks in Beirut, killing 241 American military personnel and 58 French paratroopers. On December 12 of the same year, Shiite extremists set off car bombs in front of the French and U.S. embassies in Kuwait City. Five were killed and 86 were wounded. On June 14, 1985, Shiite Muslims seized a TWA Boeing 727 and forced it to land in Beirut. Their demands included the release of 700 Arab prisoners in Israel. A U.S. Navy diver was killed, and 39 Americans were held hostage until Syria intervened to gain their release on July 1 of that year. A few months later, the *Achille Lauro* was hijacked by Palestinian militants, and a disabled American Jew, Leon Klinghoffer, was shot and his body thrown overboard. A year later, on September 5, 1986, a Pan Am jet carrying 358 people was hijacked at the Karachi airport. In the melee that ensued when a SWAT team took over the plane, 20 people were killed. The 1988 bombing of Pan Am flight 103 resulted in another 270 deaths over Lockerbie, Scotland. President Reagan had ordered the bombing of the Libyan capital of Tripoli and the city of Benghazi in 1986 as revenge for the bombing of a Berlin nightclub where two Americans died. One theory is that the Pan Am bombing was a response to this action.

It's predictable that the hard right would blame Bill Clinton for September 11. The very people who tell liberals that they ought to stop being so partisan and act more like "Americans" are the first to point fingers. Of course, when a conservative says "Why don't you act more American?" what that person is really saying is "Why don't you act like a conservative?" What's astounding is the extent to which Clinton gets blamed for even minor infractions. Former South African president Nelson Mandela had some harsh words for Bush 43 when he addressed the International Women's Forum in Johannesburg on January 30, 2003. "What I am condemning is that one power, with a president who has no foresight, who cannot think properly, is now wanting to plunge the world into a holocaust. . . . Why does the United States behave so arrogantly?" Mandela asked. "Is this because the secretary-general of the United Nations is now a black man?" he asked. "They never did that when secretary-generals were white."

Now, no reasonable person would believe that Bush 43 is a unilateralist because the head of the UN is black. In fact, I may have strong policy differences with Bush 43, but he is certainly not a racist, and to call him one is just plain wrong. But guess who got blamed for this on one well-known right-wing website? That's right: Bill Clinton. According to NewsMax.com, run by Christopher Ruddy (also known as the chief proponent of the theory that Clinton White House counsel Vince Foster was murdered), "Questions are swirling about the role ex-President Clinton may have played in encouraging one-time international human rights icon Nelson Mandela's acid attack on President Bush." Oh really? Where were these questions "swirling"? In someone's right-wing, conspiracy-laden head, that's where. NewsMax is the website of choice for conservative talk-show hosts, and they never fail to deliver red meat to their constituency. And the evidence that Bill Clinton was behind Mandela's attacks on Bush 43? Well, you see, four months before Mandela's statement, Clinton was in Cape Town and met with Mandela to form a partnership to battle AIDS, and they were both behind concerts to raise money for the cause. Furthermore, Rhodes scholars from South Africa were joining with Rhodes scholars from other countries to oppose Bush 43 on Iraq. And what a coincidence! Bill Clinton is a Rhodes scholar!

Frankly, I don't think the right wing goes far enough here. Isn't Bill Clinton responsible for AIDS in the first place? I mean this guy was so loose, who knows what diseases he's carrying? In fact, haven't they determined that Bill Clinton causes cancer in rats? And the Tawana Brawley hoax! We know Clinton was behind that because he once had a conversation with Al Sharpton. Acid rain? Well, he's been in the rain, and Lord knows he must have done acid at some point, even if he didn't inhale.

One of the juicier allegations against Clinton was that he fathered a black child, Danny Williams, allegedly the result of an affair with a black prostitute named Bobbie Ann Willams. It isn't enough to say that Clinton had an affair with a prostitute; it's so much better if you can also say it's a black prostitute with whom he had a black baby. So not only did Bill Clinton like black people, he actually *had sex* with them on occasion. On December 15, 1998, NewsMax.com asked, "Why won't the same media that chased the story of Rep. Dan Burton's love child and made national headlines out of House Judiciary Committee Chairman Henry Hyde's ancient affair report the Danny Williams story?" And the answer to that question is: because the Danny Williams story isn't true. *Star* magazine paid a private firm to compare Bill Clinton's DNA, made public by Independent Counsel Ken Starr, and the DNA of Danny Williams. Even though the test came back negative, NewsMax refused to believe it, questioning "whether the FBI Lab's Clinton DNA report was presented accurately in the Starr Report." Funny that they believed everything *else* that was in the Starr Report.

The pinnacle of the anti-Clinton garbage had to be what became known as "The Clinton Body Count." From Vince Foster, the White House counsel whose body was found in Washington, D.C.'s, Fort Marcy Park on July 7, 1993, to former Commerce secretary Ron Brown, to Clinton bodyguards, the story was that people associated with Bill Clinton in some way wound up dead. Unfortunately, we all wind up dead at some point, and we all know lots of people; but, when Bill Clinton knows people who die, he must have had something to do with it. I believe Bill Clinton has been linked to almost every death in America between his birth in 1946 and today. We have now solved the mysteries of Marilyn Monroe, JFK, and Jimmy Hoffa. Watch your back. Clinton might be coming for you next.

Not only did Bill Clinton kill people, according to some conservatives; he never really won the presidency. When he was elected president in 1992 with 42 percent of the popular vote, much was made of how his inability to attract a majority delegitimatized him. Even when he was reelected with 49 percent of the vote in 1996, he was derided for not having a mandate. That didn't stop the Bushies from crowing about their wonderful victory in 2000, even though their candidate *lost* the popular vote. Bush 43 was elected with only 47.8 percent of the popular vote. Richard Nixon won with 43.4 percent in 1968 and Abraham Lincoln a paltry 39.9 percent in 1860, but you never heard the right wing speak up about those minority numbers.

The Straw Person Hall of Fame

Hillary Clinton deserves placement in the Straw Man Hall of Fame. Okay, we'll make it the Straw *Person* Hall of Fame. Hillary can't say the word *president* without conservatives saying it's a subliminal wish that she were living at 1600 Pennsylvania Avenue again. If they take attendance and Hillary says "present" they say, "She really meant 'president'." And when conservatives say that Hillary wants to be president, what they're really trying to do is warn and alarm America. They're saying, "You'd better lock your doors, grab the kids, and hide your money. Hillary Clinton may run the country and no one will be safe." And how *dare* this American citizen, duly elected by a wide margin to the United States Senate from one of America's largest states, how dare she even *think* about one day running for the White House! Conservatives think it's bad enough that any Democrat would have ambition to run for public office, but there's something about Hillary that drives them crazy.

So worried were conservatives that Hillary might one day seek higher office that, according to Robert Novak, "A prominent conservative operative in Washington, fearing the prospect of Hillary Clinton on the Democratic ticket for vice president next year, is urging Senate Republicans 'not to do anything to help her ambitions by building a Senate record.' Specifically, he urged not co-signing letters or co-sponsoring legislation with Clinton, not getting photographed with her, and not socializing or traveling with her."

So not only should conservatives not legislate with her, even if they can agree on something in a bipartisan way, they shouldn't even be *seen* with her. This is a long way from the days of Tip O'Neill. When President Reagan wanted to know why the Democratic Speaker of the House had blasted his economic plan when they had had such a wonderful time together just a few nights before, O'Neill told him, "Ol' buddy, that's politics. After six o'clock we can be friends but before six, it's politics." But Hillary was to be treated as though she had the plague. Unfortunately, some conservatives believe that liberalism and the plague are synonymous. This can't be good for America.

Appearing on *Hardball with Chris Matthews* in November 2002, Hillary was asked about Bush's motive to go to war with Iraq. Matthews wanted to know if she thought it had to do with weapons of mass destruction or if there were other reasons for wanting to remove Saddam. She replied, "I think there a lot of reasons. I mean it is clear that a lot of people in this administration have some old scores to settle with Saddam Hussein. But I cannot discount the potential threat of weapons of mass destruction in the hands of somebody who has repeatedly demonstrated that he will do anything in order to keep and maintain his power."

All her enemies heard was, "Bush has an old score to settle." It was the president himself who said during a speech in Houston in the days leading up to the push to go into Iraq that Saddam was "the guy who tried to kill my dad." Nevertheless, Hillary was attacked for accusing the president of starting a war based on a personal vendetta. And this in spite of her vote in the Senate to authorize the president to use all necessary means to deal with Iraq.

And the Popular Vote Winner Is . . .

One great lie we still (and will probably always) hear is that Al Gore tried to steal the election of 2000. How do you steal what you've already won? If only we could do away with that obsolete Electoral College and actually allow voters to pick the president directly. The further lie is that Al Gore acted inappropriately, as though Bush 43 would have done anything differently had roles been reversed. Even before Election Day that year, here's what Andrew Miga reported in the *Boston Herald:* "The Bush camp, sources said, would likely challenge the legitimacy of a Gore win, casting it as an affront to the people's will and branding the Electoral College as an antiquated relic."

There is precedent for Republican behavior in such situations. In 1984, Democrat incumbent Frank McCloskey was unseated by challenger Richard McIntyre in Indiana's "Bloody 8th" congressional district by 34 votes. A county-by-county recount was done, widening the lead to 418 votes. Then it went to the House, where McCloskey won by 4 votes. One Republican congressman was so incensed by this he said, "I think we ought to go to war." He later added, "There's unanimity. We need bold and dramatic action [to get McCloskey's win overturned]." That person happened to be

Wyoming's Richard Cheney, a future vice president of the United States, thanks to another postelection battle. Jack Kemp, then a congressman, and a future vice presidential nominee, referred to this as "political and moral outrage at the outright theft of the seat in the 8th District of Indiana," and President Reagan called it "damned robbery."

More recently there were charges of ineligible voters casting ballots, absentee ballots being delivered illegally, groups being illegally persuaded to vote, and unaccounted-for ballots. This time, though, it was 1996, and the person making these charges and calling for a recount was Representative Bob Dornan, the Republican firebrand from Orange County, California, who lost to Democrat Loretta Sanchez by 984 votes.

As conservative columnist Kathleen Parker wrote in the *Chicago Tribune* on November 29, 2000, "We can also comfortably assume that George W. Bush's team would have done the same were circumstances reversed."

The Reagan Myth

Ronald Reagan has achieved near-mythical status in conservative America. We have heard for years that Reagan lowered taxes and deficits simultaneously, and that this is a tribute to the theory of supply-side economics.

In fact, Reagan raised taxes and increased the deficits. Congressman Gene Taylor of Mississippi, known as a Blue Dog Democrat, and one of the most conservative Democrats in Congress, accurately states: "Almost half of the increased revenues of the Reagan era came from Social Security and Medicare payroll taxes, which were *increased* by President Reagan and Congress in 1983. The Reagan Administration and the split Congress also raised taxes in 1982, 1984, and 1986, although back then they were called 'revenue enhancements'."

When Reagan assumed office in January 1981, the federal deficit was $79 billion and the debt was $908.5 billion, or 34 percent of the gross domestic product. By the end of the Reagan era, in 1988, in spite of what we were promised by Reagan/Bush 41, the deficit was $152.5 billion and the debt was $2.6 trillion, or 54 percent of the GDP. In 1992, as Bush 41 was leaving office, those figures had increased to a deficit of $255.1 billion, and a debt of $4.1 trillion, representing 67 percent of the GDP.

Reagan's final budget for fiscal year 1990 called for spending of $1.15 trillion, compared with $678.2 billion in 1981. Fifteen percent of monies allocated in this budget went to service the debt. Domestic programs were cut by $18 billion, with the agriculture budget alone down by 18 percent. At the same time, the plan called for a 44 percent increase in the "Star Wars" missile defense budget and a 50 percent pay raise for members of Congress and other federal officials. Even more troubling, $16 billion in 1990 and $9 billion in 1991 were set aside to bail out savings and loans institutions, which were damaged by Reagan's own deregulatory policies in the first place. All this, while eighty domestic programs were to be cut to save $4.9 billion.

In converse proportion to the elevation of Ronald Reagan to cultlike status is the attempted diminution of Bill Clinton. Conservatives can't even acknowledge how much better the economy was during the Clinton years, saying Clinton inherited a good economy for which Bush 41 never received credit. They've invented the term "Clinton recession" to attach our forty-second president's name to a faltering economy.

Don't conservatives preach personal responsibility? When there's a conservative Congress, a Democratic president, and a good economy, they claim credit; when there's a Democratic Congress, a conservative president (Reagan), and a bad economy, the Congress gets the blame.

Trickle-Down Thinking

For years during the 1980s and 1990s conservatives couldn't speak more than two sentences without spouting the words *balanced budget*. They even wanted a balanced budget amendment. Forget that it was

Reagan's "Star Wars" fantasy in the era of big defense overruns, double billing, and hundred-dollar airplane ashtrays that helped to drive up the deficit. Forget that it was Bill Clinton, a Democratic president who, during his first two years in office, with a Democratic House and Senate, cut the deficit in half. Any Republicans want to push a balanced budget amendment now? Anyone? On Christmas Eve 2002, the Bush 43 administration asked Congress to consider another increase in the federal debt limit. Nice that they wanted to give themselves a little Christmas present at taxpayer expense and do it at a time when they knew it wouldn't get much attention.

Republicans accuse Democrats of playing class warfare when they point out that conservative economic policies favor the rich over the poor. They can't bear to hear the phrase "tax cuts for the rich." How else do you explain a plan in which according to Citizens for Tax Justice, as reported in the *New York Times*, "the wealthiest 1 percent of taxpayers—those with annual incomes over $356,000— would receive about half the revenue the government would lose next year if dividends went untaxed and 45 percent of all the money from accelerating the rate cuts? The 80 percent of households with incomes below $73,000 a year would get less than 10 percent of the new tax breaks." At the time this plan was proposed by the Bush 43 administration, R. Glenn Hubbard, chairman of the president's Council of Economic advisors, said, "the increasing reliance on taxing higher-income households and targeted social preferences at lower incomes stands in the way of moving to a simpler, flatter system." Nothing like sacrificing the well-being of the needy in the name of simplicity and flatness.

We can all agree that the rich pay more in taxes because they make more, but in terms of who gets the most breaks according to the Bush plan, we're talking *percentages*, and that proves that it is disproportionately weighted. Republicans can yell "class warfare" at liberals all they want, but simply accusing liberals of this doesn't make it so. This is a brilliant tactic, often used by the right, of accusing the left of what they themselves are doing.

Because Congress promised that revenue loss from tax cuts would be limited to $1.35 trillion over ten years, and that it would be encoded in the budget provision, they had to include a "sunset provision," whereby the tax cuts expired after nine years. That was the only way they could maintain the $1.35 trillion figure. We couldn't afford these tax cuts, and making them permanent was fiscally irresponsible. And economic theory indicates that unless you permanently put money in someone's pocket, they're not going to spend it.

In a *Wall Street Journal* piece on November 1, 2001, Bruce Bartlett, Senior Fellow at the National Center for Policy Analysis, dispelled the right's notion that tax rebates would stimulate the economy and punched a hole in their beloved "trickle-down" theory:

> A federal tax rebate in 1974 and state tax rebates since did not raise consumer spending much, if at all. The available data from this year's rebate only confirm this conclusion. People simply socked away the money or used it to pay down debt, which is the same thing. This follows from something economists call the "permanent income hypothesis." It says that people raise their spending only in response to permanent increases in income. Temporary increases do not change spending patterns.

The Bush economic plan introduced at the beginning of 2003 was called "bold" by his supporters. I'd use the word *audacious*. The centerpiece of the plan was the elimination of the tax dividend on stock. This benefits the investor class, not the average person. According to IRS data, only 22 percent of taxpayers with income under $100,000 have any dividend income. I'm absolutely stunned that more average Americans, who didn't get much the first time around, who didn't do better under Reagan, and who have little to gain under the Republican plan, nevertheless, attack the Democrats, whose plan serves them much better.

Another phrase, used as a mantra by Republicans, is "tax-and-spend Democrats," But look who's spending. In Bush 43's State of the Union address in 2003, he offered $10 billion in new money for AIDS treatment in Africa, $1.2 billion for hydrogen-powered cars, $450 million to mentor youngsters, $600 million for drug treatment, and $400 billion to strengthen Medicare. Would the great applause he received for these programs from the right side of the aisle be as thunderous were the speech delivered by a "tax-and-spend Democrat"?

Democrats have been talking about cutting Social Security and Medicare payroll taxes (the very ones Reagan raised), which would give more Americans an opportunity to share in the tax cuts. And these are the Americans who need it most, who would spend it rather than hoard it, and for whom a few dollars would go a long way. The Democratic plan, offered to counter the Bush 43 plan to line the pockets of corporations, did two major things that the Bush 43 plan didn't: it offered to stimulate the economy sooner rather than later, and to focus on those who needed the money most. And it did so at a cost of $136 billion, not the $670 billion that the Republicans would have added to the already-mushrooming deficit. So who are the real taxers and spenders?

Another myth about Ronald Reagan concerns just what his military experience was. He loved to reminisce about his World War II experiences. Defending his unfortunate trip to the cemetery in Bitburg, Germany, where members of Hitler's SS were buried, Reagan proclaimed, "Yes I know all the bad things that happened in that war. I was in uniform for four years myself." Al Hunt wrote in the September 28, 2000, edition of the *Wall Street Journal* that ". . . in his 1965 autobiography, *Where's the Rest of Me?*, Reagan commented on the rigors of war: 'By the time I got out of the Army Air Corps all I wanted to do—in common with several million other veterans—was to rest up, make love to my wife. . . .' " Hunt went on to report that "Mr. Reagan actually spent the war years making training films and spending most nights at home. In 1983 the Gipper regaled Israeli Prime Minister Yitzhak Shamir and Nazi-hunter Simon Wiesenthal with his memories of photographing Nazi death camps at the end of the war. But Mr. Reagan never left the country during that war, period."

Dead Straw Men Tell No Lies

One of the arguments the right tries to force on the left is that President John F. Kennedy was a tax-cutter who would support the Bush 43 tax cut plan. But let's set some things straight here.

At the time of the 1963 tax cuts, the top tax rate was 91 percent, and only 6 percent of the Kennedy cuts went to those making more than $300,000, in today's dollars. Now, deficits are much larger as a percentage of the economy, and the deficit is growing. Presidents Kennedy and Johnson saw it going in the other direction. Senator Ted Kennedy may be closer to the situation than the conservatives trying to make hay with his brother's name. And he was rightfully indignant about the use of his brother's voice in GOP-sponsored advertising. "It stretches decency a bit when selling that program for Republican leaders to be using President Kennedy's voice in these several states [in radio ads] in support of his tax cut in 1961 as a suggestion that he might support this tax cut. He certainly would not have," Senator Kennedy said in 2001. "It is intellectually dishonest and politically irresponsible to suggest that President Kennedy would have supported such a tax cut. It is a dramatic misreading of history to compare President Kennedy's and President Bush's tax cut proposals."

In 1963 the national debt was $250 billion, roughly fourteen times less than what it is today. Listen, if JFK's ideas were so good for America, why did Republicans vote for Richard Nixon?

It's a phony tactic to hold up a respected dead person on the other side of the political spectrum to convince your opponent of the wrongheadedness of his or her ideas. It would be nice to be able to do what Woody Allen did in *Annie Hall*, when his character, Alvy Singer, heard someone in a movie theater line misinterpret the writings of Marshall McLuhan. Woody's character brought out the real McLuhan to face the camera and set the record straight.

In his book *The End of Racism: Principles for a Multicultural Society*, conservative author Dinesh D'Souza attempts to stake his claim as an heir to Martin Luther King Jr. on the issue of affirmative action. One line, taken from King's "I Have a Dream" speech, the dream that his children might one day "be judged not by the color of their skin but by the content of their character," is used as Exhibit A. But in King's 1963 work, *Why We Can't Wait*, King advocated "compensatory consideration" for blacks, and in his final book, in 1967, *Where Do We Go from Here?* King wrote: "A society that has done something special *against* the Negro for hundreds of years, he must now do something special *for* him." As for D'Souza, he claims that slavery, "proved to be the transmission belt that nevertheless brought Africans into the orbit of modern civilization and Western freedom." I never saw anything like THAT in the "I Have a Dream" speech. And, although, unlike some conservatives, I don't speak for the dead, I can say with a fair degree of certainty that King would not have supported D'Souza's desire to repeal the Civil Rights Act of 1964.

So, conservatives, come up with your own heroes. Stop shamelessly appropriating ours for your own political gain. And if you really want to know what the dead are thinking, get yourself some tickets to "Crossing Over" or go see the psychic George Anderson.

Contraindications of the Truth

Listening to the way conservatives attempt to eviscerate liberals, you would think everyone on the right is of the George "I cannot tell a lie" Washington ethic. But lying is not solely the province of the left. On January 26, 1987, President Reagan told the Tower Commission, created to investigate the Iran-Contra scandal, that he approved of the sale of arms to Iran in return for hostages in August 1985. This confirmed testimony by National Security Advisor Robert McFarlane. But had this story stood, White House chief of staff Donald Regan could have been brought up on perjury charges for having testified otherwise. On February 2, 1987, Reagan told the

Tower Commission that, after speaking with Donald Regan, he realized that arms for hostages were not approved in advance, thus changing what he said during his testimony one week earlier. It became obvious that Reagan was talking from prepared notes when he mistakenly read his instructions aloud: "If the question comes up at the Tower Board meeting, you might want to say that you were surprised."

As for Bush 41, he told the FBI on December 12, 1986, and testified to the Office of Independent Council on January 11, 1988, that he received regular information about arms sales to Iran and knew about 1985 Israeli arms shipments. But in an August 5, 1987, interview with David Broder at the *Washington Post*, Bush 41 said he didn't oppose the sale of arms to Iran because he never heard the objections of Secretary of State George Shultz or Secretary of Defense Caspar Weinberger: "Maybe I would have had a stronger view, but when you don't know something, it's hard to react. . . . We were not in the loop." And the September 8, 1992, Broder column states:

> According to a memo dictated by Shultz on August 7, Weinberger referred to Bush's statement in the interview and said it was "terrible. He was on the other side. It's on the Record. Why did he say that?" According to the executive summary of the Independent Counsel's report, "The Iran operations were carried out with the knowledge of, among others, President Ronald Reagan, Vice President George Bush, Secretary of State George P. Shultz, Secretary of Defense Caspar W. Weinberger, Director of Central Intelligence William J. Casey, and national security advisors Robert C. McFarlane and John M. Poindexter; of these officials, only Weinberger and Shultz dissented from the policy decision.

The Iran-Contra scandal had a very happy ending for the principals because Bush 41 gave very nice holiday gifts to his buddies as he was headed out the White House door. Independent Counsel Lawrence Walsh indicted Defense Secretary Caspar Weinberger,

CIA clandestine services chief Clair George, and Dewey Clarridge, the CIA's European Division chief, for taking part in a cover-up, but all received last-minute pardons from the outgoing president. Merry Christmas.

Good for Thou but Not for Thee

One of the issues that the Republicans rode to victory in 1994 was term limits. The issue was so hot that even the Speaker of the House, Democrat Tom Foley, was scorched. Republican George Nethercutt knocked Foley off after thirty years of service, largely by pledging to serve no more than six years. But when his six years were up, guess what? The poster boy for term limits ran again. And again. Jonathan Rauch in the *National Journal* compiled Nethercutt's arguments for breaking his promise:

> Some of them are pathetic, as when he said (to the *Washington Post*) that he had "blurted out" his promise in 1994. Others are irrelevant, as when he told *The American Spectator*, "I feel I have to finish the work I started." (He did not promise, in 1994, to stay until he felt he was finished.) Some are crass, as when he told *The NewsHour With Jim Lehrer* that in 1994, "I didn't realize I'd be in the majority. I didn't realize I'd be on the Appropriations Committee. That means something for our district—not for me, but for our district." . . . Still others are simply weird. "I'm less enamored with the idea of term limitations, and I'm the perfect example of why we don't need them," he told *The Post*.

This is the same man who said about Bill Clinton: "Your word is your bond, whether it's your public life or your private life. The honorable thing for him to do is to resign."

It's ironic that conservatives, who claim to dislike government so much, spend their lives and fortunes trying to be a part of it. And once they get there, they find out that the perks are so good, they don't want to leave. The antigovernment conservatives began to blossom during the Reagan era. These are the politicians who ran for office telling us they hated the government and that we were being overtaxed, and then were all too happy to get government paychecks funded by taxpayer dollars. Before Spencer Abraham lost reelection as a senator from Michigan, he sponsored Senate bill S. 896. This was the Department of Energy Abolishment Act, calling for the "complete abolishment of the Department of Energy." But on January 18, 2001, Abraham testified before the Senate Energy and Natural Resources Committee that the department was now necessary: ". . . a number of new developments have occurred that either significantly addressed these concerns or put them in a new light." And why was Senator Abraham testifying before his former colleagues? Why, to become secretary of the Department of Energy. While we're on the subject of staying intellectually consistent, how about applying it to adulterers? When allegations of adultery against former Louisiana congressman Bob Livingston were raised just as he was about to become Speaker of the House, he resigned. He was then widely praised by conservatives for being a man of great integrity. I suppose this means that if Clinton stepped down at that moment he would have been crowned the Heritage Foundation Man of the Year. Personally, I want a president who is sexually satisfied. Besides, if a president can't get some, who can? Eventually, it came out that not only did Clinton have sex in the Oval Office, but he did so while talking on the phone with congressmen! First they whined that he was having sex on taxpayer time and the taxpayer dime, and then they complained that he was working at the same time he was being pleasured. I, for one, am glad to know that a president can be good at multitasking.

Size Does Count

Conservatives are always claiming that they want smaller government. Ronald Reagan, who began the modern-day conservative

movement, ran on the issues of less government and tax simplifica-
tion. But tell me, did it get easier to do your taxes under Ronald
Reagan? I've yet to hear one person praise how much kinder and
gentler the IRS is. And Reagan actually *expanded* the federal payroll
by 61,000, while that big-spending, government-loving liberal, Bill
Clinton, reduced it by 373,000.

But here's the way it really is, as reported by the *Financial Times*
on September 13, 2002: "Since the 1960s, the Republican and
Democrat administrations have switched places on economic policy.
The pattern is so well established that the generalization can no
longer be denied: the Republicans have become the party of fiscal
irresponsibility, trade restriction, big government and bad microeco-
nomics." The *Financial Times* went on to compare the records of
Reagan, Bush 41, and Bush 43, reminding us that deficits tend to rise
during Republican administrations, and that Bush's policies could
leave us in the same budget hole that Reagan's did.

As for free trade, it was Jimmy Carter and Bill Clinton who
advanced it as policy, not the Republicans who served in between:
"Highlights include George W. Bush's tariffs on steel and lumber
and Ronald Reagan's voluntary export restraints on autos. And the
trend toward deregulation that most imagine began in the Reagan
administration? It began under Jimmy Carter in airlines, trucking,
natural gas and banking. Mr. Reagan continued the trend."

Here's another switcheroo. When he was running for Congress,
Senator Lindsay Graham called for the abolition of the Department
of Education, but once his own party controlled the executive
branch, he changed his tune. As the *Greenville News* reported on
January 31, 2003, "Graham and other Republicans who in 1994
promised to eliminate the Education Department last year supported Bush's multi-billion-dollar expansion of the department."

Well into the Bush 43 administration, *Fortune* magazine declared,
"The era of big government has returned," and reported spending
was up 13.9 percent for the fiscal 2002 fiscal year. And it wasn't the
reaction to the September 11 atrocities that accounted for profligate

spending. While $30 billion in spending was related to the attacks on America, $91 billion went for other goodies, like highway construction and medical research. And rhetoric doesn't always match reality. After proposing a 4 percent reduction in agriculture subsidies in 2001, Bush 43 signed the most expensive farm subsidy bill in history, calling for $190 billion in spending over a decade.

Listening to Bush 43's 2003 State of the Union address, you would have thought he was a liberal. In all, twenty new federal programs were proposed in this speech, but small-government advocates can take heart. That's down from thirty-nine proposed new initiatives the year before.

Bush 43's big government got even bigger in the wake of September 11, 2001. The Department of Homeland Security combined twenty-two agencies and a hundred seventy thousand workers into one huge bureaucracy. And I've already detailed how efforts to encroach our civil liberties by our government's executive branch make George Orwell's *1984* seem as prescient as Nostradamus.

Here Comes the Judge

Republicans have consistently whined when Democrat-controlled Senates haven't approved judges in an expeditious manner. Judges Priscilla Owen and Charles Pickering, in particular, were opposed by liberals, and became right-wing causes célèbres. But the facts don't support the level of anger Republicans have toward Democrats on this score. The Senate ended its 2002 session having confirmed 72 new judges appointed by President Bush, the best one-year record for confirmations since 1994. This 107th Congress approved 100 judges, compared to the 73 confirmations President Clinton won in the 104th Congress, 98 in the 105th, and 72 in the 106th.

A 1999 study showed that hostility toward President Clinton by the Republican-controlled Senate was a major factor in slowing the confirmation rate of judges to historic lows. The study, coauthored by political science professors Elliot Slotnick of Ohio State

University and Sheldon Goldman of the University of Massachusetts, showed that the 1992 Democrat-controlled Senate took 92 days on average to hold hearings on Bush 41's nominees for district judges, but that the Republican-controlled Senate of 1998 took an average of 160 days to act on President Clinton's nominations. And the study found that it wasn't the judges' ideology that held up the process here; Clinton's nominees, especially in his second term, tended to be moderate, not liberal. Goldman shows that Clinton faced "unprecedented delay . . . and acrimony" over his appointees. So why did Republicans hold up needed judgeships? Clearly, it was because they didn't like the tie Clinton was wearing, especially when it was the Zegna tie allegedly given to him by Monica Lewinsky.

Justice Owen was so extreme on abortion that even many Republicans, like those on the all-Republican Texas court, didn't concur with her. Texas law makes exceptions for underage girls seeking abortions who don't feel they can inform their parents, but that wasn't good enough for Justice Owen. Justice Owen voted to deny an abortion to a girl, claiming she didn't understand the seriousness of it. Alberto Gonzales, who served with Justice Owen on the Texas court and, ironically became Bush 43's White House counsel, wrote that to construe the Texas statute narrowly "would be an unconscionable act of judicial activism." Texas is one of nine states where judges run partisan political campaigns to get their jobs, and Justice Owen had the distinction of taking a political contribution of $8,600 from Enron; and then later writing a decision reversing a lower court order that saved that fine company $225,000 in taxes.

Other golden oldies from the Owen file include a ruling in favor of an insurance company that denied a benefit for a poor family after it informed the family it would pay the bill. She took a year and a half to issue an opinion that involved a young man injured in a truck accident. In the interim, the man died because his family couldn't afford nursing care because the appeal delayed the multimillion-dollar verdict. This, from the state of Texas, home of compassionate conservatism.

Judge Pickering was also opposed by Democrats, not for being a conservative, but for being outside the conservative mainstream. In 1994, Judge Pickering worked to reduce the sentence required by law and given to a man convicted of burning a cross on the lawn of a home of an interracial couple. He once referred to the "one-person-one-vote" law as "obtrusive." I have to agree with him here. If the person voting is a right-wing reactionary, it is obtrusive, indeed. According to independentjudiciary.com, Pickering, as a law student, "wrote a law review article suggesting ways the state could amend its miscegenation statute to ensure it would be found constitutional and enforceable. . . . When asked in 1990 about the article, he stated that he had no opinion at the time about whether interracial marriage *should* be illegal. He now says he does not think it should be, but he has never disavowed the content of the article."

Should we believe that Pickering had "no opinion" on whether a white could be able to marry a black? That's safe, isn't it? Imagine having "no opinion" about whether people should be allowed to marry whomever they want.

Sounds just like Clarence Thomas who, during his confirmation hearings, swore under oath that he had no opinion on abortion. Thomas claimed that when the case was decided in 1973, he was a married law student with a job. He claimed, "I did not spend a lot of time around the law school doing what all the students enjoyed so much, and that is debating all the current cases and all of the slip opinions." Okay, Justice Thomas, did you even think about current issues and have views on them? Thomas added, in an exchange with Senator Patrick Leahy, that he never mixed it up on the issue of *Roe v. Wade*. "If you are asking me whether or not I have ever debated the contents of it, the answer to that is no, Senator."

Exasperated, Leahy pointed out that Thomas had participated in a working group that criticized the *Roe* decision, and he had cited the abortion issue in more than one article. But Thomas steadfastly refused to comment, saying, "Senator, your question to me was, did I debate the contents of *Roe v. Wade*, do I have this day an opinion, a personal opinion, on the outcome in *Roe v. Wade*, and my answer to you is that I do not." Now, I know judges are supposed to be impartial on the bench, but to deny that you have a personal opinion on one of the most-often debated judicial topics? This strains credulity.

Judge Pickering's record included a few other issues that rightfully needed examination. For one thing, his rulings were disproportionately reversed on appeal. And in an effort to secure his move up the judicial ladder, he solicited letters of commendation from lawyers who practiced before him.

Not that Republicans would ever extract revenge at the expense of national security, but a request by the Judiciary Committee for $1.5 million to investigate failures in the Intelligence Committee was blocked by Senator Lott as payback for the rejection of Judge Pickering. Lott accused the committee of showing a "deliberate pattern of obstructionism" on Bush's judicial nominees and said, "I am hard-pressed to understand why the committee under its current leadership should be entrusted with further responsibilities and resources when they have failed to take action on their primary responsibilities."

But why should Republicans explore intelligence failures when they can make a political point? Maybe so that it'll take longer to analyze why we can't catch terrorists before they kill thousands of Americans, and maybe that will teach those pesky Dems a lesson!

Republicans complained that their judicial nominees were rejected in committee before they could ever have a vote in the full Senate. They may have a point when they say that it would benefit the democratic process to have nominees voted up or down by the entire body, but that didn't seem to matter when the Republicans controlled the Senate. Bill Lann Lee couldn't get a hearing when he was up for the position of assistant attorney general because of his pro-affirmative-action views. And then senator John Ashcroft was against a full Senate vote for Missouri Supreme Court Justice Ronnie White because he didn't agree with one decision White made against imposing the death penalty.

During the confirmation hearings of Miguel Estrada for appointment to the Circuit Court of Appeals for the District of Columbia, Democrats complained that, just as in the Thomas hearings, precious little information was available about the prospective judge. He gave terse answers during his hearing, and his view of the Constitution's role in the judiciary was unclear. As in the Thomas case, this was fine with Republicans. But when a Clinton nominee, Marcia Berzon, was up for a job with the Ninth Circuit Court of Appeals, Republicans wanted transcripts of every ACLU meeting that occured when she was a member, even those meetings she didn't attend. Senate Judiciary chair Orrin Hatch said at the time: "Determining which of President Clinton's nominees will become activists is complicated and it will require the Senate to be more diligent and extensive in its questioning of nominees' jurisprudential views."

The only reason there was a vacancy for Estrada to fill in the first place was because Republicans passed over many Clinton nominees, claiming there were too many judges on that court already. They were just running out the Clinton clock, waiting for their own chance to fill the seat.

It was Republican senator James Inhofe of Oklahoma who "declared . . . he'd block every administration nominee to the federal bench for the rest of Clinton's term in protest of the recent reappointment of a member of the National Labor Relations Board without Senate's consent."

In this case, the appointee was Sara Fox, and the appointment was controversial because it was a "recess appointment," one a president is allowed to make when Congress is in, of all things, recess. Clinton was raked over the coals for using this provision to make controversial appointments. But this is the same process Bush 43 used to appoint Eugene Scalia, son of Supreme Court Justice Antonin Scalia, to a post as the top lawyer in the Labor Department. Oh, I get it. Recess appointments are only valid if they're accompanied by nepotism.

Washington Post columnist E. J. Dionne pointed out the double standards in judicial appointments in a May 2002 column: "Senate Republican Leader Trent Lott, who now demands that the Senate vote on Bush's judges, is the same Trent Lott who declared in 1999 that 'getting more federal judges is not what I came here to do.' He added that there are not a lot of people saying, 'Give us more federal judges.' Except that this is exactly what Lott is saying now."

When Earl Warren was Supreme Court Chief Justice, presiding over the civil rights era, conservatives accused him of running a liberal activist court. Even if we were to concede that point, let's not be in denial about the conservative activist court run by William Rehnquist. The Warren Court struck down federal law in twenty cases over sixteen years. The Rehnquist court has struck down thirty-two laws in eight years. Eleven of these were states' rights cases in which the states' laws were upheld; and in many of these cases, the states were trying to avoid enforcement of civil rights guaranteed by federal law. And let's not forget how this states'-rights-friendly court wasn't so friendly to the Supreme Court of Florida when it decided in Al Gore's favor in the presidential election controversy of 2000.

When James Hormel was nominated by Bill Clinton as ambassador to Luxembourg, in October of 1997, the nomination was blocked in spite of the 16–2 vote of approval by the Senate Foreign Relations Committee. Senators James Inhofe of Oklahoma and Tim Hutchinson of Arkansas objected to his nomination because he advocated gay rights. Conservatives who supported this view said they didn't mind that he was gay; they minded that he was a gay activist. Does that mean it would have been all right for him to be a straight activist or a gay couch potato? Senator Inhofe went so far as to compare Hormel with former Ku Klux Klan grand wizard David Duke. At the time, Inhofe said, "I would feel the same way if it were David Duke or anybody whose agenda is more important than the country." So James Hormel wanting equal rights for gays is the same thing as David Duke saying blacks and Jews have too many rights as it is. Nice.

A month after Inhofe elevated David Duke to James Hormel's status, it was Trent Lott's turn. In an interview with Armstrong Williams, the Senate majority leader said this about homosexuality: "You should try to show them a way to deal with that problem just like alcohol or sex addiction or kleptomania." So being gay is as bad as being a thief. And it's as dangerous as alcoholism. Beware of driving while gay.

The Official Office of American Lying

It was reported in early 2002 that the Pentagon had something called the "Office of Strategic Influence." Do they have bureaucrats who get our taxpayer dollars to come up with names that mean nothing but mask insidiousness? What they wanted to do was plant false stories in the international media to help fight "The 'War' on Terror." Many of us who take American values seriously believe this disinformation campaign would undermine those values. Many in the Pentagon believed this would undermine their credibility. So when a furor erupted over this misguided effort, it was announced with great fanfare that the office would be eliminated. But was it?

The secretary of Defense was asked about it on *Meet the Press.*

Q: So you may, in fact, eliminate it?

RUMSFELD: It wouldn't be me. It would be the people who are worrying this through. I've never even seen the charter for the office.

Q: But you are the secretary of Defense.

RUMSFELD: I am. I am, but I will certainly meet with them and talk to them about it. And I know they are considering what to do about it.

In a further clarification, Rummy proclaimed, "the Pentagon has not spread lies and would never do so in the future. President Bush pledged on Monday 'we'll tell the American people the truth.'"

But by November, our Defense secretary was singing a different tune: "And then there was the Office of Strategic Influence. You may recall that. And 'oh my goodness gracious isn't that terrible, Henny Penny the sky is going to fall.' I went down that next day and said fine, if you want to savage this thing, fine. I'll give you the corpse. There's the name. You can have the name, but I'm gonna keep doing every single thing that needs to be done and I have."

Guess Who Said It

Let's play a little game. Guess who said this and when:

> "The President began this mission with very vague objectives and lots of unanswered questions. A month later, these questions are still unanswered. There are no clarified rules of engagement. There is no timetable. There is no legitimate definition of victory. There is no contingency plan for mission creep. There is no clear funding program. There is no agenda to bolster our overextended military. There is no explanation defining what vital national interests are at stake."

Gee, sounds like a Democrat criticizing Bush 43's plan for war with Iraq. But, no. It's Texas Republican congressman Tom DeLay criticizing Bill Clinton's effort in the Federal Republic of Yugoslavia. And I'd like to thank Mr. DeLay for giving cover to those of us who many disagree with what Bush 43 is doing, but who fervently support our troops. DeLay proclaimed, "I normally, and I still do, support our military and the fine work that they are doing. But I cannot support a failed foreign policy."

When liberals say they're against the war but support the troops, they're called disingenuous. Prior to the start of Gulf War II, Senate Minority Leader Tom Daschle came under great fire for saying, "I'm saddened, saddened that this president failed so miserably at diplomacy that we're now forced to war. Saddened that we have to give up one life because this president couldn't create the kind of diplomatic effort that was so critical for our country."

Conservatives went crazy that Daschle could say such a thing "on the eve of war." Imagine how crazy they would have gone if Daschle had said that to call the war a victory or great leadership on the part of the president would be a farce. Thankfully, Daschle didn't make these comments. But Republican Tom DeLay did. When opposing a resolution commending the successful Kosovo campaign, DeLay took to the floor of the House to say, "For us to call this a victory and to commend the President of the United States as the Commander in Chief showing great leadership in Operation Allied Force is a farce." Senator Richard Lugar also weighed in with this vote of support for his commander in chief during the Bosnia campaign, saying, "This is President Clinton's war, and when he falls flat on his face, that's his problem."

Criticism of military strategy during Gulf War II met with tremendous outrage on the part of those who felt that any such words during a time of hostilities showed a lack of respect and concern for the troops. But when it was "President Clinton's war," then senator John Ashcroft said, "A lackluster air campaign has given the Serb dictator Milosevic time to achieve most of his strategic goals in Kosovo." Apparently, then, one of Milosevic's goals was not to remain in power.

Oh, and here is what the *Houston Chronicle* reported in April 1999 about the conduct of then candidate Bush during "Clinton's war": "Bush, in Austin, criticized President Clinton's administration for not doing enough to enunciate a goal for the Kosovo military action and indicated the bombing campaign might not be a tough enough response. 'Victory means exit strategy, and it's important for the president to explain to us what the exit strategy is,' Bush said."

In the run-up to war with Iraq, there was great debate about how much the president should consult with Congress, the UN, and our allies. Rhetoric about the need to consult prior to the 1991 mission was a far cry from what was said in the 2002/2003 version of going after Saddam Hussein. Trent Lott, for example, had this to say prior to the first Persian Gulf War: "And I do think that whatever actions are taken or not taken should be taken after consultation with our allies, after working with the United Nations." By the time of the second Gulf War, Lott had changed his tune.

Let's play another game. What president of which political party is referred to here by what congressperson of which political party concerning an attack on Iraq? "This president is shameless in what he would do to stay in office. He will use our military and he will use our foreign policy to remain president. I do not put it past him." The quote belongs to Republican congresswoman Tillie Fowler, the president in question was Bill Clinton, and the year was 1998.

Republicans didn't want a war against Saddam Hussein when it was Bill Clinton spearheading it. But the left didn't call them "cowardly." When liberals try to find ways other than war to solve problems, that's exactly what they're called:

From: gusb
Sent: Tuesday, November 19, 2002 9:32 PM
To: colmes
Subject: Alan

Alan, I already knew you were a communist now after . . . tonight, I now know you are a yellow bellied communist.

Trent Lott was against going into Iraq when Clinton was conducting "Operation Desert Fox" in 1998: "While I have been assured by administration officials that there is no connection with the impeachment process in the House of Representatives, I cannot support this military action in the Persian Gulf at this time." Lott added that "all Americans will fully support our troops in battle."

Can you imagine what the national dialogue would have been were it Clinton who failed to knock off Saddam Hussein during the first Persian Gulf War? But it was Bush 41 who let Saddam slide, and that was hardly mentioned in all the talk about "regime change" coming from the Bush 43 administration. Do you think if Clinton were conducting a war that resulted in American's archenemy being allowed to rule his nation for the next dozen years that the Republican attack machine would have remained silent?

I have to admire the right's ability to build straw men and women, and to effectively convince the American public that what they've created is credible. But I'd like to believe that as easily as straw men can be erected, they can be destroyed, and that the truth ultimately wins. You may not agree politically with Tom Daschle, Bill and Hillary Clinton, or with any other Democrat, but let's at least acknowledge that most Americans, regardless of political stripe, want what's best for America, even if we don't agree on how to get there.

Although the right has done a wonderful job promulgating the idea that Reagan and the two Bushes were and are not only great political leaders but also paragons of truth and morality, and that Bill Clinton and the Democrats are exemplars of debauchery and deceit, let us agree that neither of these extreme sentiments are quite accurate. Lying, the kissing cousin of hypocrisy, should have no place among those who spend their time accusing their adversaries of using the very techniques they use to gain political advantage. I'll make a deal with those conservatives who care to misrepresent my side. My friend, and the dean of conservative talk radio, Barry Farber, uses this line: if you promise to stop lying about me, I promise to stop telling the truth about you.

SIX

Bill Clinton,
Our Greatest President

Bill Clinton was the greatest American president in the second half of the twentieth century and may, through the lens of a longer history, go down as one of our greatest presidents, ever. We had unheralded prosperity, as evidenced by the rising tide of jobs, the stock market, and real estate values, and falling unemployment. He forged a peace agreement in Northern Ireland after decades of turmoil, achieved the Dayton Accords to calm the Balkans, and might have actually turned water into wine if the Republicans didn't try to steal his canteen. Okay, I'm kidding about the last one. But the Republicans did try to steal away his presidency, and since they couldn't get him on Whitewater, an old, not-very-significant land deal, they went after him on sex.

"He lied! He lied!" they bellowed. When reminded that most presidents lie at one time or another, they began to bellow, "He lied under oath! He lied under oath!" It was the Republicans, many seething with hatred for Clinton, who diverted his administration from doing the business of the country because they were consumed with trying to oust him. I don't defend his personal actions, but I do defend his professional ones, and I don't believe his personal behavior rose to the level necessary for impeaching a chief executive. When Reagan and Bush lied, as in the Iran-Contra affair, they lied about things that actually mattered to the American people, like policy issues that actually affected our lives. Clinton lied, all right, but all sense of proportionality was lost in the vicious, politically driven efforts to unseat him. My defense of Clinton's right to remain president angered my political adversaries enormously.

From: dewey
Sent: Tuesday, November 28, 2000 1:43 AM
To: colmes
Subject: (no subject)

Colmes—you don't even deserve to have a Mr. or Sir put in front of your name. . . . I know it has to be because no one could be that blindly loyal to scum bags like Bill Clinton and Al Gore. I know when you look in the mirror and your all by yourself you don't believe any of the horse crap that comes out of your mouth every night on your show. Give it up Colmes, you are terrible.

Dewey
San Antonio, TX

My fondness and respect for Clinton continues to cause hypertension in Clinton-haters. The more their bile level increases, the more I care to embrace him. I did a radio song parody once to the tune "The Greatest Love of All" and called it "The Greatest President of All." This made them positively apoplectic. I just couldn't bear to see a good man vilified for being human, for making many of the same mistakes his most vicious critics have made. The unfair and mean-spirited treatment of this man was so blinding that it often obscured his real record of accomplishment, a record that would have been even better if a group of ideological fanatics had focused on what was best for America, rather than what was best for their selfish agendas. Let's examine that record.

When he entered office in January 1993, Bill Clinton inherited a $290 billion deficit and 10 million unemployed Americans. His initial economic plan was denounced by Republicans who never apologized when their criticism turned out to be inaccurate. The creation of 22 million new jobs and thirty-year lows in the unemployment rate during his presidency were meaningless to the Clinton-haters. Women experienced the lowest unemployment rate in thirty years and Hispanics and blacks had the lowest unemployment rates ever recorded. The income of the average American family increased more than $5,000 and the number of families owning stock increased 40 percent. America went from the largest deficits to the largest surpluses in history. But many Republicans couldn't be gracious enough to give Clinton a scintilla of credit: Senator Trent Lott of Mississippi claimed, "The federal government is balancing its budget, thanks to the Republican Congress." Republican senator Mitch McConnell of Kentucky, joined in: "I agree that Bill and Al are responsible for the prosperity we are currently enjoying across America. That's Bill Gates and Alan Greenspan." How magnanimous!

Although his foes are still in denial, the facts show that Bill Clinton was instrumental in creating the longest-running expansion in America's history. But this wasn't an economic accomplishment, according to Bush 43. The great gains made in the stock market during the Clinton years were called a "binge": "In order for us to have the security we all want," Bush said in 2002, "America must get rid of the hangover that we now have as a result of the binge, the economic binge, we just went through. We were in a land of endless profit. There was no tomorrow when it came to the stock markets and corporate profits and now we're suffering a hangover for that binge."

Wait a minute! I thought profits were *good*. And if you're a Republican, corporate profits are even *better*. But when the profits are the result of Clintonism, it's a "binge." In fact, during the Clinton

era, the average workweek for production for nonsupervisory workers declined while the average hourly earnings for these same workers grew by 37.1 percent, and construction jobs enjoyed their fastest
growth in fifty years, after that sector lost 662,000 jobs in the four
years leading up to the Clinton presidency. Because worker demand
was so great, companies began hiring people with less education and
trained them, leading incomes on the bottom fifth rung of the ladder
to increase more than they had in decades. In the meantime, wage
increases reflected their fastest and longest growth in more than
thirty years, and inflation was lower than it had been during those
three decades. By 1999, the federal economy was in the black, and by
2000 there was a $230 billion surplus. Oh, and by the way, 15 million
families had their taxes cut with the earned income tax credit. But it
wasn't the Republican-favored investor class that benefited, it was
families with income below $27,000, and with that 4.3 million
Americans were lifted out of poverty.

A few Republicans ought to order up some humble pie to go with
their too-expensive decaf latte cappuccinos. Their predictions concerning the evils of the Clinton economic plan should buy them
some healthy portions. Senator Phil Gramm said that with
Clintonomics, we're buying "a job killer" and "a one-way ticket to a
recession." House Speaker Newt Gingrich warned, "The tax
increase will kill jobs and lead to a recession, and the recession will
force people off of work and onto unemployment and will actually
increase the deficit." John Kasich, the former Ohio congressman,
who became the Republicans' most brilliant numbers cruncher, had
this to say: "It's like a snakebite. The venom is going to be injected
into the body of this economy; in our judgment it's going to spread
throughout the body and it's going to begin to kill the jobs." And
New Mexico's senator Pete Dominici predicted, "April Fools'
America. This Clinton budget plan will not create jobs, will not
grow the economy, and will not reduce the deficit." Want some
ginkgo biloba with that humble pie?

While we're at it, let's not forget that while the Clinton health care plan failed, it resulted in passage of less sweeping but still significant reforms, like the Family and Medical Leave Act, which enabled workers to leave or change jobs without worrying about losing benefits. It also became more difficult for insurance companies to penalize us for preexisting conditions. And this was no thanks to Bush 41, who vetoed this bill, which helped 35 million Americans after Clinton signed it. Another result of Clinton's focus on health care was the Children Health Insurance Program, or CHIP, providing insurance for 4.6 million children who are not poor enough for Medicare, but whose parents can't afford health insurance. And not since it was created in 1965 was Medicare expanded to help more Americans than it was during the Clinton years.

The COPS program put a hundred thousand more police officers on the street. Crime rates fell for eight consecutive years, and reached twenty-five-year lows. And what a coincidence! This was happening against the backdrop of the Republican-opposed Brady Bill which, since 1994, has resulted in the denial of almost a million gun purchase applications. This was another initiative vetoed by Bush 43. Oh, and by the way, violent crime dropped 27 percent during the Clinton presidency. Also during this time, twenty-nine thousand teachers were hired and classes got smaller, and tax credits made at least some college available to anyone who wanted to go.

A friend of the environment, Clinton promoted the Roadless Area Conservation Protection Rule that protected 58.5 million American acres from roadbuilding and commercial logging. Yellowstone National Park, the California redwoods, and the Florida Everglades were just some of the areas preserved for posterity, no thanks to the Republicans who didn't support their protection. During Clinton's presidency, new clean air standards were set for soot and smog, and diesel engine emissions and emissions for cars, trucks, and SUVs were more strictly regulated; and the Endangered Species Act was expanded to protect 170 plants and animals living in threatened environments.

If the Republicans had their way, they would have sold off the national parks to private interests. Would we really have wanted one of our great national treasures to be known as "The Trump Canyon"? When the Republicans got mad at Clinton and shut down the federal government in 1995 and 1996, and access to national parks was denied, the public came to understand the value of these public monuments. Carl Pope, executive director of the Sierra Club, said, "President Clinton will go down in history as one of the great defenders of the environment, not only for everything the administration accomplished, but for all the things they stopped Congress from doing." The Wilderness Society declared Clinton "one of the top conservation presidents of all time."

It wasn't long before the Bush 43 administration tried to undo Clinton's environmental accomplishments by rescinding new rules on arsenic in drinking water and loosening restrictions on mining. In fact, within ninety minutes of taking office on January 20, 2001, Bush 43 had his chief of staff, Andy Card, put out a memo to department heads to stop publishing new or pending regulations in the *Federal Register*. Based on what regulations were pending, it seemed clear that Bush 43 was trying to halt environmental initiatives that would have decreased water pollution generated by factory farms, created national monuments, and reduced harmful diesel emissions. Bush 43 seemed to think first about WWCD—What Would Clinton Do— and then he'd do the opposite. Clinton likes roast beef? I'm having the turkey. Clinton used the elevator? I'm taking the stairs. Clinton wore a yellow tie? I'm wearing red. Hey, pal, I'm *seeing* red here.

Clinton's Successful Affairs—Foreign, That Is

George Mitchell says he feels more frightened sitting between Sean and me than he does when he's in tense negotiating sessions. But the former Senate majority leader from Maine chaired talks that resulted in the Good Friday Accords, bringing peace to Northern Ireland on April 10, 1998, for the first time in twenty-nine years. On September

26, 1995, the Clinton administration achieved another huge foreign policy victory when the foreign ministers of Bosnia, Croatia, and Serbia (including the Bosnian Serbs) agreed in principle to a pact that was codified in Dayton, Ohio, on November 21 and signed in Paris in December 14, 1995. When the Serbs began "ethnic cleansing" of Albanians in 1999, Clinton, with the cooperation of NATO, initiated a bombing campaign, and the despot responsible, Slobodan Milosevic, wound up in a world court. And unlike our policy toward Iraq, there was no plan for American takeover of a foreign government and possession of its natural resources.

In Haiti, Clinton was able to peacefully achieve the removal of General Raoul Cedras, who had overthrown a democratically elected president. As the president prepared to send troops in if necessary, Colin Powell and Jimmy Carter and Georgia senator Sam Nunn convinced Cedras to step aside so Jean-Bertrand Aristide could resume his presidency. Great leadership was also shown in brokering a relationship between Ehud Barak and Yasser Arafat, which resulted in the Wye Agreements that called for a Palestinian state in the Gaza Strip. A good relationship with Boris Yeltsin and an agreement to help the former Soviet Union financially helped secure Russia's nuclear arsenal and made it possible for Russia to agree to help us dismantle their nuclear weapons.

The North American Free Trade Agreement, which opponents predicted would steal jobs from Americans, resulted in one-and-a-half times more gains than losses, according to the Library of Congress. But NAFTA's biggest success was its impact on the politics and the economy of Mexico. It helped to stabilize our neighbors to the south without the "giant sucking sound" of jobs leaving America, as Ross Perot predicted. Taking a political risk by going against the protectionist grain of his own party, Bill Clinton's NAFTA vision has proven to be correct over time. And when the Senate opposed bailing out Mexico by 81–15, Clinton did it by executive order. His prescience proved correct, as Mexico repaid the loan three years ahead of schedule.

A policy of free trade, international alliances for peacekeeping, and protection of basic human and civil rights was the basis for Clinton's "Doctrine of Enlargement," which resulted in the expansion of NATO to include Poland, Hungary, and the Czech Republic. The Clinton era provided not only enhanced prosperity but also enhanced global peace, which, in turn, fed that prosperity.

Of course, I did not always agree with Bill Clinton. Just as I was against the war in Iraq, I opposed sending forces into Kosovo. But at least my opposition has been consistent. Republicans, who have a tendency to knock the patriotism of anyone who questions a Republican president's decision to go to war, were less consistent when the commander in chief was Bill Clinton. When Clinton responded to the threat of terrorism by ordering retaliatory strikes in Afghanistan and Sudan, Senator Dan Coates offered this incisive war analysis: "I just hope and pray the decision that was made was made on the basis of sound judgment and made for the right reasons, and not made because it was necessary to save the president's job." And when Clinton responded to the threat of terrorism by ordering retaliatory strikes in Afghanistan and Sudan, Senator Arlen Specter of Pennsylvania felt the need to state, "There's an obvious issue that will be raised internationally as to whether there is any diversionary motivation." And then senator John Ashcroft, who was toying with running for president against Al Gore, greeted military action by saying, ". . . there is a cloud over this presidency." Dana Rohrabacher, the California congressional firebrand, actually blamed Clinton for terrorism in Afghanistan: "Once the fire from the retaliatory strike dies down, the American people are going to find out that it is the Clinton administration's wrongheaded policies that resulted in the creation of this terrorist haven in Afghanistan in the first place." That's a new one, especially since it was Ronald Reagan who signed National Security Decision Directive 166 in March 1985 that called for us to arm and finance the Mujahedin to fight the Soviets in Afghanistan. And the Mujahedin formed the core of what later became the Taliban.

Will His Epitaph Read "Here 'Lies' Bill Clinton"?

A complete record of Clinton's accomplishments will be available at the Clinton Presidential Center in Little Rock; but not content to allow him to construct a Clinton library unimpeded, a few of his nonadmirers announced plans for a "Counter Clinton Liebary" to open in Little Rock, a "short walk" from the real thing, "to set the record straight." John "Boot" LeBoutiller who, in spite of our political differences, has been a friend of mine since his days as the youngest congressman in the House in 1980, came on *Hannity & Colmes* to talk about it:

> COLMES: . . . next year, just six months before the official opening of the Clinton library in Little Rock, Arkansas, another library will open in the same city. The founders of the Counter Clinton library said it'll feature sixteen rooms of scandals that the official library surely won't touch, including the National Insecurity Hall, the Department of Domestic Affairs, and the Hall of Shame.
>
> LEBOUTILLIER: . . . it's the Hillary Hall of Shame is what it's called.
>
> COLMES: All right, I want to get to that, too. But first, you said your favorite room in one of the stories I read is the exit room. . . . You talk about how the Clintons trashed the White House.
>
> LEBOUTILLIER: Correct.
>
> COLMES: That's not a part—some of the misconceptions here. Let me show you what the GAO report said about this. They said "the condition of the real property was consistent with what we would expect to encounter when tenants vacate office space after an extended occupancy."

LEBOUTILLIER: Right. Now that is not the actual report that the permanent staff of the White House has written. . . . And President Bush . . .

COLMES: . . . that's what the GAO said, nonpartisan.

LEBOUTILLIER: No, but we have a report, and it's posted on our site . . . on the front page, written by the permanent White House staff. . . . It's a 78-page report describing what the Clintons did to the building. And . . .

COLMES: It was a biased report.

And, horror of horrors, we found out Clinton's library is "taxpayer funded." Somehow, the same financial model for the Reagan library failed to attract such startled responses from the peanut gallery.

Boot says the reason the "exit" room is his favorite is because it signifies the end of the Clinton presidency. It apparently hasn't signified the end of the anti-Clinton gravy train. The "Exit Room" is to be, according to the counterclintonlibrary.com press release "as the Clintons left it—trashed, damaged and defiled." As I pointed out to Boot, that is inaccurate. The General Accounting Office reported a very different story. As I said on *Hannity & Colmes*, the GAO's May 18, 2001, report stated: "The condition of the real property was consistent with what we would expect to encounter when tenants vacate office space after an extended occupancy." A later report by the GAO claimed that it couldn't verify the condition of the property because records weren't available. What? Could there have been a shredder in a Republican White House?

Conservatives salivate at the opportunity to remind you about how Clinton "loathed the military and all it stands for." Of course, that's not what Clinton said, but it's been repeated so many times that it's become common parlance. Here's what then student Clinton actually said in a letter to Colonel Eugene Holmes of the University of Arkansas ROTC: ". . . so many fine people have come to find themselves still loving their country but loathing the military, to which you and other good men have devoted years, lifetimes, of the best service you could give . . ."

In fact, many who had strong views about an undeclared war in Vietnam experienced evolutions in thinking during that time, as our government lied about body counts and the relative success of the war. Bush 43 hasn't been held nearly as accountable for his days of being "young and irresponsible," a time during which he allegedly not only inhaled, but also swallowed and who knows what else.

One of the stated goals of the "Counter Clinton Liebrary" is to warn people about the political ambitions of Hillary. How often do we hear, in shocking tones, that, oh my God, Hillary wants to be president! And she might even get elected! What are they worried about? Do they fear a democratic process in which voting citizens get to decide on government personnel? I'd be a little more upset about a dishonest electoral system that doesn't respect the popular vote.

Among the lies spread about Hillary Clinton, and promoted as part of the "liebrary," is "her Yale Law School defense of Black Panther murderers." This entry in the "Stop Hillary Now" part of the "liebrary" is based on an urban legend floating around the Internet that claims that Hillary defended Black Panthers accused of killing another Panther named Alex Rackely, and that she led a demonstration that shut down Yale in the process. The truth is, as usual, much tamer. Hillary worked as an intern in the law office of one of the attorneys defending the accused Panthers (who were nowhere near the scene of the crime), and she presided over a meeting of law students discussing the proper response to the gassing of student demonstrators. But nuances don't make good copy. And they don't fit the anti-Billary agenda.

Please buy another copy of this book. I'm going to use the proceeds to open a tribute to Ronald Reagan. I'm calling it the "Contra Contra Liebrary." Or maybe I'll go down to Texas where all those executions take place and open the Bush 43 "Frybrary."

Low Names and High Dudgeon

I guess we shouldn't be surprised at the demeaning "liebrary" Clinton's detractors are promoting. It's consistent with their use of derogatory language to insult him. One of the most amusing aspects of the Clinton years was how his enemies referred to him. Until impeachment he was either "Bubba" or "Slick Willie," but during impeachment proceedings he became known as "William Jefferson Clinton," as if to ask how a man with such a haughty-sounding name could be on trial for such low behavior. But no matter how clearly or how loudly one proclaims the accomplishments of our forty-second president, the seething hatred toward him proves, as Mark Twain once said, "Denial ain't just a river in Egypt."

From: Wally T
Sent: Monday, July 03, 2000 7:08 PM
To: colmes
Subject: Values

Mr. Colmes,
Clinton and his supporters like yourself, has for 7 long years done everything possible to undermind this republic.

Well, THANK GOD you have failed, and your reign of corruption is coming to a close. Am I still allowed to say THANK GOD on the computer??? . . .

I served 6 years in the Army defending Liberal jackoffs like yourself, I sometime wonder if it was worth it. Months at a time in the jungles of Central America. Panama, El Salvador Nicaragua, do you know these places? I think the only way you would see places like this would be on the Discovery channel.

Wally T.
Smyrna, GA

Wally, first let me thank you for serving our country, even if you did have to defend "jackoffs" like me. And let me quote my favorite president: I feel your pain. And so did Bill Clinton, even if you can't return the favor. He had a quality you've failed to display here: empathy. At a campaign event in New York on March 26, 1992, Bob Rafsky, an activist from ACT-UP who was trying to draw attention to the AIDS epidemic by accusing Clinton of not addressing the issue when he was governor of Arkansas, continually jeered him. After a few interruptions, Clinton snapped back, "I feel your pain, I feel your pain, but if you want to attack me personally you're no better than Jerry Brown and all the rest of these people who say whatever sounds good at the moment. If you want something to be done, you ask me a question and you listen. If you don't agree with me, go support somebody else for President but quit talking to me like that." The phrase "I feel your pain" may have become fodder for those who wished to mock Clinton, but it represented a candidate, and later a president, who could connect with Americans viscerally, whether addressing a large crowd or speaking one-on-one.

So What If Bill Clinton Is Black?

It was no accident that the Nobel Prize winner Toni Morrison referred to Clinton as "our first black president." During the Clinton era, minorities did especially well. Unemployment among blacks dropped from 14.1 percent to 7.8 percent between 1992 and 1999, and black teen unemployment went from 40.5 percent in January 1993 to 28.6 percent in August 1999. In that same period, Hispanic unemployment decreased from 11.3 percent to 6.5 percent. We can argue all we want about whether affirmative action is the right path; we can constantly debate whether having Condoleezza Rice and Colin Powell in highly visible positions really advances the cause of African Americans. But the true test of government policy that promotes equality in America is reflected in these numbers from the Clinton era.

Bill Clinton's gift to African Americans extended beyond the economic policies that lifted so many out of poverty. Clinton was the first president to acknowledge some of our own sordid history concerning the treatment of minorities. We presume to own the high ground when it comes to humanitarianism, but we have conveniently forgotten episodes like the Tuskegee experiments. Our government used poor, black, illiterate sharecroppers from Alabama as though they were lab animals. And this isn't ancient history. The Tuskegee experiments began in 1932 and continued until they were exposed forty years later. Three hundred ninety-nine men in the late stages of syphilis were told they were being treated for "bad blood." In fact, they were being treated for nothing. It wasn't their live bodies the government wanted, but their dead ones, so their corpses could be used by the U.S. Public Health Service to see how syphilis affected them differently than it affected whites. Because husbands who believed they were being treated were deceived, wives were infected and children were born with congenital syphilis during these experiments. When penicillin was invented in the 1940s, it was purposely denied to these men. And when asked about it, the Public Health Service claimed these people were participating voluntarily.

When President Clinton did the right thing and apologized for what the government did, his detractors accused him of pandering to the black community. Here's what President Clinton said: "The United States government did something that was wrong—deeply, profoundly, morally wrong. It was an outrage to our commitment to integrity and equality for all our citizens. . . . clearly racist."

Predictably, some conservative pundits used this opportunity to tie Clinton's good-hearted and moral gesture to his sex life. Jonah Goldberg, who became a member of the punditocracy thanks to the meddling efforts of his mother, Lucianne, to help Linda Tripp get a book deal off her friendship with Monica Lewinsky, had this to say: "Many thought that the African apology safari was a limited engagement, a sideshow to distract people from the center ring during the Year of the President's Pants."

If Bill Clinton had found a cure for cancer, they would have called it a distraction from Republican attempts to impeach him.

Hate Him at Your Own Peril

Sometimes you know how successful you are by who your enemies are and by how intensely they hate you. By that measure, Clinton is our most successful president. Hating Clinton became a cottage industry for many Americans. Not only could Clinton feel your pain, but also, if you were his enemy, he'd toss that pain right back at you. This frustrated his opponents to no end. His enemies tried to destroy his career using every trick in the book, ultimately settling on a trumped-up sex charge. But rather than achieve his resignation, it was Republicans like Louisiana congressman Bob Livingston who wound up eating his dust. More Republicans resigned than Democrats during the attempt to remove Bill Clinton from office.

Isn't it ironic that most of the House impeachment managers are no longer in Congress? And not all by their own choices. Bob Barr of Georgia, the man who started the impeachment ball rolling, lost a primary race to John Linder. George Gekas of Pennsylvania and James Rogan of California were thrown out. Ed Bryant of Tennessee lost a Senate primary bid. Bill McCollum, Asa Hutchinson, and Charles Canady all resigned their seats, the very seats they used to try to derail Clinton.

Clinton's most ardent foes begrudgingly acknowledge his prowess as a master politician. Part of his mastery of the political art was his ability to let you see him warts and all. Like all great men—check that—like all *people*, Clinton was flawed. The evildoers who were out to destroy his presidency tried to pass themselves off as unblemished, and that was their undoing. Clinton wasn't and isn't afraid to be who he is, even as his adversaries have tried to stick the "slick" label on him. Most Americans knew that he came from humble roots. In spite of the attempt to label him as money-hungry during "Whitewater," his last job before the presidency paid $35,000 a year. Hillary made six figures as a lawyer, so they weren't starving. Still, they owned no home, having spent years in a governor's mansion, and they actually lost money on the Whitewater deal. While the taxpayers ponied up

$70 million when all was said and done to investigate it, the Clintons actually lost $47,000 on the Whitewater deal.

Conservatives tend to look at the world in stark terms. People can be defined, and often demonized, by one seminal event. For conservatives, Ronald Reagan may be defined as the man who told Gorbachev to "tear down this wall," not as the man who visited the Bitburg cemetery where Nazis responsible for 642 victims of the 1944 massacre at Oradour in the south of France are buried, or the man who gave his first postconvention speech in 1980 in Philadelphia, Mississippi. This is the place where, just sixteen years earlier, three young civil rights workers, James Chaney, Andrew Goodman, and Michael Schwerner, were murdered by members of the KKK. But Reagan never paid homage to these sacrificial lambs of the civil rights movement; instead, he was using code words like "states' rights." Conservatives will forever define Bill Clinton by a dumb affair and a stained dress, not by the number of people lifted out of poverty during his tenure. President John Fitzgerald Kennedy is currently revered by conservatives for having been a tax cutter, and yet they never mention *his* legendary infidelities that made Clinton look practically celibate. Let's face it—we are all complex beings, and we can all find moments in our past that we would prefer not to appear in our epitaphs. It's a shame that sometimes we don't see the whole person but pick and choose how we view someone based on our own biases. If we don't agree with someone politically, we'll try to use personal weaknesses as evidence of professional failures. We demand a level of honor and morality in our leaders that we rarely exercise ourselves.

As for that dumb affair and the stained dress: Bill Clinton paid a huge price for his indiscretion. He suffered the ignominy of being the first elected president ever to be impeached. And I'm guessing things were not too rosy at the Clinton household when his attention was needed for important domestic and global matters. Yes, he brought this upon himself. But he fought back and didn't give in to the forces that wanted to do him in. And in the end, he was able to leave office with an admirable record on the issues that mattered. Most important for him personally, he was able to keep his family together, a fight he had to wage against the backdrop of constant public snorting by those who attacked him in the name of "family values."

A Legacy Up on the Competition

You probably noticed my earlier jab about the popular versus the electoral vote. Al Gore received more votes than any other Democratic presidential candidate, ever, but lost the presidency because of the odd electoral system we have, and because of a Supreme Court that suddenly decided it was no longer a "states' rights" court. But the Clinton legacy continues with his former adviser, Rahm Emanuel, whose Clinton ties didn't hurt his ability to win a congressional race in Chicago, by a wide margin, and with Bill Richardson, the former UN ambassador and Department of Energy secretary, who was handily elected governor of New Mexico. And let us not forget that the person to whom he is closest in life became a senator from New York, garnering 55 percent of the vote, 12 percentage points more than her opponent, Congressman Rick Lazio.

But even without bright lights from his administration to carry on Clinton's work, the fact is that at the end of the Clinton era we had a country that was financially in the black, a world mostly at peace, a booming stock market, and better lives for America's working poor. Sure, we have a few angry conservatives who continue to vent steam to this day that Clinton has the gall to walk the planet. And while that hot, polluted air is bad for us, I know we'll have a Democratic president one day who will clean up this pox on the environment.

Clinton continues to fight for the causes he championed as president, whether offering to mediate racial tensions in Cincinnati or speaking, as he did in February 2003, to scientists involved in AIDS research in Boston. He is especially active in developing countries, where he works to implement care, treatment, and prevention programs in order to help stem the AIDS epidemic. The Clinton Foundation is helping to build infrastructures to address this crisis, including acquiring the necessary pharmaceuticals so proper care can be offered.

It's true that politics makes strange bedfellows, but post–political life can make even stranger ones. Clinton has teamed with Senator Bob Dole, his 1996 challenger, to cochair the Families of Freedom Scholarship Fund, which helps to fund higher education of children whose families were victimized by the September 11 attacks.

As the former president continues his journey on the world stage and enhances his presidential accomplishments, his enemies will only grow angrier. Good. He'll continue to do what he's always done: work for the public good. And they'll do what they've always done: be angry with Bill Clinton.

Greatness isn't judged by one event, by an isolated moment in time, or by a set of statistics. It's not quantifiable, objective, or even verifiable. It's more of an "I-know-it-when-I-see-it" experience. We should be defined not by the mistakes we make, but what we make of our mistakes. Our actions are often less significant than our intent. Clinton held great promise for America. He didn't live up to every inch of that promise. Nobody could. But his love of his country, his desire to do good, his actual accomplishments, and his continued activism on behalf of causes he holds dear continue to define him.

I can understand how onetime Clinton supporters may have become former supporters, how both admirers and former admirers alike might feel let down by some of his behavior. And I don't exempt the former president from the need to take personal responsibility for the self-inflicted damage to his presidency. But we should look at the record objectively and not allow our understandably emotional reactions to his bad personal behavior obscure our sense of fairness and justice. Bill Clinton felt our pain for eight years. Can we be big enough as a nation, compassionate enough, and even Christian enough to feel his? Let's applaud him for his accomplishments and forgive him for his shortcomings, which is the same treatment we'd all want. It's not only the right thing to do. It's the American thing to do.

SEVEN

OJ Is Innocent

Orenthal James Simpson was found "not guilty" during his criminal trial for the murders of Nicole Brown Simpson and Ronald Goldman. In America, you are innocent until proven guilty in a court of law. Nevertheless, OJ went on to be held liable for these murders in a civil trial stemming from the same alleged crime. I'm amazed that more people didn't point out that this should be a violation of the Fifth Amendment of the United States Constitution that prohibits the government from trying us twice for the same crime, sometimes referred to as "double jeopardy." It will forever be debated why he was found not guilty, but that was the verdict. Some conservatives love to use the term "convicted felon" when it comes to former assistant attorney general Webster Hubbell, Susan McDougal (who went to jail in the Whitewater case for refusing to testify against President Clinton), and anyone else associated with Clinton; but in the OJ case, when they found themselves with a jury verdict they didn't like, they refused to abide by the "innocent until proven guilty" bedrock of our criminal justice system.

There was a good reason the prosecution never proved that OJ was guilty in the first place. The glove that didn't fit was found by former LAPD detective Mark Fuhrman at Simpson's home the day after the murders. It was described as "wet and sticky." But why would it be wet and sticky a day later? And since there was a Caucasian hair on the glove, might not a DNA test prove once and for all whether that glove had been planted? It wasn't just the gloves that didn't fit. Timing was off, as well. Dogs began barking at 10:35 or 10:40 p.m. The forensic experts said the struggle took between five and fifteen minutes. Simpson lawyer Johnnie Cochran put it all into perspective during his closing argument:

> Consider everything that Mr. Simpson would have had to have done in a very short time under their timeline. He would have had to drive over to Bundy, as they described in this little limited time frame where there is not enough time, kill two athletic people in a struggle that takes five to fifteen minutes, walk slowly from the scene, return to the scene, supposedly looking for a missing hat and glove and poking around, go back to this alley a second time, drive more than five minutes to Rockingham where nobody hears him or sees him, either stop along the way to hide these bloody clothes and knives, et cetera, or take them in the house with you where they are still hoisted by their own petard because there is no blood, there is no trace, there is no nothing. So that is why the prosecution has had to try and push back their timeline. Even to today they are still pushing it back because it doesn't make any sense. It doesn't fit.

Furthermore, blood scrapings from beneath Nicole's fingernails were EAP type B. According to the serology report by Greg Matheson, the LAPD scientist, "Problem, no match to anyone." It didn't match Ron Goldman, OJ, or even Nicole herself. But the fact that it didn't match OJ's blood was most significant. Now, let's look at Simpson's Ford Bronco. They couldn't find Ron or Nicole's hair or clothing fibers in the car. And there was no DNA matching OJ found on the glove at Rockingham or the one found at Nicole's Bundy home.

It's troubling that certain common police procedures weren't followed. For example, blood was washed off Ron's and Nicole's bodies and never tested. Soil samples at Bundy were never tested to see if OJ had left any hair or fibers. There was a piece of paper at the crime scene that disappeared. Detective Tom Lange said that based on what he saw of the paper it was of no value. Since when is this kind of thing determined just visually? And since when is forensic evidence disposed of at a crime scene?

It was no secret that OJ was black, and it was no secret that he married and dated white women. And according to witnesses, this was something that didn't sit too well with Mark Fuhrman. Kathleen Bell, a Los Angeles real estate broker who met Fuhrman in 1985 and knew him socially, sent a letter to the defense, claiming, "When he sees a 'nigger' (as he called it) driving with a white woman, he would pull them over. I asked would he if he didn't have a reason, and he said that he would find one."

The famous Fuhrman tapes were recorded by Laura McKinny, who was a learning skills counselor for high-risk athletes at UCLA at the time she met Fuhrman in February 1985. She interviewed Fuhrman as part of her research for a screenplay she was writing about the Los Angeles Police Department. There are a number of places on the tapes where Fuhrman brags about defying police procedure. For example, when asked about arresting someone for an outstanding traffic warrant, he said:

FUHRMAN: . . . he's probably gotten several tickets from policemen, and he hasn't taken care of them. He's going to go to the station, because he won't have any identification because when he gives me his driver's license, I'll just rip the fucker up.

MCKINNY: Have you done that before?

FUHRMAN: (Nods.)

Fuhrman also admitted he didn't follow department procedure on whether to shoot to kill:

FUHRMAN: I listen to liberals talk, and I can't believe that someone who is educated, or even just opens their eyes for one day can think what they think.

MCKINNY: What are some of the things that really annoy you when you hear liberals talk?

FUHRMAN: Do you people—don't you shoot to wound 'em? No, we shoot to kill 'em. Now the department says we shoot to stop, not kill, which is horseshit. The only way you can stop somebody is to kill the son of a bitch. And what's the big deal? If you've got a reason to shoot somebody, you've got a reason to kill him.

According to these tapes, Fuhrman was no fan of females on the force:

FUHRMAN: They don't do anything. They don't go out and initiate contact with some 6'5" nigger that's been in prison for seven years pumping weights.

Fuhrman has claimed that these tapes don't represent his views, but rather that he was acting to help create a fictional story. Unfortunately these tapes came out after Fuhrman claimed he hadn't used the word *nigger* in ten years.

If Respect You Lack, You Must Be Black

The OJ trial was prosecuted against the backdrop of black versus white and liberal versus conservative. Many are troubled that OJ was treated differently than most murder defendants, but conservatives tend not to be as troubled by the number of blacks in America who are regularly tried, convicted, and put to death, often because of incompetent attorneys appointed by the state. The injustices to these indigent Americans are the flip side of the injustices of the OJ trial, but that rarely gets attention from the very people who were outraged by "The Trial of the Century." Why is a verdict troubling only when a black man goes free? Why is it that the federal criminal code and the laws of fourteen states allow a sentence of five years for selling five grams of crack, but to get five years for selling cocaine, you need to be found with five hundred grams? Could it be because cocaine is considered more of a white person's drug by the authorities? Contrary to those who whine that the white man is an endangered species in America, our nation continues to abide a tremendous amount of racism, sexism, and ageism.

Leo Terrell, a Los Angeles civil rights attorney, has been a frequent guest on *Hannity & Colmes* (and is an OJ friend and defender). During one of Terrell's appearances, we discussed how Congressman Jesse Jackson Junior referred to Bush 43's State of the Union address as "The Police State of the Union," After that show, this love letter arrived:

From: kevin235
Sent: Wednesday, February 06, 2002 10:29 PM
To: colmes
Subject: (no subject)

You and Leo Belong Together! . . . Leo Terrell is a Militant Racist Left-Wing Radical Hateful Nigger. Look up his name in the dictionary. It's listed under "Hate."

You and Leo should spend the rest of your lives in Hell. . . . You and Leo are "The Best Example of the Worst we have to Offer in America."

kevin235
Canton, OH

When you start to think about how far we've come in terms of equality in America, it's a reality check to see how some people still think on this issue. Then you'll realize how far we still have to go.

The Right's Race Problem

Racism may never be fully expunged from American life. But I hope that racism as a political tool will be. Each party has its race demons, but it's the left that has spearheaded the civil rights movement, and it's the right that's had to play catch-up.

When the *Washington Post* reported in 1998 that Trent Lott had addressed the Conservative Citizens' Council, a group formed in the 1950s to fight the Supreme Court's ruling on desegregation of schools, Lott said he "had no firsthand knowledge of the group's views." As the story persisted, the *Post* reported Lott saying, "I have made my condemnation of the white supremacist and racist view of this group, or any group, clear. Any use of my name to publicize their view is not only unauthorized, it's wrong." How could Lott not have known their views as he claimed? He wrote for the CCC's publication, *The Citizens Informer*, and was the keynote speaker at a 1992 event where he said, "The people in this room stand for the right principles and the right philosophy."

When Bob Jones University was embroiled in an effort to keep its tax-exempt status in 1981, which was threatened by its policy that bans interracial dating, Trent Lott stepped in to defend the institution. Writing to the Supreme Court, Lott said, "If racial discrimination in the interest of diversity does not violate public policy, then surely discrimination in the practices of religion is no violation."

It's true that racial discrimination doesn't always violate public policy. But it seems as though Lott's statement excuses racial discrimination if it doesn't violate public policy and is offered in the name of religion. So perhaps I should suggest a policy to ban inter-political dating. Maybe liberals shouldn't get anywhere near the DNA of conservatives. It wouldn't violate public policy and would keep my political party "pure."

Lest you think America is without the fumes of a racist past, every so often an ugly statement rears its head that reminds us of our less-than-stellar civil rights background. This was the case at the one hundredth birthday party for the late Strom Thurmond on December 6, 2002, when Trent Lott got in some hot water for making this statement: "I want to say this about my state: When Strom Thurmond ran for president we voted for him. We're proud of it. And if the rest of the country had of followed our lead we wouldn't of had all these problems over all these years, either."

What wasn't said was that when Strom Thurmond ran for president in 1948 he did so as a Dixiecrat, on the platform of segregation. One of the Stromster's comments during that campaign was: "All the laws of Washington and all the bayonets of the Army cannot force the Negro into our homes, our schools, our churches." The great Lott controversy revolved around the Mississippi senator's implication that this is the America he wished a Thurmond presidency would have spawned.

Lott apologized the next day: "A poor choice of words conveyed to some the impression that I embraced the discarded policies of the past. Nothing could be further from the truth, and I apologize to anyone who was offended by my statement."

At first I was outraged that Lott could have been so reckless at Thurmond's party, especially when it was revealed by the *Jackson Clarion-Ledger* that he made a similar, almost word-for-word statement back in 1980 when, as a congressman, he told a crowd at a Strom Thurmond rally, "You know, if we had elected this man 30 years ago, we wouldn't be in the mess we are today."

But, to his credit, Lott went on Hannity's radio show and said he regretted his words, that they were "terrible," and that it was "a mistake of the head, not the heart."

I said on *Hannity & Colmes*, on December 11, 2002, that I was actually starting to feel badly for Senator Lott as this story was developing a life of its own:

COLMES: I think he went as far as one could go. I'm no fan of some of the things he says politically. I'm troubled by a series of statements and events that are like this. But I think on

Sean's radio show he said—what more could he possibly say after this?

I even went on *The O'Reilly Factor* two days later and defended Senator Lott:

COLMES: . . . I think there's too much piling on on Trent Lott. I've been defending Lott. And I think there's just too much already. Let it go.

My e-mail reaction to this episode was revealing. The lesson was that if you're defined as "liberal," you will be vilified for taking the liberal position even when you don't take the liberal position. Here I was, defending Senator Lott from a "piling on" effect, and yet I was receiving hate mail from people assuming I said something else:

From: patriciawomn
Sent: Thursday, December 12, 2002 9:40 PM
To: Colmes
Subject: (no subject)

Mr. Colmes, It's always good to hear the nasty comments like against Sen. Lott especially from a left winger like you. He made a mistake and I am sure he regrets it, but why harp on him so much? Is this the only way liberals make browny points?

Patriciawomn
Rochester, NY

Lott went even further in yet another apology during a news conference on December 13, when he said that segregation was wrong and immoral then, just as it is now, and that he had learned from his own mistakes. The senator asked for forbearance and forgiveness and said he would dedicate himself to undoing the hurt that resulted from his remarks. And I went further in defending Lott that night. After all, what are liberals about if not forbearance and forgiveness? I couldn't stand the blood sport that the Clinton episodes became, and I sensed the thirst for Lott's blood that I found so repugnant during the Clinton-capades. Conservatives didn't accept Clinton's apologies and that riled me. I wanted to accept Lott's. Once a person says they're wrong, shows that they want to learn from their mistakes and take full responsibility for what they said or did, the controversy should end.

The night of Lott's news conference, during my appearance on *The O'Reilly Factor*, Bill wanted to know at what point an advocate of a particular political party jumps off that platform and doesn't support it anymore.

> O'REILLY: Let's go over to Colmes. You're a radio guy. You were on the radio before television. You know that most of the radio talk-show hosts, who aren't journalists, by the way, will now basically get up in the morning, get the talking points from whatever party they are in, and just parrot that.

> COLMES: I think that's often the case. I don't—I—look, I get the DNC talking points. They e-mail them to me. . . . But you know what? I don't look at them. And I am less of a cheerleader for the Democratic Party than I am for the ideals I believe it should uphold.

I tried to emphasize, and I firmly believe, that one must be true to one's beliefs and ideals, even if it means taking an unpopular position with one's own party as, in the case of Senator Lott, saying, "Enough is enough."

Lott's most effusive apology came during his appearance on Black Entertainment Television with Ed Gordon on December 16. By that time, Lott was coming out in favor of affirmative action. At this rate, he was soon going to be promoting reparations and becoming a replacement singer with the Temptations. The roller coaster had begun its descent and there was no way to climb back to the top of the curve.

But it wasn't those evil Democrats who threw Lott down the stairs; it was the Bush administration. When 43 spoke in Philadelphia on December 12, he said, "Any suggestion that the segregated past was acceptable or positive is offensive and it is wrong!" Bush said what he had to say to put a game face on his party, but he did so without acknowledging that Lott had apologized. That was it for Lott. If that weren't enough, 43's brother, and the man who would be 44, Florida governor Jeb Bush said, "Something's going to have to change. . . . This can't be the topic of conversation over the next week." Bye-bye Lott. Done in, not by the libs, but by the cons.

So, the Bush administration got what it wanted when Lott stumbled. But if Republicans truly want to cleanse themselves of the kind of taint that Lott highlighted, they need not look much further than the chief law enforcement officer of the land, Attorney General John Ashcroft. During his time as both governor and attorney general in Missouri, a racial storm was brewing. Federal courts decided that students in both St. Louis and Kansas City were not receiving equal education, and desegregation was ordered. In 1991, when Ashcroft testified before the Senate Judiciary Committee after his nomination to become U.S. Attorney General, he defended his opposition to a voluntary desegregation plan for St. Louis. As the *Washington Post* reported on January 18, 2001, "court documents show that a federal district judge ruled that the state was a 'primary constitutional wrongdoer' in perpetuating segregated schools in St. Louis, both by denying blacks an equal education in the past and doing little to remedy the situation later." A U.S. District Court threatened to hold then Missouri attorney general Ashcroft in contempt of court for "continual delay and failure to comply" with a court-ordered desegregation plan. Even worse, according to *Time* magazine, were "charges that Ashcroft worked to suppress black voter turnout by twice vetoing laws that would have promoted voter-registration efforts in the city of St. Louis."

And what are we to make of Ashcroft's comments to *Southern Partisan* magazine, a publication that has referred to Abraham

Lincoln as a "consummate conniver, manipulator and a liar," and to John Wilkes Booth as someone whose behavior was "not only sane, but sensible." Was ending slavery some "perverted agenda"? As we like to say at Fox: You decide. Ashcroft told *Southern Partisan*: "Your magazine also helps set the record straight. You've got a heritage of doing that, of defending Southern patriots like [Robert E.] Lee, [Stonewall] Jackson and [Confederate President Jefferson] Davis. Traditionalists must do more. I've got to do more. We've all got to stand up and speak in this respect, or else we'll be taught that these people were giving their lives, subscribing their sacred fortunes and their honor to some perverted agenda."

Ashcroft also campaigned against the nomination of Ronnie White to serve as a federal district judge. Ashcroft convinced the Senate that White, the first black to sit on the Missouri Supreme Court, had a history of overturning death sentences, and even called him "procriminal." This was ostensibly because of one case in which White did not want the death penalty for a convict because he didn't think the man had adequate counsel. But in forty-one of fifty-nine cases, White affirmed the death penalty. When Ashcroft, as a member of the Senate Judiciary Committee, had the chance to question White as a nominee for a judgeship, this didn't even come up. But during a Senate campaign against Mel Carnahan, who appointed White, Ashcroft used that one anti-death-penalty decision as a club on Carnahan. Even though Carnahan won this ugly campaign posthumously, Ashcroft was rewarded with a cabinet post.

Lott's comments on race seem mild compared with those of another senator from Mississippi, the late James Eastland. In *Master of the Senate: The Years of Lyndon Johnson*, Robert Caro recounts a speech Eastland gave to the White Citizens' Council in 1956: "In every stage of the bus boycott we have been oppressed and degraded because of black, slimy, juicy, unbearably stinking niggers.... African flesh-eaters. When in the course of human events it becomes necessary to abolish the Negro race, proper methods should be used. Among these are guns, bows and arrows, slingshots and knives...."

All whites are created equal with certain rights, among these are life, liberty and the pursuit of dead niggers." But rather than get demoted, as Lott did, Eastland was appointed head of the powerful Senate Judiciary Committee and served in the Senate until 1978. Lott worked to get what had been the Federal Post Office and Court House in Jackson, Mississippi, renamed the James O. Eastland Federal Building where, I presume, the black granite and the white granite do not touch. Given Lott's mea culpas, though, Eastland makes him look like a one-man Rainbow Coalition.

It's one thing to look at the history of America's political parties and argue over which has the most embarrassing history of racial insensitivity, if not downright bigotry. It's more depressing to realize there are still incidents that reflect poorly on where we are in America in the twenty-first century. In Louisiana's runoff election that put Democrat Mary Landrieu back in the Senate, it was imperative that Landrieu get out the African American vote. Some in Louisiana didn't think that was a good idea. An unsigned pamphlet was distributed in housing projects that it was okay to vote on December 10 if they didn't feel like voting on December 7. "Bad weather? No problem!!! If the weather is uncomfortable on Election Day, remember you can wait and cast your ballot on Tuesday, December 10." I'm sure the defenders of such racism would claim they were urging those folks to vote even though they were giving them the impression they could do so three days after the actual election.

On the day Louisiana residents went to the polls, December 7, 2002, the Republican Party hired black youths to hold signs in black neighborhoods urging their neighbors not to vote for Landrieu, with placards saying, "Mary, if you don't respect us, don't expect us." And so as recently as 2002 some Republicans were trying to suppress the black vote. There is no other way to interpret this.

In more than one state, the Confederate flag was still an issue in the elections of 2002. In Georgia, Republican challenger Sonny Purdue ousted Governor Roy Barnes by, among other things, promising to hold a referendum on whether the state flag should once again feature a large Confederate battle emblem, as it did before Barnes's efforts to make it smaller. During the campaign Purdue put out fliers that asked voters to "remember who changed your flag."

Just before the 2002 election, the Associated Press reported that South Carolina's incumbent governor Jim Hodges "has been dogged by his failure to deliver an auto plant and the decision to remove the Confederate flag from the statehouse dome." Hodges, a Democrat, lost his seat to former three-term Republican congressman Mark Sanford.

Each political party is busy claiming its heritage as the true progenitor of civil rights. Republicans love to rail against Ernest Hollings because, as governor of South Carolina, he raised the Confederate flag over the statehouse; against Al Gore's father because of his vote against the Civil Rights Act of 1964; against Harry Truman because of allegations of KKK membership; against Robert Byrd because of his KKK roots and his "white niggers" comment.

Ernest Hollings, it turns out, helped integrate Clemson University as governor. He also provided funding for law enforcement to go after the Klan. As a legislator, he was the only southern senator to vote against weakening the 1982 Voting Rights Act. Senator Gore Sr. said his vote against the Civil Rights Act of 1964 was the biggest mistake of his career. Al Gore Jr. argued vehemently with his father about that vote. But Gore Sr. was one of only three southern senators who refused to sign Strom Thurmond's "Southern Manifesto" that repudiated the Supreme Court decision that integrated schools.

The Civil Rights Act of 1964 and the Voting Rights Act of 1965 defined Lyndon Johnson's Democratic Party and pushed southern anti-civil-rights Democrats like Strom Thurmond out of the party. The party of Lincoln underwent realignment as those who just couldn't brook the toleration of nonwhite Americans found a friendlier place with the Republicans. The so-called southern strategies of Richard Nixon and Ronald Reagan of appealing to white Democrats who were uncomfortable in an increasingly nonwhite America helped them win their respective presidencies. Their ability to simultaneously appeal to Eisenhower Republicans and Thurmond Democrats provided them with broad bases of support.

Harry Truman paid $10 to join the Ku Klux Klan in 1922 when he needed its support in his run for judge in Jackson Country, Missouri. When he was asked not to hire Catholics shortly thereafter, he quit the group and got his money back. As president, Harry Truman desegregated the armed forces. So, do we judge him by a brief, but misguided foray into a group he immediately quit upon learning of its views, or by his overall accomplishments?

Playing a game of word association with Senator Byrd on the March 4, 2001, edition of *Fox News Sunday,* my Fox News colleague Tony Snow threw out the term "race relations" and got this response: "There are white niggers. I've seen a lot of white niggers in my time. I'm going to use that word. We just need to work together to make our country a better country, and I'd just as soon quit talking about it so much."

Robert Byrd has renounced his racist past, but that doesn't excuse his "white niggers" comment. On that show with Tony Snow, Byrd said, "We all make mistakes. I made a mistake when I was a young man—it's always been an albatross around my neck in joining the Ku Klux Klan."

We don't know what is in another's heart, so how do we judge except by one's words and actions?

Republican senator Conrad Burns of Montana has a long way to go if he's to catch up to Lott in the mea culpa department. An editor from *The Hotline* interviewed Burns in 1994, when the senator regaled him with a story of a rancher who said to him, "Conrad, how can you live back there [in Washington] with all those niggers?" Burns's reply: "It's a hell of a challenge."

Once, during a speech to the Montana Equipment Dealers Association, Burns decried the dependence of America on Mideast oil and referred to the Arabs as "ragheads." He later offered a feeble apology by claiming he got too "emotionally involved" in the issue.

In 1991, right after a Senate vote on a civil rights bill, Burns invited a group of civil rights lobbyists who were there to an auction. The *Washington Post* reported that when he was asked what was being auctioned off, Burns's answer was "Slaves." None of this has stopped the Senator from winning multiple reelections.

It's surprising that Louisiana governor Mike Foster got little national attention when he bought a list of supporters from David Duke for $100,000 in 1995. I'm guessing the names on that list were not exactly veterans of marches in Selma, Alabama, or people who know the words to "We Shall Overcome." But Foster has had a good long run in Louisiana thanks to some of those supporters. Now, I'm not calling Foster a racist, but this is a manifestation of the "southern strategy" that Republicans have used when they needed certain votes to get elected.

Ward Connerly is an interesting case: he's a black man who has spent his public career fighting affirmative action. Maybe Trent Lott can call him and convince him to think otherwise. As a member of California's Board of Regents, he promoted an initiative that resulted in ending affirmative action in the state's university system, and he went on to work to end affirmative action in California's state government.

But William F. Jasper wrote in *The New American*, a publication of the right-wing John Birch Society, "[Connerly] concedes that in a few cases new laws and regulations have forced him to certify his company as a minority-owned enterprise in order to keep previous contracts with public agencies." That's the JOHN BIRCH SOCI-ETY! They were trying to argue FOR Connerly and against affir-mative action. In the *New York Times*, Bob Herbert quotes Ward Connerly as saying, "Supporting segregation need not be racist. One can believe in segregation and believe in equality of the races." Okay, Ward, let's go back to how equal the black schools were before *Brown v. the Board of Education*. Let's talk about how equal black bathrooms and water fountains were. I can understand arguing for solutions that are not race-based, and Connerly was an eloquent spokesman for the idea of ending affirmative action. But why then try to say something that sounds like a defense of segregation?

Bush 43 had a program in Texas called "Affirmative Access." Affirmative Access guaranteed a spot in state colleges for everyone who finished in the top 10 percent of their high school graduating class. It promotes diversity in places like Texas, where the Latino population is spread out around the state, and minorities from many areas get to continue their education. In most states, however, minority populations are not as widespread, so not as many would get the benefit. This, however, is a very clever way of being against affirmative action. Pick something that sounds like what you're against, make it *seem* like it accomplishes the same thing, and that way you seem sympathetic to the other side's cause. Conservatives did this with welfare by christening it "workfare." It reminds me of the wonderful character created by Gilda Radner, "Roseanne Rosannadanna," who would talk about something until she actually found out what it meant, like the time she waxed poetic on the issue of "Soviet Jewelry," only to be forced, upon being set straight, to conclude, "Oh, never mind!" By using this technique folks on the right can appear to be supporting minorities reaching higher goals by advocating the "civil heights" movement. They don't want you to spit out objects you're chewing, which enables them to claim they favor "gum control." And, of course, the rich should get their fair share of tax cuts, making them "proapportion."

This kind of double talk was evident when the Bush 43 administration tried to define its position on the case regarding the University of Michigan's admission policy. The idea of using anything other than academic scores to advance a student academically seems to bother conservatives, especially if it's race that's advancing that student. But how many schools accept students for reasons other than how well they did on their SAT scores? Bush 43's admission to Yale didn't have anything to do with Bush 41, did it? Now *that's* "Affirmative Access."

Bush 43 spoke to the nation on affirmative action on Wednesday, January 15, 2003, saying, "At their core, the Michigan policies amount to a quota system that unfairly rewards or penalizes prospective students based solely on their race." But what Michigan was doing did not involve quotas at all. Prospective students were given twenty points for race, but they could also receive points for other factors like socioeconomic disadvantage, for example (and could not receive points for both race *and* socioeconomic disadvantage).

Also contradictory were the comments of Condoleezza Rice, who is often held up as proof that Bush is race-friendly. On one hand, she claimed to support the Bush position on the Michigan case during her *Meet the Press* appearance on January 19, 2003. On the other hand, she stated, "It is important to take race into consideration if you must, if race-neutral means do not work." She went on to acknowledge that she, herself, benefited from affirmative action when she was hired to teach at Stanford. "I think they saw a person that they thought had potential, and yes, I think they were looking to diversify the faculty." She went on to use the very argument liberals have used for years in defending affirmative action: "I think there's nothing wrong with that in the United States. It does not mean that one has to go to people of lower quality. Race is a factor in our society." So, she was *defending* Bush's opposition to affirmative action while pointing out it was responsible for her own success, and telling us why affirmative action is such a good idea. I have to stop writing for a moment. I'm scratching my head.

Yes, race is still a factor in our society. And it's often played, as was suggested at the OJ trial, "from the bottom of the deck." And the deck is still stacked against African Americans. There is no doubt that some Americans still have a negative perception of minorities, and that there is a special reluctance to accept relationships between black men and white women. In OJ's case, there was an immediate national conclusion of guilt. That was the assumption from the Bronco chase on, and many Americans never even considered that there could have been another explanation for the deaths of Ron Brown and Nicole Simpson.

Simpson had an even stronger case than was presented. There was much testimony favoring the defense that the jury never got to see. Rosa Lopez, the maid who lived next door to OJ, made a videotape on which she said that OJ's Bronco was parked in the same spot before, during, and after Ron and Nicole were killed. She didn't want to testify at the trial because she wanted to leave the country. Defense attorneys were threatened with sanctions if they played her testimony because it hadn't been turned over to the prosecution as required by law. Mary Ann Gerchas, a jewelry store owner, never got to testify. She claimed to have seen four men near the crime scene at 10:45 p.m., and that two were carrying something before they all sped off in a car. But Gerchas was arrested for allegedly failing to pay thousands of dollars in hotel bills and was considered too damaged a witness. Kary Mullis was going to testify for the defense about how the police handled DNA evidence. Mullis won a Nobel Prize for developing something called polymerase chain reaction. PCR is a form of DNA testing that can get information from very small fragments. But prosecutor Rockne Harmon said he would go after Mullis for drug use if he ever took the stand. The jury did not hear many of the allegations of Mark Fuhrman's misconduct. And many Simpson friends and associates never took the stand.

It's a shame that race had to play a role at the Simpson trial, just as it's a shame that race has been a factor in issues that, in a truly just society, would have no racial component. I look forward to the day when each political party stops using race as bait in the game of "gotcha," to when affirmative action is no longer argued because it's no longer necessary, to when we accept blacks and whites, even when they're married to each other, and to when it matters not how many blacks are on a jury.

Some Americans think OJ was not convicted because of the racial makeup of the jury. How about the plain truth that the defense put forth a better case than the prosecution? The fact is, the verdict did come in "not guilty." In America you are innocent until proven guilty. OJ is innocent.

EIGHT

Jesus Was a Liberal

> Do not seek revenge or bear a grudge against one
> of your people, but love your neighbor as yourself.
>
> —LEVITICUS 19:18
> (New International Version)

From: Susan L
Sent: Friday, April 11, 2003 9:29 AM
To: colmes
Subject: God is right!

When the righteous are in authority, the people rejoice: but when the wicked beareth rule, the people mourn. (Proverbs 29:2) Have you seen the poll results? Can you argue with GOD? The democrats are toast . . . Praise The Lord!!!!

Susan L Lexington, KY

Listening to today's conservatives, you would think that Jesus is a member of the Republican Party, hates Bill Clinton, and wants no Democrats in office. You might even believe that God anointed George W. Bush to rule us at this time in our history. The gospel of the right would also have you thinking that our forefathers were all good Christians who envisioned a Christian nation, not to be besmirched by religious beliefs that did not reflect their own. How Jesus became co-opted by the right, and how the left has allowed this to happen, boggles the mind. I have it on good authority (the highest) that Jesus attends both Republican and Democratic conventions, that he is in the voting booth regardless of who is voting, and that he himself doesn't pull the lever. Let's examine just what Jesus did and what he stood for, and we'll let his actions speak for themselves.

Jesus ate with prostitutes, threw out the money changers (capitalists), believed the rich should give to the poor, and preached the golden rule. He had a problem with the conservatives of the day, the Pharisees, and opposed their stoning sinners and quoting from Scripture. The tendency conservatives have to see the world in black and white is very palatable to those who have no need for critical thinking. Hence the gay issue, for example, is handled by phrases like, "God made Adam and Eve, not Adam and Steve." This is very bad news to every conservative named Steve. God didn't make you. Sorry! Better luck next time.

The love Jesus offered during his short life was not dictated by economic status, religious belief, racial background, or sexual identity. Jesus was a champion to all. He spoke truth to power, even as he respected history and tradition, much as today's patriotic liberals do. Jesus preached love, compassion, justice, and peace. Let's take one of Jesus' basic tenets: "Love thy neighbor as thyself." So why do some conservatives insist on being less than loving toward neighbors not like themselves?

From: MindTravlr
Sent: Tuesday, September 11, 2001 4:44 PM
To: colmes
Subject: (no subject)

I pray that Jesus Christ will soften your cold and sick mind before He comes back to get all of the Republicans.

Yes, I realize it will take Democrats longer to get there, but that's because they'll be using public transportation and hydrogen-powered vehicles.

White Like Me

Conservatives would also have you believe that Jesus was the world's first advocate for the white man and that he looked like David Duke. In fact, he was of Mediterranean complexion and looked more like Ricardo Montalban. In April 2001, the Discovery Channel created a digitized version of what Jesus probably looked like. The look can be described in one word: Jewfro.

Reverend Paul Scott of the "New Righteous Movement" came on *Hannity & Colmes* on December 4, 2002, to rail against the misuse of Jesus as a paragon of whiteness.

COLMES: He was most likely dark-skinned, correct?

SCOTT: Of course. The image of the blue-eyed, blond-haired Jesus that is on many walls and even in many black churches is not even historically correct ... we believe he was a black man.

Scott posed an interesting question during his appearance on our show:

SCOTT: Let me ask this, if the person you call Jesus was around during the Jim Crow days in Alabama, at a restaurant that segregated against black people ... would he have been served ... or would he have been asked to leave the restaurant? He would have been kicked out of the restaurant because of his color.

That show prompted this e-mail exchange:

From: Margaret
Sent: Wednesday, December 04, 2002 9:43 PM
To: colmes
Subject: (no subject)

This a comment for your guest Reverend Paul Scott. Jesus was Jewish and white. Facts are facts, and it has nothing to do with race. I would tell Mr. Scott to study his History because if he would have done his homework, then there would be no speculation about who and what Jesus was.

From: Colmes
Sent: Wednesday, December 04, 2002 10:28 PM
To: Margaret
Subject: RE: (no subject)

Jesus was from the Mediterranean and was olive skinned, more like an off-white, maybe a mocha or latte.

Jesus on the Issues

Jesus said, "Love thy neighbor as thyself." He didn't say, "Love only thy conservative neighbor as thyself." "Thy neighbor" includes the poor, the sick, the emotionally disadvantaged, the illegal immigrant who just snuck across the border and, yes, even liberals. At the Sermon on the Mount, speaking to the largest gathering of his ministry, Jesus spoke words that are considered central to Judeo-Christian tradition. The Beatitudes bless those who mourn, those who hunger and thirst for righteousness, those who are merciful, and those who are pure of heart. "Blessed are the peacemakers," says Jesus, "for they shall be called Sons of God." Evil dictators like Saddam Hussein aren't getting blessings here, but neither are those who would initiate war against them. And I'm guessing Jesus is endorsing the Nuclear Test Ban Treaty. "Blessed are the meek, for they shall inherit the earth," it says in Matthew 5:5. Sorry, all you loud, right-wing talk-show hosts, but we nice, easygoing liberals are inheriting beachfront property.

If you help the poor, the needy, and the infirm, you are doing it for Jesus. Matthew 25, says:

> Then I, the King, shall say to those at my right, "Come, blessed of my Father, into the Kingdom prepared for you from the founding of the world. For I was hungry and you fed me; I was thirsty and you gave me water; I was a stranger and you invited me into your homes; naked and you clothed me; sick and in prison, and you visited me." Then these righteous ones will reply, "Sir, when did we ever see you hungry and feed you? Or thirsty and give you anything to drink? Or a stranger, and help you? Or naked, and clothe you? When did we ever see you sick or in prison, and visit you?" And I, the King, will tell them, "When you did it to these my brothers you were doing it to me!"

So when the government clothes and feeds the needy; when the government gives Medicare and Medicaid; when Head Start can help otherwise-neglected children, and when housing is made available to those who would otherwise have no shelter, the government is doing it for Jesus. This does not comport with the policies of conservatives who continue to demonize those who need a helping hand. Even though welfare takes up just 2 percent of the federal budget (compared with 16 percent for defense, for example), many taxpayers resent that their dollars go to help the less fortunate among us. But given how so much of social policy is in keeping with Jesus' teachings, you'd think conservatives would applaud these government programs because they make more porous the impenetrable wall between church and state.

Jesus encouraged us to sell everything we have and give the money to the poor. Tell that to conservatives fighting to erase the estate taxes, which affect only the wealthiest Americans in the first place. Only the richest families are taxed on what is actually a gift, and many of them resent that these tax dollars go to help those who need it most. When you support a tax plan that favors the investor class, remember Matthew 19:23–24, where Jesus says, "Again I tell you, it is easier for a camel to go through the eye of needle than for a rich man to enter the kingdom of God."

On the issue of equal opportunity, Luke 11:9–10 says "For everyone who asks receives; he who seeks finds; and to he who knocks, the door will be open." Affirmative action, anyone?

Jesus was antigun. You'd think, listening to the National Rifle Association, that Jesus' actual words were "from my cold, dead hands," but no. Here's what Jesus actually said in Matthew 26:52: "Put your sword back into its place; for all who take the sword will perish by the sword." Jesus would be very upset with current gun show loopholes. He would be disturbed by all of the lobbying against the use of safety locks to protect our children. But when liberals talk about the modern-day equivalent of turning swords into plowshares, they're committing NRA blasphemy.

Why is it that conservatives think that liberals have never met Jesus Christ?

From: UncleJoe
Sent: Saturday, February 15, 2003 3:39 PM
To: colmes
Subject: Accept Christ

Mr. Colmes, John 3:16—I pray, that you will accept Christ as your personal savior, Mr. Colmes, he is the only answer . . . Once you give your heart to Jesus, Mr. Colmes, you'll understand Mr. Hannity, and all the others like me, too. Hope to see you in Heaven, and eat at the table of Christ. Sincerely; UncleJoe

That's Me in the Spotlight, Losing My Religion

REM's song "Losing My Religion" wasn't about losing his religion.

It's an old southern phrase about being at the end of one's rope, which is where I am in trying to defend what our founding fathers really had in mind when they called for separation of church and state. It was an effort to protect the *church* from *state* interference, not the other way around. It is true that at the time of our founding most Americans considered themselves Christians. But our founding fathers realized that religious differences, which might become more pronounced down the road, could lead to division, as they did when the Puritans left England to form the Massachusetts Bay Colony, or even violence, as they did during the English civil war in the seventeenth century.

James Madison eloquently expressed the theory of separation of church and state in his undated essay, "Monopolies, Perpetuities, Corporations, Ecclesiastical Endowments." He warned not to deviate from "the sacred principle of religious liberty, by giving to Caesar what belongs to God," and to "make the example of your country as pure and compleat, in what relates to the freedom of the mind and its allegiance to its maker, as in what belongs to the legitimate objects of political and civil institutions." Advocating passage of the Virginia Bill for Religions Liberty, Madison fought against those who wanted to insert the name of the savior and stated that the best proof of reverence for the holy name "would be not to profane it by making it a topic of legislative discussion."

The Treaty of Tripoli, which affirmed our friendship with the Barbary Coast nation, was negotiated during the administration of our nation's founder, George Washington, and signed on June 10, 1797, by our second president John Adams. Article XI of the treaty states, "As the government of the United States of America is not in any sense founded on the Christian Religion . . . no pretext arising from religious opinions shall ever produce an interruption of the harmony existing between the two countries. . . . The United States is not a Christian nation any more than it is a Jewish or a Mohammedan nation."

Our third president was also known to believe in the value of church and state separation. The Danville, Connecticut, Baptist

Association wrote to Thomas Jefferson on October 7, 1801, to express its concern about religious liberty in our new nation. In his reply of January 1, 1802 (snail mail), Jefferson explained the basic tenets of the relationship between church and state:

> Believing with you that religion is a matter which lies solely between man and his God; that he owes account to none other for his faith or his worship; that the legislative powers of the government reach actions only, and not opinions, I contemplate with sovereign reverence that act of the whole American people which declared that their legislature should "make no law respecting an establishment of religion, or prohibiting the free exercise thereof," thus building a wall of separation between church and State.

Jefferson devoted years to writing what became known as *The Jefferson Bible*. Formally known as *The Life and Morals of Jesus of Nazareth*, Jefferson's goal was to get at the heart of Jesus' message, free from political spin and agenda-driven interpretations. In 1800, Jefferson wrote a letter to his friend Dr. Benjamin Rush, in which he described his disdain for clergy, forswearing "eternal hostility against any form of tyranny over the mind of man." On organized religion, Jefferson wrote to Mrs. Samuel H. Smith on August 6, 1816, "The artificial structures they have built on the purest of all moral system, for the purpose of deriving from it pence and power, revolts those who think for themselves."

The writer Michael Novak tries to make the case for the Christian basis of our nation in *On Two Wings: An Alternative to the Secular Myth of America's Creation*. But the historian Zachary Karabell, reviewing Novak's book in the *Los Angeles Times*, makes the point that there was a different concept of religion in eighteenth-century America than there is today. "The problem," Karabell explains, "is that no one in 18th century America or Europe understood 'religion' quite like it was thought of in the late 20th century. To claim, as Novak does, that the religious dimension of the founding has been given short shrift is both defensible and valuable, but to imply, as he seems to, that the founders were men of religion as we understand religion today risks replacing one myth with another."

Some of our founders were deists, not Christians. Deism rejects revealed scripture but does acknowledge a God that created the universe and then left the rest up to us. Deist James Madison declared, "Religion and government will both exist in greater purity, the less they are mixed together." Madison also had this to say about Christianity: "During almost fifteen centuries had the legal establishment of Christianity been on trial. What have been its fruits? More or less in all places, pride and indolence in the Clergy, ignorance and servility in the laity, in both, superstition, bigotry and persecution."

In his book *Washington and Religion*, Paul F. Boller Jr. quotes a minister and contemporary of our first president who asserted, "while Washington was very deferential to religion and its ceremonies, like nearly all the founders of the Republic, he was not a Christian, but a Deist."

Ethan Allen, the champion of Vermont statehood and the man who led the battle at Fort Ticonderoga, the Revolutionary War's first colonial victory, proclaimed, "That Jesus Christ was not God is evidence from his own words." He said he was "denominated a Deist . . . being conscious that I am no Christian." During his wedding to Fanny Buchanan, he stopped the service when he was asked if his marriage would be "agreeable to the laws of God," refusing to answer until the judge allowed that the God here was the God of nature and the laws were those "written in the great book of nature."

Benjamin Franklin, also considered a Deist, mentioned Jesus of Nazareth in a letter to his friend, Yale president Ezra Stiles, by saying, "I have, with most of the present dissenters in England, some doubts as to his Divinity; tho' it is a question I do not dogmatize upon, having never studied it, and think needless to busy myself with it now, when I expect soon an opportunity of knowing the Truth." Franklin may well have soon found out the truth, for he died a month later.

Why is it so important for some Americans to insist this is a Christian nation? Are they so insecure in their beliefs that they need government sanction for their faith? They decry the lack of religious imagery around us, as though our country would be better served if there were crosses, pictures of Jesus, and plaques of the Ten Commandments everywhere we turn. Everyone should believe what they believe, and think like they think, but don't insist that I believe what you believe or think like you think in order to justify your own beliefs.

The Real Chosen People

Defending the view that God put Bush 43 in the White House and Republicans in charge of both houses of Congress, a number of conservatives sent me this passage from the New King James Version of the Bible, Romans 13:1: "Let every soul be subject to the governing authorities. For there is no authority, except from God, and the authorities that exist are appointed by God."

There you have it. Our authorities are appointed by God. I've asked many who e-mailed me this passage if this means we should stay home from the polls on Election Day, but I have yet to receive a satisfactory reply. Perhaps each election is good versus evil, and Satan guides the hands of Democrats while God guides the hands of Republicans.

From: Michelle W.
Sent: Tuesday, November 12, 2002 9:37 PM
To: colmes
Subject: did God use -call Politicians

On your show tonight . . . you asked if God chooses people in the political world—you bet He does. How do you think George Bush became President???

All of us Christians prayed for someone who was morally good and loved God and we got him. We still pray for him everyday, and you just wait and see if God doesn't win. George Bush is going to be one of His best disciples.

Michelle W. ND

Some true believers hold the notion that George W. Bush was chosen to be president by God. This view was enhanced after September 11, 2001, when many sensed that Bush 43 exhibited a sense of mission that seemed fervent and religious in nature. On the July 11, 2002, *Hannity & Colmes* I asked Dr. James Dobson, the highly respected head of "Focus on the Family" who has a huge following among Christian conservatives, if he believes George W. Bush was chosen by God.

COLMES: Do you think God chose George W. Bush to be president?

DOBSON: Well, I think an awful lot of people were praying about that last election, not that God is a Republican, but I think that he does influence the affairs of men, especially when people are asking him for guidance, and so—I don't really know. We'd have to ask him directly, but I suspect that maybe he did.

So I did eventually get a yes on how Bush ascended to the presidency, but the good doctor was a bit more hesitant to give God credit for our previous president:

COLMES: Let me ask you then—if that's the case, did God then choose Bill Clinton at one time to be president? I mean, is that how it works?

DOBSON: You know, you have to talk to God about that, which might be a good idea, you know.

COLMES: We communicate regularly, Dr. Dobson.

Ironically, for those who believe in the marriage of evangelical Christianity and Republicanism, our first modern-day evangelical in the White House was a Democrat—Jimmy Carter. He is a devout Southern Baptist, taught Sunday school while president, and read the Bible daily. He is a Christian of unquestionable faith who continues to pray daily. Speaking to Terry Gross on NPR's Fresh Air program in 2002, Carter shared his practice, "I never prayed for popularity, never prayed to be re-elected, things of that kind. I prayed that I could keep my nation at peace; I prayed that I could extend the advantages of peace to other people; say between Egypt and Israel at Camp David. When the hostage crisis came along, the prayer that I made was that all the hostages would come back home safe and free, that I would not betray the principles of my nation or do anything to embarrass it. And I think in all those cases my prayers were answered."

While Jimmy Carter walked the walk, it was Ronald Reagan who was embraced by conservative religious activists, even though Reagan was less openly religious. Yet Carter is denounced by many on the religious right for being one of our worst presidents, ever, and an anti-God liberal. In fact, when Carter was a Georgia state senator, he proposed an amendment to remove a paragraph in the state Constitution stating that all citizens have "the natural and inalienable right to worship God according to the dictates of his own conscience." Carter preferred that Georgia's Constitution have the same wording as our U.S. Bill of Rights, which states, "No law shall be passed respecting an establishment of religion or prohibiting the free exercise thereof." His political opponents seized on this to describe him as an "ultra-liberal who had once worked to delete the word 'God' from the Georgia Constitution."

I wonder if those who believe that Bush is God's choice can bring themselves to the view that if God guides hands as they pull levers in voting booths, he doesn't guide them only toward "Row A." On April 12, 2002, Tom DeLay, then house whip, spoke at the First Baptist Church of Pearland, Texas, and said that God was using him to promote "a biblical worldview" in American politics and that Bill

Clinton had to be impeached because he had "the wrong world-view." I have no quarrel with Congressman DeLay's belief that his prominence came at the hands of God, as long as he will acknowledge that it cuts both ways.

James Dobson, like Tom DeLay and Bush 43, believes that God chose him for a special kind of ministry. While I disagree with Dr. Dobson politically, I don't doubt his dedication and sincerity. Dobson really wants government to reflect his religious and moral views. On February 7, 1998, he threatened to bolt the Republican Party if it didn't give higher priority to conservative social issues, saying he'd take his flock with him: "If I go, I will do everything I can to take as many people with me as possible," And its a considerable flock, given that his radio listenership is estimated at 200 million listeners in 98 countries.

I enjoyed telling Dr. Dobson, on our November 22, 2002, broadcast, that I'm where I am, too, because of God's will:

DOBSON: But I think there is free will. I think that's what happened in the Garden of Eden, where God allowed . . .

HANNITY: Like Alan chooses to be a liberal. I mean, he chooses that path.

COLMES: God has made me a liberal.

DOBSON: That's kind of hard to understand, but you know I love him anyway.

COLMES: God has made me who I am and I'm proud of it.

The Blame Game

I don't believe Jesus played the blame game, but that can't be said of many of Jesus' most visible disciples. Even though conservatives love to tag liberals as the "Blame America First Crowd," I heartily reject that designation. Two days after the September 11 attacks, it was

Reverend Jerry Falwell on Reverend Pat Robertson's *700 Club* who implicated liberals for God's decision to remove the aura of protection over America. Falwell blamed "the Pagans, and the abortionists, and the feminists, and the gay and the lesbians who are actively trying to make that an alternative lifestyle, the ACLU, People for the American Way—all of them who have tried to secularize America." Who's pointing fingers here? Read on: "I point the finger in their face and say, 'You helped this happen,'" Falwell said. The "Moral Majority" founder went on to say that these Americans "make God mad." Here was a self-proclaimed religious American blaming his *fellow Americans* for allowing September 11 to happen. At the same time, liberals who asked that we not only fight terrorism, but look within for the causes of hatred, were accused of not putting the blame where it belonged—on foreign-bred terrorists. We were branded "the Blame America first" crowd. See if you can grasp those concepts at the same time without your head exploding.

Now, let me get this straight: if we had prayer in schools and the Ten Commandments adorning federal walls, bin Laden would have said, "I can't fly into buildings in *that* country. Their children say prayers on public property and their federal building walls display what Moses handed to God on Mount Sinai!"

To his credit, when asked by Geraldo Rivera if that was the "real" Jerry Falwell who spoke on the *700 Club*, the reverend replied, "I want to tell you that I regret those comments . . . I wrongly blamed others, misrepresented my own beliefs."

Muslims, both foreign and domestic, became easy prey after September 11. Reverend Franklin Graham, the harder-edged son of Reverend Billy Graham, called Islam "a very evil and wicked religion" in an interview with former Charlotte television reporter Bruce Bowers that was sold to NBC. Trying to clarify his comments, Graham wrote in the *Wall Street Journal* on December 3, 2001, "I do not believe Muslims are evil people because of their faith. I personally have many Muslim friends. But I decry the evil that has been done in the name of Islam, or any other faith—including Christianity."

Graham then went on to say, "The persecution or elimination of non-Muslims has been a cornerstone of Islamic conquests and rule for centuries." He condemns "the ultimate goal of an Islamic world." But many Christians have the ultimate goal of a Christian world, with Graham as one of the leading proponents of this view.

Franklin Graham appeared on the February 19, 2002, edition of *Hannity & Colmes*, and I asked him about his controversial comments:

COLMES: You believe Islam then is an evil religion, and—do they—that's what you're saying. Do they worship the same God as the Judeo-Christian God? Is it a different God?

GRAHAM: No, it's a different God. The God that we worship is a god that has—that's a father, and he has a son, and his name is Jesus Christ, who came to this earth to die for the sins of mankind. And of course, in Islam, their God is not a father. He—it does not have a son, and, of course, if you said that he has a son, that's blasphemous to a Muslim . . .

Again, on August 5, 2002, the issue of Islam as evil came up with Reverend Graham:

COLMES: But is the religion itself evil, in fact?

GRAHAM: Well, you tell me. I mean, just what you see. When people go up and blow themselves up and the religious leaders of this religion say nothing, something's wrong here. And two plus two doesn't add up.

It's amazing to me that this religious scion, dedicated to carrying on the works of his father, said the things he did after September 11. He placed himself squarely in the center of the "Blame America First" crowd.

I was raised to believe that we each have our own way, that we are all struggling to find the right spiritual path, and that it doesn't matter which path you use to get there. And I have no vested interest in increasing the traffic on my particular path; in fact, I rather enjoy an uncrowded one. Graham, however, prefers the divide and conquer technique: "The God of Islam is not the same God. . . . It's a different God and I believe it is a very evil and wicked religion."

Funny how these good, caring, compassionate souls, while they're busy demonizing Mohammed, never bring up those little periods of Christian history known as the Crusades, the Inquisition, or the Thirty Years War. Just a slight omission, I'm sure.

Former television evangelist Jimmy Swaggart's response to September 11 was to call for expelling all Muslims with visas, and Reverend Pat Robertson referred to Islamic anti-Semites as "worse than the Nazis." Swaggart, like Falwell, later said he regretted his comment and Robertson said he should have said "*some* Muslims."

But Robertson hasn't backed off comments he made in his 2002 book *Bring It On*. He was clearly implicating those who favor a woman's right to choose when he wrote, "It is logical to assume that any nation that has willingly slaughtered more than forty million innocent unborn babies, as we have done in the United States, would be subject to the wrath of God. Indeed, any nation that has embraced sodomy, adultery, fornication, and all manner of debauchery as we in America have done should live in terror not from Islamic fanatics, but terror at what Almighty God will do when His patience is exhausted. At minimum, God is no longer bound to protect such a nation from its enemies."

So, God is off the hook, but he's really, really pissed. Maybe if everyone were faithful to his and her spouse, restricted sexual activity to the missionary position, and did so only within the confines of marriage, September 11 would have been just another sunny day on the East Coast. Maybe, but I doubt it.

On his *700 Club* broadcast of February 21, 2002, Robertson didn't exactly call the Welcome Wagon lady to greet new Muslims to the neighborhood. "The fact is that our immigration policies are now so skewed to the Middle East and away from Europe that we have introduced these people into our midst and undoubtedly there are terrorist cells all over them." He went on to accuse some Muslims of not wanting to live here peacefully, saying, "they want to coexist until they can control, dominate and then if need be, destroy." Can you imagine anyone talking so publicly about an American religion in that manner?

Pat Robertson's appearances on *Hannity & Colmes* have been provocative, to say the least. I must say, that in spite of our differences, I've thoroughly enjoyed the many back-and-forths I've had with him. We've argued often and vociferously. On September 18, 2002, he referred to Mohammed as "a wild-eyed fanatic, a robber and brigand." The conversation then turned to politics, and I asked Robertson to explain a statement he'd made previously on *Hannity & Colmes* when he said, "Liberals always lie":

COLMES: What—Pat, what would Jesus say about that kind of a comment. Liberals always lie?

HANNITY: Amen.

COLMES: Jesus has spoken. Ladies and gentlemen, Jesus has spoken.

HANNITY: He'd say "Amen."

COLMES: He's come back! He's sitting next to me! We have just seen the second coming. Go ahead.

ROBERTSON: You know, Jesus spoke to the Pharisees. He called them whitewashed tombs. And he said you know, you always speak a falsehood. So he talked about the devil being a liar and the father of lies. So he said some pretty rough words as well.

COLMES: All right. Is that—do you want to interpret that as antiliberal bigotry? You make a blanket statement: liberals lie. That's not a Christian-like thing to say.

ROBERTSON: Well, it's not Christian, but it's true.

Some of the staunchest supporters of Israel reside on the Christian right, but not for reasons that would warm the heart of Jews. Many evangelical Christians believe that the second coming of Christ can occur only after the temple in Jerusalem is rebuilt. And they believe that on the last day, Jews will suddenly find Jesus and be saved. I don't think that's quite what Israelis fighting for survival have in mind.

I addressed this with Reverend Robertson on the April 10, 2002, *Hannity & Colmes:*

COLMES: I know you are a very strong supporter of Israel and the Jews. You have historically been very supportive of Israel's right to exist and its biblical prophesy. But these are people who do not accept Jesus Christ.

ROBERTSON: The Bible says that Israel is going to be converted in a single day. There is going to be an event that is going to bring them to the point where they say, "Blessed is he that comes in the name of the Lord." . . . And we've seen many many Jewish people who are responding and becoming so-called messianic Jews.

COLMES: So the Jews who accept Jesus will be okay.

ROBERTSON: Well, I think the whole nation, in the not-too-distant future, is going to recognize their messiah.

John Ashcroft, that paragon of Christian love, gave us all a theology lesson, courtesy of an interview with my Fox News colleague and friend Cal Thomas, during which he said, "Islam is a religion in which God requires you to send your son to die for him. Christianity is a faith in which God sends his son to die for you." Ashcroft may have just read Franklin Graham's book, *The Name*, in which a similar statement appears. Although Cal Thomas had packed up his tape recorder by the time this comment was made, the quote was read back to the attorney general before he left the interview, and the words stood. And when the words were made public, Thomas, a man of impeccable virtue and journalistic ethics, was accused of misquoting the attorney general. Now, wait a minute: *which* administration said it would be the most ethical one, ever?

I'm curious, would God really back out of our lives because there is a separation of church and state? If God is really all-powerful, do we have the power to expel him? I'm fairly certain that God doesn't need government to show how powerful he is.

The Bible Tells Me So

From: LandRk
Sent: Saturday, November 23, 2002 8:12 PM
To: colmes
Subject: (no subject)

Colmes,
You support separation of Church & State etc. Well, fine continue on your liberal viewpoints! That just means that Christ'll be coming sooner. Refer to (Rev. 9:13–19) does that sound like what might be ready to take place in a chemical with Saddam in Iraq? So, then it will be down to the 4 Hoursemen-Plagues. / And, then the Return of Christ after the 7th Trumpet!

It's an easy but intellectually dishonest game to pull a quote from the Bible and use it to justify your view on a particular topic or a particular religion. I've read both the Old and New Testaments, but I must confess that my classes did not do so in the original Aramaic. The Bible is full of inspirational readings and wonderful morality tales that can help one develop a code for living, but to try to take every word literally is a recipe for confusion. Since September 11, 2001, Islam-bashers have offered up violent passages from the Koran as if to prove that the religion it represents is itself violent. I don't recall the Islam-bashers quoting these passages from the Koran:

Thus, if they let you be, and do not make war on you, and offer you peace, God does not allow you to harm them. (4:90)

. . . whoever took a life, unless it be for murder or for spreading disorder on earth, it would be as if he killed all mankind; and whoever saved a life, it would be as if he saved all mankind. (5:32)

And wouldn't it be nice to know what the Koran says about waging war on non-Muslim countries?

After the Prophet and his authorized Companion, no individual or group or state has the right to wage war against any non-Muslim country for the propagation of Islam. Now *Jihad*, or *Qital* to be more precise, can be done by an Islamic state only for purpose of ending oppression. (4:75)

Those who argue that the Koran is violent sometimes incorrectly imply that the Jewish/Christian Bible is less so. While they point out how the Koran promotes war, they omit some very unpleasant biblical passages:

. . . when I sharpen my flashing sword and my hand grasps it in judgment, I will take vengeance on my adversaries and repay those who hate me. (Deut. 32:41)

And the Lord said, "Go through the city, and smite: let not your eye spare, neither have you pity. Slay utterly old and young, both maids and little children, and women." (Ezek. 9:5)

Now I know why John Huston's 1966 movie, *The Bible*, wasn't a musical.

The Christian Right versus the Right Christians

We see time after time how the Bible is used to promote particular political and social agendas. The Reverend Al Sharpton crossed a picket line for the first time in his life on the thirtieth anniversary of *Roe v. Wade.* Antichoicers were protesting the National Abortion and Reproductive Rights Action League [NARAL] dinner at the Omni Sheraton Hotel in Washington, but that wasn't going to stop Sharpton from addressing the crowd. When one young woman challenged him, as a minister, to boycott the dinner, he told her, "Young lady, it is time for the Christian right to meet the right Christians."

According to some conservatives, the Christian right is a myth created by liberals. In her book *Slander,* Ann Coulter considers the "Christian Right" an artificial creation of the liberal media and democratic politicians. She writes, "Like all propagandists, liberals create mythical enemies to justify their own viciousness and advance their agenda. There is no bogeyman that strikes greater terror in the left than the apocryphal 'religious right.' The very phrase is a meaningless concept, an inverted construct of the left's own Marquis de Sade lifestyle."

Honestly, I can't imagine what the liberals' view of the religious right has to do with the Marquis de Sade, but it wasn't the media that created the religious right (although it's fashionable on the right to blame the "liberal media" for everything). Years of direct mail campaigns by and contributions to groups like the Moral Majority were not a fantasy of the left. While John F. Kennedy said, "I believe in a president whose views on religion are his own private affairs," Ronald Reagan invited religious right groups like the Moral Majority (which some say is neither) to participate in the political process. Bush 41 declared to a conference of National Religious Broadcasters on January 27, 1992, "You cannot be America's president without a belief in God or a belief in prayer." Pandering to the religious right, Bush 43 proclaimed that Jesus was his favorite political philosopher, "because he changed my heart." Bush 43 wants to lower the wall between church and state separation with school vouchers and faith-based initiatives. It's as though Bush 43 were saying, to paraphrase Reagan's plea to Gorbachev, "Mr. Jefferson, tear down this wall!"

A *Financial Times* article, "Preaching to the Converted," quotes Karl Rove responding to a question about how big a role Christian communities play in politics: "Not big enough." The article points out, "Bush scooped up 82 percent of the conservative Christian vote in the 2000 elections. When Saxby Chambliss shocked the Democratic establishment in the South in November by taking the Georgia Senate seat for the Republicans, he owed a debt of thanks to charismatic Christian communities—74 percent of conservative Christians voted for the Republican candidate in Georgia." And you may not know that in the White House Office of Public Liaison there is a special assistant whose focus is Christian outreach.

Coulter declares, "Liberals hate religion because politics is a religion substitute for liberals and they can't stand competitions." And she compares liberals who expose the Christian right to the agents of the Spanish Inquisition "rounding up right-wingers and putting them on trial for hate crimes."

Conservatives also like to argue that being gay is anti-Christian. They invoke their favorite biblical passages like, "Man shall not lay with his fellow man." Peter Gomes, Christian morals professor at Harvard, wrote an op-ed piece in the *New York Times* on August 17, 1992, called "Homophobic? Re-read your Bible." He points out that Leviticus 18:19–23 and Leviticus 20:10–16 are part of what scholars refer to as the "holiness code" that bans homosexual acts. Gomes goes on to write, "But it also prohibits eating raw meat, planting two different kinds of seed in the same field, and wearing garments with two different kinds of yarn. Tattoos, adultery, and sexual intercourse during a woman's menstrual cycle are similarly outlawed." So, let me put it to you this way: you're just as guilty of sin, whether you're engaging in gay sex, or wearing a cotton-poly blend. And while you're at it, get "My heart belongs to Cathy" off your chest.

Homosexuality doesn't come up in the four Gospels of the New Testament. Jesus wasn't that concerned about it. St. Paul's quotes in the Bible are often cited by those seeking to denounce homosexuality (Romans 1:26–2:1, I Corinthians 6:9–11, and I Timothy 1:10), but that's because, as Gomes explains, St. Paul was against all lust and sensuality, regardless of sexual orientation. Gomes adds some inspiring words that put the Bible in perspective for me and help me understand how the Good Book can be both properly used or disastrously misused:

> The same Bible that the predecessors of Mr. Falwell and Mr. Robertson used to keep white churches white is the source of inspiration of the Rev. Martin Luther King, Jr. and the social reformation of the 1960s. The same Bible that anti-feminists use to keep women silent in the churches is the Bible that preaches liberation to captives and says that in Christ there is neither male nor female, slave nor free.
>
> And the same Bible that on the basis of an archaic social code of ancient Israel and a tortured reading of Paul is used to condemn all gays, includes metaphors of redemption, renewal, inclusion, and love—principles that invite gays to accept their freedom and responsibility in Christ and demands that their fellow Christians accept them as well.

Jerry Falwell sounded the alarm as early as 1984. In a fund-raising letter he talked about "militant homosexuals plotting a dangerously different future for America." The solicitiation for funds went on to read, "It is clear they intend to recruit our children to their perverted life style . . . and they do have their eyes on our children!" I've got really bad news for you if you're a concerned parent. Heterosexual adults also have their eyes on your children, and they're a much bigger threat, since there are so many of those heteros out there these days. In fact, heteros have their own bars, their own dating services, and are often quite open about their "relationships." Be careful.

It fascinates me when I hear that supposedly intelligent adults are worried that others in our society are going to be "recruited" or "turn gay." They must have some enticing brochures and training films. I understand that some gay groups offer free toasters or long-distance telephone service. But you have to promise to like the same sex for at least a year.

We now know a toy can be gay. Jerry Falwell expressed alarm about an allegedly gay Teletubby when he said this about Tinky Winky: "The character, whose voice is obviously that of a boy, has been found carrying a red purse in many episodes and has become a favorite character among gay groups worldwide." Falwell told Katie Couric on the *Today* show that his senior editor, not he, wrote that in the *National Liberty Journal* newspaper. But he didn't disabuse anyone of that sentiment; and the day before he was quoted by the Associated Press on the incident, saying, "As a Christian, I feel that role modeling the gay lifestyle is damaging to the moral lives of children." Falwell was really on a roll in early 1999. Just a month earlier, he declared that the Antichrist was a Jewish man who is currently alive. To soothe the situation, Falwell explained that the Antichrist is Jewish because Jesus was. I was a little concerned when I heard this, as I fit these qualifications; plus, like Jesus, I'm a liberal. And I did once receive a copy of this e-mail that was sent to warn Hannity about me:

From: Jasper
Sent: Thursday, October 03, 2002 1:45 PM
To: Hannity
CC: Colmes
Subject: Alan

Hi Sean!
My wife and I were watching your show the other night and I was explaining to her how Napolian may have been the first antichrist. Hitler the 2nd, and Sadam or Bin Ladin is probably the third. She looked at me and said, "No, Alan is."

Jasper

Fortunately, this commotion died down, and I am now living a normal (relatively, for someone in my profession) life. I attend church regularly with my bride and, in spite of the characteristics laid out by Reverend Falwell, I have not been the victim of profiling.

In His Name

God created us in His image, not the other way around. Similarly, our forefathers had a vision for America, and rather than try to live up to that vision, conservatives often twist what they said and who they were to meet their own ideological needs, just as they've done with Jesus. The fire and brimstone tele-reverends spend more time telling us what they're against than preaching what they're for. Where is the message of tolerance and love that is truly what should be offered in God and Jesus' names?

Ray Dubuque, on his fabulous website liberalslikechrist.org, asks, "What are liberals, anyway?" Listed are a variety of historical figures, all of whom battled the conservatives of their day, from Gandhi, one of the great practitioners of forging change through nonviolence, to Abraham Lincoln (a liberal Republican), to the brave early feminist activists like Susan B. Anthony and Elizabeth Cady Stanton, who stood up at a time when women were supposed to sit in the corner and be quiet, to Jesus Himself.

Years ago there was a memorable ad campaign for Levy's Real Jewish Rye. The concept was, "You don't have to be Jewish to enjoy Levy's Real Jewish Rye," and a series of commercials created by Bill Bernbach showed a variety of ethnic groups enjoying what had previously been marketed as a New York Jewish product. Learning about the life of Jesus, it's obvious you don't have to be Christian to be Christlike. This makes a lot of sense since, after all, neither was He.

As you do unto the least of them you do unto me. (Matthew 25:45)

NINE

Conservatives Say the Darndest Things

Ever since James Watt had to resign as interior secretary in the Reagan administration for bragging about a federal commission he appointed consisting of "a black, a woman . . . two Jews, and a cripple," the hits have just kept on coming. This was proof enough for me that conservatives say the darndest things.

Art Linkletter hit on a gold mine when he discovered that talking to children could elicit some astounding responses. The beauty of what he discovered lies in the innocence of childhood, and children's total lack of guile. I wish the same were true for adults. What we have here are statements and actions by fully grown human beings, some highly educated in both school and life. And these are Americans who have reached the highest rungs on the professional, social, and economic ladders. That is why it is actually adults who say the darndest things, especially *conservative* adults.

Presidents Say the Darndest Things

Time for another pop quiz:

"There ought to be limits to freedom," was a declaration of

1. Adolf Hilter
2. Benito Mussolini
3. Kris Kristofferson
4. George W. Bush

If you picked (1) or (2) you're wrong. Nice try with Kris Kristofferson, but you may be confusing, "There ought to be limits to freedom," with "Freedom's just another word for nothing left to lose." George W. Bush was peeved that a website called gwbush.com had the nerve to appropriate his name. At a press conference in Austin on May 21, 2000, his peevishness got the best of him when he complained about this website. But free speech in America works beautifully. George W. Bush is president and gwbush.com is still in business.

All national candidates wax eloquent about how they're going to get along with the opposition party and represent *all* Americans. During his first trip to Washington as president-elect, Bush 43 met with the four top congressional leaders to talk about how they could work together. "I told all four that there were going to be some times where we don't agree with each other. But that's OK. If this were a dictatorship, it'd be a heck of a lot easier, just so long as I'm the dictator."

I know it's a joke. You know it's a joke. Not everyone who heard it thought it was a joke:

From: Laurie C
Sent: Thursday, November 29, 2001 9:28 PM
To: colmes
Subject: Can't stand it. Can You????

For your information we do need a dictator to rule this country instead of that pervert we had for eight years. You just can't stand how well the President is doing can you? You know darn well that the economy was falling while Clinton was in the office. Laurie

Yes, Laurie, I remember going into the voting booth and seeing the choices as "pervert" or "dictator." Frankly, I'll take a pervert over a dictator any day. I mean, whom would you rather have rule the country, Saddam Hussein or Hugh Hefner?

Cabinet Secretaries Say the Darndest Things

Paul O'Neill was as popular as the nation's Treasury secretary as Yasser Arafat would be at a B'nai Brith meeting. Maybe it's because of some of his comments during his two-year tenure. Among the hit parade: "If you set aside Three Mile Island and Chernobyl, the safety record of nuclear [energy] is really very good."

And if you set aside the concentration camps during World War II, Germany was really Fun City.

During a trip to Africa with the pop star Bono to underscore the plight of underdeveloped nations, then secretary O'Neill engendered some criticism for touring the globe while the economy at home wasn't doing well. His rejoinder? "If people don't like what I'm doing, I don't give a damn. I could be off sailing around on a yacht or driving around the country."

That's what I like so much about rich Republicans. They really have the common touch. During the fall of Enron, O'Neill showed equal sensitivity to those who lost their jobs, their livelihoods, and their 401k's: "Companies come and go. It's part of the genius of capitalism." That "genius" has made 401k's into 101k's.

In an interview with the *Financial Times* of London on May 22, 2001, O'Neill pined for an America devoid of Social Security, Medicare, and Medicaid: "Able-bodied adults should save enough on a regular basis so that they can provide for their own retirement and for that matter for their health and medical needs."

When asked about whether we should eliminate the corporate income tax, he replied, "Absolutely. In economic logic there is no reason to have this phony process as though somehow individual human beings didn't pay the taxes that are embedded in the prices of goods and services."

As for O'Neill, well, to quote the great John McLaughlin: "Bye-bye!"

Who says the Republicans care only about benefiting the rich?

Paul O'Neill was a Washington outsider, which is the way Bush 43 braggingly described himself during his campaign for the presidency. It was supposed to be a positive that he couldn't stand the Beltway mentality. The next thing you know, his administration is conducting secret meetings with Republican donors, lobbyists are writing legislation, and the NRA is bragging that they'll have more access to the White House than legal immigrants have to government services. Kane Robinson, first vice president of the NRA and Iowa State Republican chairman, told an NRA gathering in February 2000: "If we win we'll have a Supreme Court that will back us to the hilt. . . . If we win, we'll have a president where we work out of their office—unbelievably friendly relations."

Fighting Words

Dick Cheney, one of the more hawkish voices in the push to go to war with Iraq, is on record as having said, "I had other priorities in the '60's than military service." Bill Clinton is still referred to as "a triple draft dodger" by my friend and political adversary Bob Dornan. In 1995, with presidential aspirations of his own, Congressman Dornan said, "Our young men and women around this country were killed in Somalia and are about to be killed in Bosnia by a triple draft dodger, an adulterer, a man whose background is financial corruption in Little Rock." Dick Cheney, meanwhile, the man whose priorities pointedly did not include defending his nation, received five—count 'em, five—deferments. And when the Selective Service expanded the draft to include married men without children, guess who got pregnant? The Cheneys' bundle of draft-resistant joy entered the world nine months and two days after that rule change. With that kind of timing, you have to give the man credit for knowing how to pull off a money shot.

Joining hawk Cheney in finding ways to avoid serving in the military are the other major prowar members of the Bush 43 administration, Paul Wolfowitz and Richard Perle. If you did a word association test with them and said "Army," they'd respond with, "Oh, you mean the former congressman from Texas." And they wouldn't even have their spelling right.

Richard Perle and Paul Wolfowitz spent the Vietnam years at the University of Chicago. Perle then joined the staff of Senator Henry "Scoop" Jackson, perhaps the last Democrat to back our incursion into Vietnam. But neither Perle nor Wolfowitz ever donned a U.S. military uniform. Unless they did so in a school play.

One, then, has to wonder, how Donald Rumsfeld would regard Perle and Wolfowitz in his military caste system. According to our Defense secretary, if you fought in a war because you were drafted, your efforts were meaningless. Rumsfeld was commenting on a bill introduced by Congressman Charlie Rangel to bring back the draft. Rangel's true agenda was to make the point that if members of every socioeconomic class had an equal chance of being drafted, politicians would be less likely to send their own children off to war. A third of the military is composed of minorities, who make up approximately a quarter of the general population, so war puts minorities more at risk. Furthermore, when a legislator must think about whether a decision will personally affect his or her family, the process may have a different result. Rummy first said that under the draft there were too many exemptions. He went on to add, "what was left was sucked into the intake, trained for a period of months, and then went out, adding no value, no advantage, really, to the United States armed services over any sustained period of time, because the churning that took place, it took enormous amount of effort in terms of training, and then they were gone."

Nice to know that the injuries sustained and lives lost by those who were drafted because they had no choice in the matter, by those who valiantly served our country, are so appreciated by our war minister. If this remark had been more widely circulated, it would have caused more pain to the families of those who have served and sacrificed.

The War on Nonwhite Non-Christians

"The 'War' on Terror" brought out some beauts. "We should invade Muslim countries, kill their leaders and convert them to Christianity," wrote conservative pundit Ann Coulter. What a nice, clean three-step program. Ludicrous as this sounds, Bush 43 is already on steps one and two. Rich Lowry decided to stop publishing Coulter at the *National Review Online* for that outrageous piece of loveliness, prompting her to call him and his colleagues there "girly boys." Got a problem with estrogen? Coulter also wants to look at men with a color chart: "We should require passports to fly domestically. Passports can be forged, but they can also be checked with the home country in the case of any suspicious-looking swarthy males." Nice to know that only "swarthy males" can look suspicious. If you look like Tim McVeigh, perhaps you can blow up a building with impunity. Ms. Coulter also reminded us: "Congress could pass a law tomorrow requiring that all aliens from Arabic countries leave." Sure they could. They could also try to overturn the Bill of Rights, and the Thirteenth Amendment to the Constitution that ended slavery. But, no thanks.

And how about this Coulter Classic: "My only regret with Timothy McVeigh is he did not go to the *New York Times* Building," a remark she made to interviewer George Gurley in the August 23, 2002, *New York Observer*. Gee, I kind of regret that 168 people actually *did* die at the hands of Tim McVeigh. I guess, Ann, they're all liberals, so it's no big loss. Sadly, Ann is not alone in her view about who should be victimized by terrorists.

Saxby Chambliss, the Republican who defeated incumbent Max Cleland for the Senate in Georgia by impugning his patriotism, remarked that officials in Valdosta, Georgia, should "just turn [the sheriff] loose and have him arrest every Muslim that crosses the state line." What a nice thought. A religious exam for everyone entering the state. Or maybe we can just stop cars and search for copies of the Koran, followed by a book burning. But I do have to hand it to Saxby. This is much cheaper than invading their countries and killing their leaders. Leave it to good, conservative legislators to come up with money-saving devices.

John Cooksey, a Louisiana congressman, gave an interview to a Louisiana radio network in which he said, "If I see someone come in and he's got a diaper on his head and a fanbelt wrapped around the diaper on his head, that guy needs to be pulled over and checked." In "the excuse is worse than the act itself" department, Cooksey later claimed he was talking only about Osama bin Laden. So maybe we would have captured OBL right away had we just looked for the proper apparatuses on his head at traffic stops.

North Carolina congresswoman Sue Myrick, in a speech to the conservative Heritage Foundation in January 2003, said that we have domestic security threats and backed that up by adding, "Look at who runs all the convenience stores across the country." She said she didn't mean to offend anyone by this remark. How nice of her. But you have to ask what they're putting in slurpees in the Tarheel state. Her fellow North Carolina congressman, Howard Coble, went on a North Carolina radio station and said he agreed with Franklin D. Roosevelt's policy of putting Japanese in internment camps during World War II. Finally, a Republican agrees with something FDR did, and look what it is. Coble seemed moderate compared with the caller to whom he was responding, who suggested that Arabs ought to be put in camps now. As Coble spoke, it only got worse. "Some probably were intent on doing harm to us," the congressman explained, "just as some of these Arab Americans are probably intent on doing harm to us." Coble went on to say that he was concerned about the safety of the Japanese, because they were not safe in the streets of America at a time of war. Maybe anyone who isn't with the majority opinion-wise ought to be put in prison for his or her own safety. Here's a fun little parlor game: every time you hear some negative comment about someone who is Arabian, French, or Muslim, for example, substitute the words *Jewish*, *black*, or *conservative Christian*, and see how it makes you feel.

From: Victor
Sent: Tuesday, February 04, 2003 9:41 PM
To: colmes
Subject: LEFT-WING TRAIITORS

Fox News:
Be sure and keep the Jew Colmes on daily TV. It is a constant remainder, and maybe America will wake up to the Jewish syndrome, which always and consistently opposes anything that would benefit America and without question, sides with any enemy, at home or abroad. Colmes is no different than any other Jew. His hatred for this country is palpable. In any other country he would be beheaded. In this country we should castrate him so he can't propagate any more Jews.

Better put me away, Mr. Ashcroft. My own safety depends on it.

I Thought Conservatives *Hated* Political Correctness

Shortly after September 11, Bill Maher said on *Politically Incorrect*, "We have been the cowards, lobbing cruise missiles from 2,000 miles away. That's cowardly. Staying in the airplane when it hits the building—say what you want about it, it's not cowardly." This was the beginning of the end of his brilliant and groundbreaking television show. Even Rush Limbaugh defended Maher, questioning what it was Maher said that was incorrect. Politically incorrect? That it was, no doubt. And I'm not the first to observe that Maher was only living up to the name of his show.

When White House spokesman Ari Fleischer was asked about press reports of Maher's comment, he said, "they're reminders to all Americans that they need to watch what they say, watch what they do. This is not a time for remarks like that; there never is." Fleischer also said he didn't hear Maher's remarks firsthand, but that didn't stop him from warning Americans to "watch what they say." Pretty chilling when coming from the spokesmouth of the country's chief executive. Did Fleischer actually mean to suggest that the free speech rights of Americans should be curtailed? I don't think this was the case at all. But when these words come from the lips of the person whose words represent the policies and ideas of the president and his administration, a very false impression could be given about the level of respect the Bush 43 White House has for our Bill of Rights. This ought to be a reminder to all presidential spokespeople that "they need to watch what they say, watch what they do."

It's Not Just Academic

Some self-appointed guardians of our well-being took Ari Fleischer's words literally. Daniel Pipes founded campus-watch.org, whose mission statement says, "Campus Watch will henceforth monitor and gather information on professors who fan the flames of disinformation, incitement and ignorance." In other words, Pipes will keep an eye on academics he doesn't agree with. Pipes is a widely published author with a PhD in history from Harvard. His writings include a July 22, 1999, piece in the *Los Angeles Times* in which he suggests there are two kinds of Muslims in America, those who want to abide by our democratic institutions, and those who don't. He fears the latter group is prevailing, and that its goal is to "make the United

States a Muslim country, perhaps along the Iranian or Sudanese models." In the *National Review* on October 22, 2001, he wrote, "every fundamentalist Muslim, no matter how peaceable in his own behavior, is part of a murderous movement and is thus, in some fashion, a foot soldier in the war that bin Laden has launched against civilization." And he doesn't have much respect for professors, either. He says on his website, "Academics seem generally to dislike their own country and think less of American allies abroad." Is that the kind of critical thinking we expect from a Harvard PhD? Unfortunately, Pipes has gone way beyond just thinking. On his website, he singles out at least fourteen professors for scrutiny. Other professors have spoken up about what they view as a Campus Un-American Activities Committee.

Robert Jensen, a tenured professor of journalism at the University of Texas at Austin, wrote in the *Houston Chronicle:* "My anger on this day is directed not only at individuals who engineered the Sept. 11 tragedy but at those who have held power in the United States and have engineered attacks on civilians. . . . For more than five decades throughout the Third World, the United States has deliberately targeted civilians or engaged in violence so indiscriminate that there is no other way to understand it except as terrorism." Thankfully, the president of UT-Austin, Larry R. Faulkner, defended not Jensen's words, but his right to say them.

At Brown University, Professors William Keach, who teaches English, and John Tomasi, a political scientist, dismissed their students early on October 9, 2001, so students could attend a rally protesting our bombing of Afghanistan. They were bombarded with hate mail, many from parents demanding they be fired for, among other things, teaching "radical leftist reactionary propaganda." One angry response accused Tomasi of being anti-American because he was antiwar and opened that he should be tried and shot.

Academic McCarthyism hit both the left and the right. Ken Hearlson, a political science professor at Orange Coast College in Costa Mesa, California, was falsely accused of calling four Muslim students "terrorists," "murderers," and "nazis." A transcript of his class one week after the terrorist attacks, provided to *Hannity & Colmes* by "The Foundation for Individual Rights in Education," reveals that Hearlson asked, "Why are everyday Muslims celebrating in the streets for the World Trade Center bombings and supporting Osama bin Laden?" Without a hearing, and simply on the word of four Muslim students (from a class where there were six other Muslims who knew the truth), Hearlson was placed on paid leave and barred from the Orange Coast campus. Hearlson was reinstated for the second semester in January 2001, but not without a letter of reprimand from his college president.

Judith Butler, a professor who teaches gender theory at Berkeley, was among a hundred or so academics so outraged by Campus Watch's attempt to intimidate that she asked to be included on the list. This was a wonderful strategy and should be considered whenever someone decides to publish a "list" for public opprobrium. As Butler said, according to the *San Francisco Chronicle*, "If a group establishes a website and says, 'We are watching you,' that has a very chilling impact on academic freedom. The more people who actively volunteer themselves for such a list, the less that power of intimidation works."

Do we want an atmosphere in America in which students hoping to graduate and professors hoping for tenure have to, in the words of Mr. Fleischer, "watch what (they) say"? And must the phrase "academic freedom" become an oxymoron? I pray not. And if you feel we need a "watch list" of peace-preaching academics, just what are you afraid of? Yes, they are going to rise up with their pens or, shall we say, keyboards, and challenge those wielding swords. It was the British cabinet member and novelist Sir Edward Bulyer-Lytton who told us which was mightier.

Single-Issue Zealots Say the Darndest Things

The two issues that elicit the most emotion are abortion and gun control, and many people vote solely on the basis of where a candidate stands on these issues. There is even a political party called the "Right to Life Party" that revolves around a sole issue. If you tell a single-issue abortion-focused person that you're against the death penalty, they will immediately point out that you're a hypocrite because you want to kill the unborn child. When these people ask me when life begins, I often reply, "At forty." As we've seen at abortion clinics in Massachusetts and Florida, and in the murder of abortion provider Dr. Barnett Slepian, the most ardent antiabortion crazies can take the most extreme action if they think you are not "pro-life": they kill you.

I have seen almost every topic imaginable linked to abortion by one-issue zealots, who can think of nothing else. Many of these monomaniacs are men who would be very happy to outlaw pregnancy if they had to experience it. And don't tell me I don't know what a pregnancy is like. I've had kidney stones. I am the proud parent of at least four grains of sand.

From: maryjane
Sent: Thursday, February 20, 2003 9:34 AM
To: colmes
Subject: consistency

Allen,
   . . . How can the same liberals who protest against military action to remove a dangerous regime from Iraq with a murderous reputation rush to the aid of mothers who want to kill their unborn children? . . . "Save the guilty of Iraq" and "Murder the innocent in the womb" just doesn't make sense. Even "Save the innocent of Iraq" and "Murder the innocent in the womb" is convoluted. But I'm sure the liberals in question will find a way to rationalize it.

Maryjane
Idaho Falls, ID

So now war with Iraq is linked to abortion. Talk about the death penalty: they bring up abortion. Mention slavery: they tie it to the unborn fetus, enslaved in a womb. To once again quote my good friend, the brilliant linguist Barry Farber, this is "the running broad jump."

"Good morning, Mr. Terry, it's a lovely day today isn't it?"

"It's not a lovely day for the never-to-be born child."

"Let's discuss forest fires."

"You want to save the forests, but you don't care about the baby in the womb."

"I believe in free speech."

"Sure, you love the First Amendment, but you hate the Second Amendment."

The Second Amendment, by the way, should be rewritten; no one knows what the hell it means. "A well regulated Militia, being necessary to the security of a free State, the right of the people to keep and bear Arms, shall not be infringed." Funny how those who support unlimited gun rights begin this Amendment thirty-one words in. If it's just "the right of the people to keep and bear Arms" that shouldn't be infringed, what does "a well regulated Militia" have to do with it? Is it "A well regulated Militia" that should not be infringed? In that case, only militia members can bear arms which, in colonial times, meant only men of military age. Are they the only ones who can have guns? And if it's a free state that needs to be protected, does that mean that the guns should go to the professionals whose job it is to protect the state? Antiabortion activists advocate for the rights of the unborn, but just what rights should fetuses have? Freedom of speech? Assembly? Okay, I'll concede these. Fetuses should be allowed to speak, and the government shouldn't get in the way of fetal groups that wish to congregate. Yes, fetuses should have all the rights in the world, but once they're born, let's deny them proper health care, day care, properly paid teachers, a livable minimum wage, and while we're at it, let's privatize Social Security so the financial services industry can benefit from them while we remove government guarantees.

I suspect it won't be long before the NRA and Operation Rescue get together to support fetal gun rights. I do see a fetal problem with the size of assault weapons, so there might have to be *some* controls on this. I mean, the womb is only so big. I've always wondered if some of the antigay whack jobs, like Reverend Fred Phelps (this is the "Reverend" who had the good taste to picket the Matthew Shephard funeral with "God Hates Fags" signs), would support abortion if they could isolate a gay gene and predict it prior to birth. And if we could accurately predict which babies would grow up to be liberals and run for office, don't you think at least some antiabortion believers would suddenly join the pro-choice camp?

Kathy Ireland, the former supermodel and current entrepreneur, came on *Hannity & Colmes*, on July 10, 2002, and we got into it on the abortion issue.

COLMES: Where are you liberal? Give me an example of where you're liberal.

IRELAND: I'm very liberal when it comes to protecting the human rights of the unborn.

COLMES: Unfortunately the government has no place in having anything to say about what women do with their bodies, because . . .

IRELAND: Is it her body? . . . the evidence I see tells me that the unborn is a human being. If you can show me any evidence that the unborn is not a human being . . .

COLMES: When? When does it become . . . I mean, is it at conception? Is that when it happens?

IRELAND: At the moment of conception, a new life comes into being with the complete genetic blueprints. The fingerprint is determined, the blood type is determined, the sex is determined.

Throwing around words like *life* and *human being* and equating them with a zygote is disingenuous. Sperm is life, too. Should we be outraged every time some sperm is allowed to die? If a fetus is the same thing as a human being, why is it that our laws, when abortion was illegal, didn't treat the destruction of the fetus as a felony? As long as a fetus is dependent on another human being, the host body, for survival, and is part of that human being, what sense does it make to advocate for government control of that part of a woman's body? (And by "dependent" I'm not referring to what that word means on a W2 form.) A fetus is not an "individual," it is part of a woman's body that may, eventually, become another human being. Eventually. Should there be separate rights for my arm?

Kathy Ireland reappeared on *Hannity & Colmes* on September 30, 2002, to continue the argument, and this time we delved into the legal aspect:

COLMES: Well, we have a system of laws and a Supreme Court decision that does not define life the way you do. So legally, that's not how it would be defined. If you want to define it that way for your personal—that's how you want to do it, that's fine, but that's not the standing law of this country.

IRELAND: If you can, Alan, if you can show me evidence that the unborn is not a human being, I will gladly join the pro-choice side. If you can show me any evidence. It's very clear and simple.

Welcome aboard, Kathy. Just see the paragraph above.

From: Samuel O.
Sent: Monday, September 30, 2002 11:06 PM

To: Colmes
Subject: Kathy Ireland got it right!

Alan:
Shame on you for trying to hide behind the law! At one time the law of the land was; only landowners could vote, a slave was not a human but property, and if you were a woman you did not have the right to vote.

How *dare* I "hide behind the law"! I don't know how to quite break this news to those who like to use the old, tired, slavery argument to deny a woman a right to make a personal choice, but, and let me speak very loudly here: SLAVES WERE ALREADY BORN! There is a difference between the born and the unborn. That's why the born are called "born." Former surgeon general Joycelyn Elders incurred the wrath of the right when she said, "We would like for the right-to-life and antichoice groups to really get over their love affair with the fetus and start supporting the children." In some cases, she was right. If conception begins at birth, why don't they celebrate "birthdays" nine months earlier than they do? Can a fetus get life insurance? Why don't lovers coo, "Fetus I Love You?" I can't get that Supremes song out of my head, "Fetus Love." I fully expect that one day the word *baby* will become obsolete and upon seeing newborns we'll exclaim, "What a beautiful postpartum fetus you have there." Of course, if I were to refer to antichoicers who come on our show as "overgrown fetuses," I don't think they'd like it very much.

And, yes, it's "choice" and "antichoice," not "life" and "pro-life." Since when do *they* get to dictate the language? I'm for a woman's right to choose. They're not. They have cleverly injected the word *life* into the argument to make those who support women's rights appear to be heartless "antilife" scolds. And yet they have no problem supporting a death penalty culture that has likely snuffed out innocent lives since the death penalty was reinstated in 1976. This culture accounts for 4.5 innocent Americans reaching death row each year and that has seen more than a hundred people released from prison since 1973 after being wrongly convicted. They'll say a baby is innocent and a criminal isn't. But they're still supporting death for the already-born, and in extreme cases they're not supporting life for mothers who have to make a torturous choice for themselves. But those choices should belong to them and not to the government.

Here's another argument I love from the antiabortion crowd: "A woman has a 'choice' every time she opens her legs and has sex with a man. That's where she's made her choice." Yes, and you have a "choice" not to be a sexist male who takes no responsibility for a man's role in lovemaking. You probably think birth control is purely a woman's responsibility, as are the laundry and dishes.

From: specialtalk
Sent: Sunday, January 07, 2001 9:38 AM
To: Colmes
Subject: What are you?

Are you a homo? Do you molest children? Are you married to a black woman? Would you donate more of your income to the govt.? Do you help women get abortions? If you answered no to any of these questions then you are indeed a liar and a first rate hypocrite about being liberal.

I actually have great empathy with those who disagree with me on abortion, and I realize that to many it is literally an issue of life and death. It is a great debate that will continue, regardless of what the courts eventually decide about *Roe v. Wade*. Changes in the law, however, will not result in changes in behavior, as evidenced by the fact that women sought abortions even before they were legal in America, albeit under less safe and more emotionally trying conditions.

We all occasionally say the darndest things. That is our right, even if there are some among us who abuse the privilege. Speaking of which, will someone please tell our commander in chief that it's "nuclear" and not "nucular"? Thanks.

TEN

Conservatives Are Downright Mean

Liberals are nicer than conservatives. They just are. They want to give to the poor, help the homeless, and fight corporate greed. And what do they get for all this? Mocked. Conservatives love to make fun of liberals by joking about how they sit around all day singing "Kumbaya." We're alternately called "naïve," "out of touch" and "idealistic." During wartime, you can throw in "traitors," "appeasers," and "anti-American."

It would be ideal if we could actually agree to disagree and disagree without being disagreeable. It would be especially nice if those who conduct the dialogue on the national stage could maintain such decorum. This was definitely not the case when Indiana congressmen Dan Burton, during Clinton's Monica Lewinsky troubles, declared: "If I could prove 10 percent of what I believe happened, he'd [Clinton] be gone. This guy's a scumbag. That's why I'm after him." Not an example of the milk of human kindness coursing through the veins.

Wouldn't it be nice if we were truly "America united"? The most insightful and profound statement of the last decade was uttered by

Rodney King: "Can't we all just get along?" Is this something to be mocked or something to be celebrated as an ideal toward which to strive? (The second greatest statement was made by the former mayor of Washington D.C., Marion Barry, when he proclaimed: "Bitch set me up." You just don't get such pith every day.)

Conservatives and Me

My e-mail inbox is usually overflowing with messages from conservatives who tell me, in no uncertain terms, how they feel about me. Maybe this means I'm doing my job. Some of them are concurrently sad and comical.

> **From:** Taylor
> **Sent:** Wednesday, September 06, 2000 6:18 PM
> **To:** Colmes
> **Subject:** (no subject)
>
> I have never listened to anyone or any liberal who could piss me off more than you. Even looking at you I can tell your mother must of Bitched slapped you at birth. Yours & all your little liberal constituents way of thinking is so irrational . . . you are a Disease in this society. . . . I hope someday that this country will come to it's senses and open season on all Liberals & put a bounty on all of you.

Does this e-mail prove conservatives are mean people? Not at all. How about a barrage of these, daily? Not proof, but certainly an indication.

Even a conservative who writes me an ostensibly positive e-mail can have a mean streak:

From: Ned
Sent: Wednesday, January 01, 2003 10:15 AM
To: colmes&foxnews.com
Subject: (no subject)

Dear Alan,
As a staunch conservative, liking you annoys me.

Ned
East Haven, CT

Or how about Oscar's early Valentine to me?

From: Oscar
Sent: Saturday, February 08, 2003 11:02 PM
To: Colmes
Subject: Just a thought

Hey Mr. Colmes;
You probably piss me off more than any one person I can think of lately.

But, in your defense, someone has to ask the hard questions to keep the other side in touch with itself.

So, begrudgingly, good job!
Oscar
Jersey City, NJ

I know conservatives *think* they're nicer than liberals and that liberals are the mean ones. That's delusional. And I speak from personal experience. My e-mails and some personal encounters with conservatives have not always been heartwarming. Liberals are more open to change, including changing their minds; conservatives have a certainty about their views that liberals don't often display. And conservatives are much better at vilifying their enemies. And while conservatives may truly believe their policies are better for America, it's my view that liberal policies help the greater number of people, especially those who need it most.

Every day I am confronted by strangers who candidly express their feelings about my job performance. It is surreal. When *Hannity & Colmes* first started, I was known primarily for my radio work. I love the intimacy of radio and its ability to paint pictures with sound, and I appreciated the irony that while it got my name and my views out there, it kept me relatively unrecognized to the outside world. Being seen on television nightly has changed all that. Although the e-mails I receive lean toward the vituperative, when I unexpectedly come face-to-face with viewers, they're generally pleasant and polite. But there have been a few notable exceptions. These exceptions show that some people *can* be downright mean.

My first face-to-face encounter with a less-than-satisfied viewer came one day, early on, when I was merrily walking along Manhattan's Sixth Avenue, not far from Fox News, minding my own business. A well-dressed businessman stopped me and said, "You're Alan Colmes, aren't you?" This was going to be fun—a little acknowledgment for my work, now that I was a little more recognizable. "Well, you're awful," blasted my admirer. And he quickly walked away. Most people don't have to face such direct analysis of their work. Tool and die makers don't have to hear, "This equipment is just awful." Even restaurant cooks don't get told off so boldly, although too many waitpersons have to bear the brunt of disgruntled customers.

More recently I was headed to work on a New York subway train when a man looked at me and shouted, "You're too liberal." This seemed mean. I responded by saying, "Thanks for letting me know," but then wondered if I should have responded at all or tried to talk to him about why he felt he could heckle a total stranger. If he had said, "I really think you're wrong about Bush 43," or "Your views on affirmative action really put me off," I could understand that as an effort to communicate a point of view. But shouting "You're too liberal" is not quite an invitation to further dialogue. What am I supposed to say? "You're right. You've convinced me. I'm changing my liberal ways"? Once, while I was on the short boat ride between the Caribbean islands of St. Martin and Anguilla, a gentleman remarked that he watched my show. Wow, not only was I being recognized, but so far from Sixth Avenue! I thanked him, shook his hand, and then offered my hand to his wife. She curtly protested that she didn't care to shake my hand, as I was too liberal for her. I hope she stays away from weddings, bar mitzvahs, and confirmations. You never know when some liberal DNA might rub off on you when you're walking the receiving line.

Not *all* conservatives are mean. I'd like to believe that most of them are like Sal here:

From: Sal
Sent: Saturday, January 18, 2003 2:48 AM
To: Colmes
Subject: Thanks Alan!

Dear Alan,
I try and watch your show every night because even though I seldom agree with anything you say, . . . I am still very impressed with your intelligence, devotion, and articulation in presenting the opinions you believe in. Fortunately we are blessed with living in this great country and have the ability to respectfully agree to disagree.

You are one of the few people with far left beliefs that I would love to kick back and have a cold adult beverage with . . .

Best Regards,
Sal

Where Right Couldn't Be More Wrong

Many conservatives aren't only mean, they're smug. They truly believe they're wiser, better informed, and smarter than liberals. Then House majority leader Dick Armey, during a campaign event for Katherine Harris in Florida on September 20, 2002, was asked why the Jewish community is divided between liberals and conservatives. Of course, the proper answer is that every community is divided between liberals and conservatives (okay, maybe not certain parts of Idaho). Instead, Armey replied, "I always see two Jewish communities in America, one of deep intellect and one of shallow, superficial intellect." He said conservatives have a deeper intellect and tend toward "occupations of the brain" like engineering, science, and economics and that liberals work in "occupations of the heart."

In a September 24 news conference, during which he tried to defend his Jewish comments, Armey was kind enough to invoke my name:

> You can go back, Richard Diamond found me on *Hannity & Colmes* with Mr. Colmes discussing this same point. Mr. Colmes didn't like it. I can't help you. Liberals are, in my estimation, just not bright people. They don't think deeply. They don't comprehend. They don't understand a partial derivative. They have a narrow educational base as opposed to the hard scientists.

Richard Diamond was his press secretary, so it's good that he was able to find his boss on *Hannity & Colmes*.

Dick Armey, of course, is the same man who called fellow congressman Barney Frank, "Barney Fag," and chalked it up to a slip of the tongue. How does one glide from "Frank" to "fag" by just a slip of the tongue? I have never, ever said to someone, "Let me be fag with you." And I never went to a ballpark and in the sixth inning ordered a "fagfurter."

On the issue of whether liberals or conservatives are smarter, strong opinions abound:

From: Marie
Sent: Monday, April 02, 2001 2:04 AM
To: Colmes
Subject: (no subject)

You're actually worst than the whore you partner with.

From: Colmes
Sent: Monday, April 02, 2001 2:10 PM
To: Marie
Subject: RE:(no subject)

Marie,
I think you mean "worse," not "worst." "Worst" pertains to three or more, while "worse" is used when you are comparing two items. I am "worse" than the whore I partner with, not "worst."

Thank you.
Alan

Treason versus Reason

From: Nighthawk
Sent: Tuesday, October 29, 2002 9:19 PM
To: Colmes
Subject: (no subject)

I HATE YOUR GUTS LIB!! YOU AND THE REST OF YOUR TREASONOUS BUDDIES NEED TO DO THE REST OF US REAL AMERICANS A FAVOR. LEAVE AND DONT COME BACK!!

And your point is . . . ? I'm not sure, but maybe a few more exclama-
tion points will help. And while we're at it, Nighthawk, you might
want to know what treason is before you accuse your fellow
Americans of it. Here's the constitutional definition in Article III
Section 3: "Treason against the United States, shall consist only in
levying War against them, or in adhering to their Enemies, giving
them Aid and Comfort. No Person shall be convicted of Treason
unless on the Testimony of two Witnesses to the same overt Act, or
on Confession in open Court."

Entire books have been written about how rotten liberals are,
most notably the book *Treason* by Ann Coulter. Witness this piece of
inclusive loveliness: ". . . liberals are always against America. They
are either traitors or idiots, and on the matter of America's self-
preservation, the difference is irrelevant. Fifty years of treason hasn't
slowed them down." If that isn't specific enough, how about,
"Liberals relentlessly attack their own country, but we can't call
them traitors, which they manifestly are. . . . The inevitable logic of
the liberal position is to be for treason."

On June 25, 2003, Coulter appeared on *Hannity & Colmes* to
defend her thesis. I tried to find out exactly who today is an
American traitor:

COLMES: Are you prepared to accuse any liberal of treason?
You want to point the finger to anyone in particular and say
this person is guilty of committing that crime?

COULTER: Keep talking. I might be able to point the finger at
you.

COLMES: Am I guilty of it?

COULTER: What was your position on the war in Iraq?

COLMES: That we shouldn't have gone there.

COULTER: Don't you think we're in the middle of a civil liberties emergency every time John Ashcroft talks to a Muslim? . . .

COLMES: If you're going to say treason—I would be curious to know if there's anybody in particular you would accuse of treason.

COULTER: Oh, sure. A whole book on it. How about the Rosenbergs? How about Alger Hiss?

COLMES: Who that is alive today on treason?

COULTER: As I was saying, how about the man who advised Franklin Roosevelt of Yalta. After Roosevelt was warned that Alger Hiss was a Soviet spy.

COLMES: And who that is alive today would you accuse of treason?

COULTER: Look, I wrote the book, let me answer the question. I understand what the question is. I'm sorry, we're going to have to wait to get the cables from Saddam Hussein of the traitors today. . . .

COLMES: I ask you, is there anybody today you accuse of treason? Probably, you don't want to make that accusation against anyone in particular, liberal or Democrat.

COULTER: You're consistently missing the point of this book. . . . But my question to you is how would liberals behave differently if they were in Saddam Hussein's pay? How would they behave differently if they were in Osama bin Laden's pay? Answer that question.

COLMES: When you say treason, it is a very serious charge. . . . If somebody is guilty of treason, they should be tried and executed, right?

COULTER: I am saying liberals consistently root against their own country.

COLMES: Name who. Name one who should be accused of treason.

COULTER: This a silly game to be playing. I keep trying to name them and you interrupt me.

As you can see, there were only a half dozen or so opportunities to answer the question. Certainly not enough time to come up with one name. Coulter's previous book, *Slander*, claims liberals lie and don't want what's best for America. In the final line of her book she calls liberals "savagely cruel bigots who hate ordinary Americans and lie for sport." Now, this may amaze and annoy some of my liberal brethren: I actually like Ann Coulter. She has been nothing but kind to me personally. It's when she starts ranting about liberals that I see an unrecognizable Ann Coulter. I can only surmise that this is good shtick to get liberal blood boiling, and not the reasoned views of a sane person.

Kenneth Timmerman devoted his book *Shakedown* to just one liberal, Jesse Jackson, and accused him of shaking down corporations for his own profit. But we have a White House that holds private meetings with energy executives—who also happen to be big campaign contributors—and those meetings result in policy decisions. I don't hear the Jesse Jackson critics complaining about *that*. Conservatives have spent an inordinate amount of time trying to define liberals as liars who are bad for America, rather than acknowledging that while liberals may think differently, they are just as well intended.

Paul Wellstone

Conservatives think they're smarter than liberals, and they also believe they're nicer. I found out just how "nice" some conservatives are in the aftermath of the tragic death of Senator Paul Wellstone of Minnesota:

From: Howard
Sent: Friday, November 15, 2002 10:03 PM
To: Colmes
Subject: misc

Alan:

It's a real shame that you were not with Wellstone on his last
flight.

Why don't you renounce your citizenship and move anywhere in
the middle-east since you are so enamored with these filthy
bastards?

People like you will assure Republican dominance for the
foreseeable future. Keep up the anti American ideas.

From: Colmes,
Sent: Friday, November 15, 2002 10:05 PM
To: Howard
Subject: RE: misc

How kind of you to wish that I die in a plane crash. Very American
to want someone with whom you disagree on an issue dead.

Many people on both sides of the political aisle agreed that Paul
Wellstone was one of the nicest people in Washington. It's an outrage that the Republicans politicized his memorial service for their
own political gain. Yes, I am accusing the Republicans of doing the
very deed they tried to pin on Democrats. They knew very well that
it was the Wellstone family that organized the event, not the
Democratic Party. For one thing, if the Democratic Party had
organized it, it wouldn't have been as well organized. (It was Will
Rogers who once said, "I'm not a member of any organized political
party. I'm a Democrat.") If this had been intended as a political
event, Bill Clinton, Al Gore, Hillary, Jesse Ventura, and other top
politicians would have been on the dais and would have spoken.
Mark Wellstone, Paul's son, was criticized for his rallying cry, "We
will win! We will win!" spoken in grief a few days after his father's

death. Critics who blasted this grieving family for what they said at an emotional memorial service ought to be ashamed of themselves.

You might wonder how Senator Wellstone would have regarded the controversy surrounding his memorial. But you don't really have to scratch your head on this because Peggy Noonan told us. Incredibly, the talented former Bush 41 speechwriter wrote a "memo" from Paul Wellstone to Democrats that was published in the *Wall Street Journal*'s "Opinion Journal," so that we could rest easy knowing what Paul was thinking. The memo from, I'm hoping heaven, states, "I know what you were trying to do the other night, or what you sort of meant to do. But it was bad." Thanks for telling us, Pegg . . . er, I mean Paul. After "Paul" chastised Democrats for using his death to score political points, he imagined what it would have been like had things been different, and Senator Lott had been the victim: "Imagine Trent Lott died in a plane crash last week. Please—stop cheering. That's the problem. Knock it off. Imagine Trent Lott dies, and there's a big memorial back home in Mississippi in some big auditorium . . . I walk in— Paul Wellstone walks in, out of respect—and the 30,000 people in the auditorium jeer me."

This is truly amazing. Not only did Ms. Noonan know what Senator Wellstone would have been thinking, but she also knew that Democrats would cheer if Trent Lott, God forbid, died in a plane crash. Before you can speak for the dead, at least be fair in your characterization of the living. I know there are trance mediums who claim to speak to the dead, and I also know there were many Americans of all political persuasions who loved Paul Wellstone and may have had some insight into what his thoughts would have been. But Peggy Noonan? I mean, I love the woman, even though I don't agree with her; but Edgar Cayce she's not.

At the 2000 Democratic Convention in Los Angeles I had the chance to meet Senator Wellstone for the first time. We talked about how both of our families are Russian-Jewish, that we both had a parent born in the Ukraine, and that we came from similar roots. He also told me that he wanted to get together again and talk about our similar backgrounds because family was so important to him. I regret that that day can never come. But not everyone in America feels the same way I do about Paul Wellstone:

From: Vorganis
Sent: Saturday, October 26, 2002 10:02 PM
To: Colmes
Subject: Paul Wellstone

If you think for one minute, I care that Paul died "I DON'T." He got what was coming to him the Leftist Socialist Scum bag, America Hater.

. . . OH what a relief he won't be in HEAVEN what a SHAME, but in HELL . . . FINALLY FINAL JUSTICE have a good time Paul in HELL.

I must say that Vorganis impresses me. He, she, or it is able to divine who goes to heaven and who goes to hell. I don't think John Edward was ever this accurate on "Crossing Over." While Vorganis might wish to use his dancing shoes on Paul's grave, were he to try on the senator's shoes, I doubt he could walk an inch.

Within hours of the crash of Senator Wellstone's plane, the name "Mondale" was immediately floated as a possible replacement. But even before the former vice president had a chance to consider a run, the Republicans began producing television ads in which their candidate, Norm Coleman, contrasted Mondale and himself. And while these ads were being produced, the right was criticizing Democrats for "scheming" to put up a candidate before the body was cold. So it's improper for the Democrats to think of their options when a candidate dies five days before an election, but it's perfectly acceptable for Republicans to produce commercials attacking that yet-to-be named candidate.

Switchers versus Fighters

After the 2002 election I got a lot of e-mail that said, essentially, "We won, you lost, you're a jerk." Some people think it's more important to be with the winning party because to the winner go the spoils. But to the person who is steadfast regardless of which way the winds are blowing go a good conscience and a good night's sleep. Some people look at political parties as they would a sporting league. They want to be in first place and they want to be on the winning team. I love the people who write to me and say, "I was a Democrat all my life, but Bill Clinton is so morally reprehensible I'm going to become a Republican now." Or, "I'm peeved that the Democrats put up Frank Lautenberg at the last minute to run against Torricelli; I'm leaving the Democratic Party." That's like saying you don't like some of your fellow males, so you are changing genders and becoming a woman. Men can really be bastards. They think with their genitals, declare war, are poor listeners, and keep very messy rooms. Women are more compassionate, intuitive, and kind. I think I'll become one.

I always get annoyed at the postelection party-switchers. I can understand an evolution in thinking that may lead one from right to left or, God forbid, left to right, but to switch party affiliations right after an election because your party lost is circumspect. After the Republican rout in 1994, when Newt Gingrich's "Contract With (On?) America" swept conservatives to victories in both houses of Congress, guess which way the party-switching went? House Democrats Nathan Deal of Georgia, Greg Laughlin of Texas, Billy Tauzin of Louisiana, Mike Parker of Mississippi, and Jimmy Hayes of Louisiana all defected in 1995. On the Senate side that year, the same move was made by Benedict, er, I mean, Ben Nighthorse Campbell. In fact, in the past twenty years, among members of Congress, fourteen Democrats have become Republicans, and only one Republican has become a Democrat. That Republican-turned-Democrat was Long Island congressman Michael Forbes, who lost his seat after he party-switched. Good. We lefties know real Democrats when we see them. Let the other side accept the fair-weather friends. Senator Bob Smith of New Hampshire left the Republican Party when it didn't look like he'd get the presidential nomination in 2000, saying, "I want my party to stand for something." He returned to the Republican fold once his presidential ambitions were dashed and then realized he was in a political no-man's-land. I guess the Republican Party, at that point, did stand for something: committee appointments.

When Vermont senator Jim Jeffords left the Republican Party, it wasn't at a time when Democrats were the majority. The move did give the Democrats a majority in the Senate for a short time, but by the slimmest possible margin; and he became an Independent, not a Democrat. When Jeffords refused to support President George W. Bush's $1.6 trillion, ten-year tax cut, he helped to hand the new president his first big defeat. As a result, Bush 43 refused to invite him to the White House to honor a Vermont resident who was named National Teacher of the Year. Bush 43 was probably thinking, "Payback's a bitch." Jeffords proved that payback is also a switch.

Classless Warfare

When Republicans gained the White House in 2000, the conservative crowing was intense, and then they tried to get liberals to eat crow after the election of 2002.

> **From:** Lilly
> **Sent:** Tuesday, November 12, 2002 12:57 AM
> **To:** Colmes
> **Subject:** The end of days
>
> Colmes,
> Hehe!!! You a Dem and you lose . . . GOP in the house . . . GOP in the senate . . . we go kick some a**!!! Yippie skippie!!!
>
> Liilly
> Wilmington, DE

With conservatives controlling all branches of government, here are some things we have to be "yippie skippie" about.

Pennsylvania Senator Rick Santorum actually said he'd fight for the right to discriminate against certain groups to promote the Republican's faith-based agenda. On November 25, 2002, the *Washington Post* reported, "Santorum has told the White House that, during the debate over welfare reform, he will fight for a provision to allow religious groups to discriminate against certain people— gays for instance—when hiring if they don't share their religious beliefs. 'I will make that stand,' Santorum said."

Santorum gained more notoriety for an April 22, 2003, interview he gave to Associated Press reporter Lara Jakes Jordan. During an hour-long discussion, Santorum commented on a case before the Supreme Court involving a Texas antigay sodomy law. Houstonians John Lawrence and Tyron Garner were arrested and jailed after police officers, responding to a false alarm, found them enjoying consensual sex in Lawrence's home. Apparently, it's permissible to have some kinds of sex in Texas if you're straight, but not if you're gay. Amazingly, some consensual behaviors even between straight, married couples have been illegal in Idaho, Utah, Louisiana, Mississippi, Alabama, Florida, South Carolina, North Carolina, and Virginia. But let's see them try to enforce *that* one. Asked about the pending case, Santorum said, "If the Supreme Court says that you have the right to consensual sex within your home, then you have the right to bigamy, you have the right to polygamy, you have the right to incest, you have the right to adultery. You have the right to anything. . . . I would argue, this right to privacy that doesn't exist, in my opinion, in the United States Constitution."

What's amazing about this statement was missed by most of the pundits who attacked Santorum for making it. He didn't just blast the concept of gay consensual sex; Santorum doesn't think *anyone* has that right. Most of the coverage of Santorum's comments put the modifier *gay* in parentheses after the word *consensual*, but the truth is he didn't make that distinction in the interview with Jordan.

Conservatives tried to excuse Santorum on the grounds that Ms. Jordan is married to an adviser to Senator John Kerry, who was busily seeking the Democratic nomination for president at the time. But this was not a "gotcha" interview, and the only agenda seemed to be Santorum's.

I was particularly amused by Santorum's explanation that "I have no problem with homosexuality—I have a problem with homosexual acts." I attracted some negative e-mail when I flippantly questioned one night on *Hannity & Colmes* whether this meant that he didn't like Siegfried and Roy.

Conservatives, in addition to being mean, can also be clueless. In a November 20, 2002, *Wall Street Journal* editorial called, "The Non-Taxpaying Class," the conservative paper, usually in favor of tax relief, pined for a system where the poor could pay more. It referred to those who make $12,000 or less a year as "lucky duckies": ". . . almost 13% of all workers have no tax liability and so are indifferent to income tax rates. And that doesn't include another 16.5 million who have some income but don't file at all. Who are these lucky duckies?"

It's disingenuous to say that almost 13 percent of workers have no tax liability. What do you call payroll taxes and sales taxes? In the December 3, 2002, issue of the *New York Times*, Paul Krugman helped us further understand the charmed lives of these "lucky duckies": "If you include payroll and sales taxes, a worker earning $12,000 probably pays well over 20 percent of income in taxes. But who's counting?" Conservatives carp about how the rich pay so much in taxes and how the poor don't pay because they can't. But the working poor do pay the very taxes that should be cut, the payroll taxes, which take a proportionally higher bite out of their paychecks, while barely putting a dent into the incomes of the wealthy.

While the right sees those who don't pay income taxes as lucky beneficiaries of government subsidies for education and child care, the people who don't owe federal income tax are people who basically can't afford to pay that tax. They also can't afford to pay their rent, clothe their children, or eat three squares a day. Providing a basic net for decent Americans who, for whatever reason, can't live the American dream right now, is the very least a good-hearted society should do. Why is it we never compain about the price of guns, but we balk at the price of butter?

What's wrong with caring for the poor, the downtrodden, the infirm, and the needy? In a capitalistic society, not everyone has luck fall his or her way. Conservatives love to brag about America being the greatest, the biggest, the richest country in the world. Then why do they begrudge the small percentage of their fellow Americans who need a helping hand? Only 2.3 percent of Americans were on welfare in 1999, down from 5.5 percent in 1993. It's not socialism to demand that everyone in America have the right to a warm place to sleep at night, proper nutrition, and the right to a living wage. We can afford it. When an administration decides to go to war, not enough hard questions are asked and answered, and cost is never an issue. Only 2 percent of the federal budget goes to welfare, compared with 16 percent for defense.

But years are spent haggling over the few who need assistance, as though the welfare rolls are rife with fraudulent users who only want to live off our taxpayer dollars. And you know what? There are people like that, and there always will be, but statistics show that these people are a very small minority of those getting help. Seventy percent of welfare recipients are off the rolls within two years, although there is a 58 percent rate of recidivism. But the average family on welfare winds up in the system for about six years, not a lifetime. Nevertheless, Americans who have fallen on hard times have been victims of increasingly hostile rhetoric from ideologues who needed to add the modifier "compassionate" because the word they had been using to define themselves didn't speak for itself.

Ronald Reagan often told the story of a "welfare queen" who went to pick up her welfare checks in a shiny, new welfare Cadillac. This woman had either thirty or eighty aliases, depending on when Reagan was telling this story. But the real problem with this "welfare queen" was that she didn't exist. This was a figment of Ronald Reagan's imagination, but one that defines those who need government assistance in the minds of many to this day.

Class warfare isn't always based on money. One influential organization in creating public policy is the conservative Heritage Foundation, replete with its "abstinence guru" Robert Rector, who actually wrote part of the 1996 Welfare Reform Bill. Rector handily created a "sexual pecking order" to help determine who should receive government benefits. "Marriage holds the place of highest regard, followed by virgins until engaged, virgins until they met someone they wanted to marry, virgins until they fell in love, and on down to the bottom." The "bottom" is something Rector refers to as "extremely dysfunctional, extremely destructive bar-hopping with casual partners to whom they have no commitment."

Can you imagine a government policy that defined the sexual pecking order of men, right down to those who cruise singles bars looking for one-night stands? Only a male-dominated government would have the gumption to categorize women this way, while being oblivious to how it would appear if the roles were reversed.

The Bush 43 administration came up with the brilliant idea of spending $300 million to encourage single mothers to get married, thereby institutionalizing Rector's sexual pecking order. But as Barbara Ehrenreich points out in "Prodding the Poor to the Altar" in the *Progressive*, low-income moms are unlikely to marry CEOs or members of conservative think tanks, and they wind up not with someone who brings home the bacon, but rather another mouth to feed. By Ehrenreich's estimates, a woman in such straits would have to marry 2.3 men to lift her out of her circumstances. Wade Horn, a big name in the fatherhood movement in America, wrote a paper in 1997 in which he said the government should "give preference to two-parent married households" when doling out goodies. This ode to the nuclear family earned him a job serving in the Bush 43 White House as the assistant secretary for the Health and Human Services Department under Secretary Tommy Thompson.

Despite the effort to "end welfare as we know it," families continue to suffer in America. According to Ann Withorn, professor of
social policy at University of Massachusetts–Boston and author of
For Crying Out Loud: Women's Poverty in the United States, "Welfare
rolls dropped by more than half nationally since 1996, but poverty
for single mothers is only down 0.7 percent." Reporting on
Connecticut's "Jobs First" program on February 20, 2002, the *New
York Times* reported that participating families "remained poor, with
low wages and high levels of hardship, like lacking money to buy
food."

Health and Human Services secretary Tommy Thompson came
on our show on January 14, 2003, to talk about the Republican effort
to reform welfare again. When Republicans say "reform welfare,"
what they really mean is "end welfare." They crow about how it
worked in 1998 (oh, you mean when *Clinton* was president? No, they
say, when Republicans ran Congress), but they refuse to acknowledge that the reason it worked so well was because the Clinton economy was so robust.

I pointed out to Secretary Thompson that we're no longer in the
Clinton economy and that, at least as of his January 2003 appearance
on *Hannity & Colmes*, the Bush 43 numbers were not all that impressive:

COLMES: All right, you—tougher work requirements as part
of this welfare plan. This is at a time when 1,673,000 jobs
have been lost since President Bush entered the White
House, according to the Bureau of Labor Statistics.
Unemployment has jumped 4.2 percent to 6.2 percent, a 42
percent jump. So how appropriate is it if we're talking about
more work when there isn't more work available and people
are losing their jobs?

THOMPSON: Well, Alan, basically you know that people need
to work. Everybody else has a forty-hour workweek. And
under this forty-hour workweek that we are proposing, the

individual that's on assistance is getting off assistance, will work for twenty-four hours, and then will have sixteen hours in which they can go to school, go to job training, get some job improvement so they can get some advancement. I think it's a very laudable program and it's very compassionate.

COLMES: But there aren't those jobs available. As I just pointed out, people are losing in this administration. Jobs have been lost, over a million jobs.

As Secretary Thompson and I were having this conversation forty-three states were operating in the red, and the Republican plan didn't increase the $17 billion the states were getting in block grants, or the $4.8 billion for child care.

Conservatives position their welfare policies as being helpful to the less fortunate, but what the statistics don't show is those who have given up, who are no longer eligible for help, or who are marginalized by a system in which they have no clout and no options. For a country that brags about its wealth and its might, this is a mean outcome.

P.S. You are Ugly Too!

Much of what I say truly upsets conservatives. It's never my goal to annoy, but the truth is, if you really are passionate about what you believe, your views are going to rub some people the wrong way. E-mail gives my viewers and listeners an opportunity to respond candidly and immediately. It gives some the mistaken notion that there is license to behave in ways they never would in person. I hope. The ability to communicate our immediate thoughts is unbuffered by the time it takes to stuff a piece of paper in an envelope, address and stamp it, and go to a mailbox; and it's aided by the false sense of anonymity that electronic communication provides. I've included some of my most entertaining and provocative exchanges through-out this book. Here are a few more:

From: Galloway
Sent: Saturday, September 28, 2002 3:57 AM
To: Colmes
Subject: You owe me a TV

Dear Mr. Colmes:
You owe me a 27-inch Sony TV. Let me explain why . . . I watch
and listen Mr. Hannity but when it Colmes to you Mr. Colmes, I
press my "MUTE" button . . . because . . . my blood starts boiling
by listening your left-wing comments. I went . . . to get a cup of
coffee and I forgot to press the mute button. You start with your
left wing, liberal, and communistic BS. I lost my temper and threw
my mug toward the TV. Sadly, it was a direct hit and the TV blew
up. I would like you to pay for my TV, Sir. It was your fault . . .

Sincerely;
Galloway
Fredericksburg, MD

Galloway, thank you for hitting the mute button rather than the
channel selector. That way, I still get ratings credit. Oh, and why not
use that good money in your Bush tax rebate check to replace your
television? That'll really trickle things down.

From: Fstnfurious
Sent: Monday, February 10, 2003 6:02 PM
To: Colmes
Subject: RATINGS

YOU HAVE NOW SURPASSED J.R. EWING AS THE MOST
HATED MAN IN AMERICA

From: Parker
Sent: Tuesday, January 15, 2002 9:56 PM
To: Colmes
Subject: (no subject)

Alan, I am sorry to say but sometimes I think you are gay the way you defend those people.

From: Colmes
Sent: Tuesday, January 15, 2002 10:15 PM
To: Parker
Subject: RE: (no subject)

and when I stand up for women's rights, do you think I'm a woman?

From: Ravi
Sent: Friday, June 13, 2000 10:04 PM
To: colmes&foxnews.com
Subject: Plethora of Nonsense

Dear Mister Alan Colmes:
How in the world can you stand to have a right hand, right ear, right eye, right foot, right side of your body, since everything abou you is so left?

yours truly, Ravi, Butte, MT

From: PhilB
Sent: Tuesday, February 11, 2003 10:39 PM
To: Colmes
Subject: Closet Conservative

Mr. Colmes—

You are a great actor, but as a Goldwater conservative (are we still allowed to say that?) I think *down deep* you are really one of us.

Phil B, Columbia, SC

From: Lawrence R.
Sent: Friday, October 11, 2002 2:41 AM
To: Colmes
Subject: marriage

Several weeks ago you announced that you were getting married, but I dooooon't recall your ever mentioning his name or how you won him over. You sly rascal, I'll bet you must have shown him how you could lick your eyebrows.

Lawrence R.

From: Colmes
Sent: Friday, October 11, 2002 1:27 PM
To: Lawrence R.
Subject: RE: marriage

sorry, Larry, I'm already taken.

From: Donald
Sent: Monday, October 21, 2002 2:59 PM
To: Colmes
Subject: Question

Hey Alan,

I watch Hannity & Colmes quite a bit and one question has been nagging me for a very long time. How do you hold up that massive head of yours? Do you work out your neck muscles or something. Your massive NOGGIN dwarfs all other heads on the show. It must weigh at least 60 lbs. I was also curious as to whether or not you served in the Navy. I figured that with a truly expansive skull like that the wind resistance on deck would give an aircraft carrier at least 10 extra knots.

Thanks a bunch, angel.
Donald

Among my favorite give-and-takes are those involving viewers who do a 180 on me and become my friend after the initial vituperative e-mail. Sometimes, all it takes is my acknowledgment for them to soften up.

From: LB Catering Co.
Sent: Monday, October 28, 2002 9:55 PM
To: colmes
Subject: I Can not watch you when I am eating dinner

Mr. Colmes
You are so liberal and so disgusting that you make me throw up.

LOVE,
Brent

From: Colmes
Sent: Monday, October 28, 2002 10:16 PM
To: LB Catering Co.
Subject: RE: I Can not watch you when I am eating dinner

Brent,
If your catering company is any good, your food will overcome your disgust at me.

Love,
Alan

From: LB Catering Co.
Sent: Monday, October 28, 2002 11:54 PM
To: Colmes
Subject: RE: I Can not watch you when I am eating dinner

Mr. Colmes,
Throwing up or not, I would not miss your show!!
Love,
Brent

This viewer chose to cc me on something he wrote to Sean:

From: Charles
Sent: Friday, January 17, 2003 12:20 PM
To: Hannity
Subject: I Refuse to Purchase or Wear "Hannity & Colmes" Gear for a very Good Reason!!

Hi Sean!
I'd love to purchase some of those nice polo shirts, but I refuse to wear anything with Alan's name on it! . . . Alan is a complete joke in my view (and in the view of countless others). He's lucky to have a job there.

Sincerely,
Charles
Springfield, MA

From: Colmes,
Sent: Wednesday, January 22, 2003 11:26 AM
To: Charles
Subject: RE: I Refuse to Purchase or Wear "Hannity & Colmes" Gear for a very Good Reason!!

so, Charles, you won't wear anything with my name on it, but you'll watch our show for Sean's point of view. Do you want to hear only those views you agree with? . . . Do you disdain all liberals so much that you want nothing to do with them? . . . Why not buy some H&C gear and put a communist flag by my name? That might help people understand how you feel.

From: Charles
Sent: Wednesday, January 22, 2003 12:47 PM
To: Colmes
Subject: RE: I Refuse to Purchase or Wear "Hannity & Colmes" Gear for a very Good Reason!!

Thanks Alan!
EXCELLENT IDEA! Yes, I really do believe that the liberals would ruin this country completely if they had their way . . . I have chosen to break friendship with most of my pathetic liberal friends since 9/11/2001 . . . Regardless of all this, I do wish you a happy and healthy new year.

From: Colmes
Sent: Wednesday, January 22, 2003 12:47 PM
To: Charles
Subject: RE: I Refuse to Purchase or Wear "Hannity & Colmes" Gear for a very Good Reason!!

. . . To hear that you choose friendships based on whether they're liberal is truly sad.

From: Charles
Sent: Wednesday, January 22, 2003 2:32 PM
To: Colmes
Subject: RE: I Refuse to Purchase or Wear "Hannity & Colmes" Gear for a very Good Reason!! (Alan, I apologize for insulting you).

Alan,

Let's put on the brakes here! You've got the wrong picture of me . . . I did insult you personally, and I now sincerely apologize for that. There is no excuse for my harsh tone . . . I'm sure that you are truly a kind and wonderful person . . . Most of my liberal friends are history . . . but not all! I do have liberal friends that I deeply care for . . . I'm really not a bigot or anything remotely close . . . I would gladly risk my life to save your life, Alan Colmes. I'll try to be more polite with my comments in the future. . . . I promise!

She likes me! She really likes me!

From: Dorrie
Sent: Thursday, November 21, 2002 12:26 PM
To: colmes
Subject: mistake

Dear Mr. Colmes,

I made a mistake again by watching your show last night. As usual I was upset by some of your kooky stuff but then I really became scared because some of your drivel started to make sense.

Dorrie
Wheeling, WV

From the Oh, that explains it! file:

From: rstr201
Sent: Tuesday, January 21, 2003 9:39 PM
To: Colmes
Subject: (no subject)

Alan

I have put up with your stupidity for years, but you have exceeded my ability to not comment on how outraged you make me feel . . . I believe that you appear homosexual so maybe that explains it all.

From: Mr. S.
Sent: Tuesday, December 10, 2002 10:16 PM
To: Colmes
Subject: athiest

you hate jews, you hate christians, you love muslims, I dare you to admit on the air that you are an athiest. If you were an honest journelist you would admit that you are an athiest and love to see a birth canal baby die with with a shot of fermaldihide in the brain. Worship your master, SATIN, or dashel or clinton you are a disgrace to all Americans.

From: Colmes
Sent: Tuesday, December 10, 2002 10:37 PM
To: Mr. S.
Subject: RE: athiest

my master is not Satin, it's Polyester

From: LSW4
Sent: Thursday, December 12, 2002 9:15 PM
To: Colmes
Subject: (no subject)

I cannot see how a decent man like Hannity can stand to be in the same room with you without continuously throwing up!

Your pal

Thanks for being a pal. Too bad you didn't sign your name so I can know who my friends are.

> **From:** Pat
> **Sent:** Friday, March 14, 2003 12:01 PM
> **To:** Colmes
> **Subject:** book?
>
> Mr. Colmes,
> Are you really writing a book? I will buy your book if funny and up beat . . .
>
> P.S. loved you last nite . . . Keep talking for us, ok? and I will for sure buy your book. (as know you care about everyone.)
>
> Pat
> Portland, OR

Thanks, one sold!

> **From:** Lester
> **Sent:** Wednesday, December 04, 2002 10:42 AM
> **To:** Colmes
> **Subject:** Amazed
>
> Colmes,
> You are consistently amazing to me!! Something I should have suspected, but didn't. Last night a long shot of your set showed you writing with your LEFT hand. Did that happen naturally or did your brain receive it's instruction from the Daily Worker, the NY Times or the DNC?
>
> Lester
> Norfolk, VA

From: Rachel
Sent: Wednesday, March 12, 2003 2:22 PM
To: Colmes
Subject: Just wondering!

Mr. Colmes
. . . What I am wondering about, is do you sometimes feel uncomfortable having to always be the other side.

Rachel, Hartford, CT

From: Colmes
Sent: Wednesday, March 12, 2003 2:46 PM
To: Rachel
Subject: RE: Just wondering!

. . . I'm not on the "other side."
Sean is.

From: Brad
Sent: Wednesday, November 6, 2002 5:14 PM
To: Colmes
Subject: mid-term elections

Dear Alan ~ You are the main reason this country went Republican.

Brad, Philadelphia, PA

Thank you, Guy, for reminding me of one of the greatest titles of any country song ever: "You're the Reason Our Kids Are Ugly." And thanks for imbuing me with far more power than I possess.

From: Scott
Sent: Thursday, March 13, 2003 10:06 PM
To: Colmes
Subject: Alan Colmes

Alan,

... You did not make me curse once tonight. There is a god. ...

Scott
Columbus, OH

From: Vera
Sent: Thursday, February 27, 2003 10:00 PM
To: Colmes
Subject: I Can't stand you!

... Why don't you take a Poll and find out how many people ...
like you. On a scale of 1 to 10, I give you a 3. And that's only
because I have had a couple of drinks. Make something out of
that, you always do.

Seriously,
Vera
Silver Spring, MD

From: Colmes
Sent: Friday, February 28, 2003 2:35 AM
To: Vera
Subject: RE: I Can't stand you!

only a "couple" of drinks?

From: Steve
Sent: Wednesday, January 08, 2003 9:15 AM
To: Colmes
Subject: Vanishing H&C T-Shirt

Alan—For a Christmas gift I received a Hannity & Colmes
t-shirt . . . After laundering the t-shirt once or twice, I noticed
that the logo lettering was beginning to fade. Finally, after the
third laundering, the words "and Colmes" had totally faded from
the t-shirt . . . I submit to you that this incident . . . proves the
existence of a vast right-wing conspiracy in our nation's garment
industry.

Steve
Appleton, WI

From: Catherine
Sent: Monday, March 17, 2003 8:50 PM
To: Colmes
Subject: To Alan

Dear Alan,
You are so wrong so often it is sometimes painful to hear you
BUT, you are so gracious that it is possible to watch you and to
listen to you. Can't ask for more than that. And, your are cute,
too.

Catherine, Seattle, WA

From: Edward
Sent: Sunday, February 21, 1999 12:03 PM
To: Colmes
Subject: Why are you un-American?

Mr. Colmes,
According to you:

Good: gun control (2nd amendment, what 2nd amendment?)
Bad: honest citizens using arms to defend themselves (concealed carry laws)

Good: black racism (quannel x, sharpton, etc.)
Bad: the police (imagine that, human beings sometimes make a mistake!)

Good: killing babies (choice?! Whose choice, not the babies!)
Bad: killing murderers (anti death penalty except for the victims death that is)

Good: Sean Hannity
Bad: Alan Colmes

S.
P.S. you are ugly too!

ELEVEN

Where Right Is Right

I don't wake up in the morning, try to figure out what a good liberal would say about whatever is in the news that day, and then spout the party line. I strive to look at each issue and then figure out where I stand. It's true that in most cases I fall left of center, but not always. Someone who is *always* liberal or *always* conservative is a nonthinking person. And, let's face it; we live in a world that tends to polarize. There is a rush to define every issue in left versus right terms, even when an issue may defy categorization. Is it liberal or conservative to want our children to have a better future, for our loved ones to have better health care, for our taxes to be as low as possible, and for our country to be protected? If you are a conservative, I hope you'll give some thought to where some of your beliefs may be "liberal."

The truth is that most rational people, regardless of ideology, want what's best for America. There are wingnuts on both sides who do a disservice to the many committed liberals and conservatives they purport to represent. And in the center are the vast numbers of Americans who don't define themselves as either left or right, just as good Americans. A Harris poll conducted from January through

December of 2002 shows that 34 percent of Americans regard them-selves as Democrats, 31 percent Republicans, and 24 percent Indepen-dents. But when it's couched in liberal versus conservative terms, 35 percent say they're conservative, only 17 percent admit to the liberal moniker, and 40 percent of respondents say they're moderate. A sim-ilar survey by the Republican-oriented Winston Group, conducted on December 29 and 30, 2002, had 33 percent claiming to be con-servative, 19 percent liberal, and 46 percent regarding themselves as moderate.

No side has the market cornered on truth, and no truthful person could believe that his or her side is always correct. Yes, I believe that left is right. Usually. But I also strive to be, as we say at Fox News, "Fair and Balanced."

He's My President, Too

Even though Bush 43 has had to endure the "Reagan II" moniker, that branding is unfair. With Rumsfeld, Cheney, former Treasury secretary Paul O'Neill and his replacement, John Snow, as key play-ers in this White House, let's call this group by its rightful name: the Ford administration. Gerald Ford is the best president we never elected. (We also never elected Chester A. Arthur, Millard Fillmore, Andrew Johnson, and John Tyler.) Ford was the only president who was never elected to either the presidency or the vice presidency. Unfortunately, many liberals continue to try to argue that President Bush is an illegitimate president who, like Ford, was never elected. It's a shame that some on the left feel compelled to devote their time to tearing down a president, even if it was the Supreme Court of the United States that made the ultimate decision that resulted in his White House residency. But he is and should be called the "President," not the "Resident," as some liberals insist on doing. I have been castigated by my fellow liberals for daring to suggest that their energies are best spent fighting on the issues and not on the bitter aftertaste of Election 2000. We should be looking forward, not backward, and liberals do themselves a disservice with their lack of graciousness in defeat.

During the antiwar demonstrations before and during the 2003 war with Iraq, many liberals held placards with the vilest language toward our president. Outside the UN office in Damascus, signs called Bush 43 a "criminal" and a "butcher." In Bahrain's capital, Manama, some banners read, "Death to America." Outside the Edwin Andrews Air Force Base in the Philippines, where hundreds of U.S. troops are stationed, one sign read "Bush No. 1 Terrorist." Walking along Broadway during a peace march on March 22, 2003, I blanched when I saw a sign that read, "Bush: The Real Butcher of Baghdad."

Liberals, and anyone else in the antiwar movement, need to do a better job of distancing themselves from these whack jobs and make sure that their political adversaries understand that this does *not* represent the liberal position. Let the conservatives do the name-calling. I'd rather be angry at the other side for their behavior than at my own side. Let the conservatives be the ones who are perceived as mean-spirited and overly emotional. Liberals need to base their opinions on fact and logic, not emotionalism. That is the only way they will disabuse a large number of their fellow Americans of their antiliberalism.

Some antiwar liberals decided to go to Iraq and proclaim themselves "human shields." They thought that by positioning themselves at hospitals and schools they could put human faces on war and prevent casualties. But when they got to the land of the not-free, they were ordered to do their shielding at water, power, and oil installations because that served Iraq's purposes better. Did these useful idiots believe they'd really be useful to the United States or to the effort to stop war? When they couldn't act as shields in their chosen locations, many of them left Iraq, complaining about Iraqi interference with their mission. Did it ever occur to them that freedom of movement and assembly didn't exist in Iraq? Just some things to think about the next time you want to go to a hostile nation without the guarantees of the U.S. Constitution.

The 2003 antiwar movement also spawned protesters who decided that lying down in front of traffic in San Francisco or staging a "die-in" to disrupt rush hour in New York would make some brilliant statement about the evils of war. Instead, these wrongheaded exercises in futility used up valuable resources at a time of high terror alerts, and prevented hardworking Americans from going about their daily business. Much as I opposed this war, I couldn't live with myself if my actions resulted in a sick child or an elderly person unable to get to a hospital quickly because their ambulance was caught up in a demonstration. Why not protest an illegal and immoral war by doing something positive for America? Go en masse and feed the homeless, bring meals to invalids, or mentor a child. The opposition would then have little ground upon which to denounce your cause.

Reasonable conservatives want a loyal opposition, but when that opposition is perceived as disloyal there can be no honest debate. When the other side sees only irrational and illogical behavior and rhetoric, we make it easy for them to rail against what they see as the paucity of liberal ideas.

The Message Is the Message

Frankly, I think the Democrats are not as smart as the Republicans at using talk radio and cable news to get their message out. *Hannity & Colmes* in particular and Fox News in general historically have had a more difficult time getting Democrats to come on our shows than we've had getting Republicans to come on. Even if we were as biased as some Democrats claim, they'd be much smarter to come into the lion's den than to avoid the zoo entirely. Republicans have been braver about going on shows and fighting the good fight. Trent Lott; Newt Gingrich, even when he was Speaker; Lynn Cheney; Denny Hastert; and other top Republicans have never shied away from us. I won't embarrass the guilty by telling you the laundry list of people who say things like, "Well, is Sean going to be nice to me?" Sean gets the same questions about me from some on his side, too, but this is more of a Democrat whine. Some Democrats came on only after long weeks and months of requests; others have still yet to appear. I hope they'll come to realize that you accomplish more when you preach in the other church than to your own choir.

A good attitude about this was expressed to me by then candidate Bush. While running for president, the Texas governor addressed the *Talkers* magazine New Media Seminar in New York City. In the middle of a tough campaign, he took a Saturday, flew to New York to talk to a bunch of radio hosts, and then went back to Texas. Lots of travel for a half-hour talk to a cynical crowd. Michael Harrison, the publisher of *Talkers,* introduced me to the man who would become the next president, and I told him that I hoped he'd consider coming on *Hannity & Colmes.* I offered that I was a reasonable liberal and would give him a fair shake. "If I can't face you on television," Bush told me, "I have no business being president." And he was right. Let's see, who's tougher to face down: Alan Colmes or Saddam Hussein?

Good Enemy Lines

I've spent enough time showing you things conservatives have said that I deem inappropriate at best and false at worst. Here are some things I agree with that have been said by my otherwise political opposites.

That old joke that even a stopped clock is right twice a day applies here. It has to if I'm going to agree with Jesse Helms. In fact, it's the far right that is often correct on our misuse of power abroad and the need to prioritize our resources toward our domestic needs.

In 1991, during the Gulf War, the *Los Angeles Times* reported on the issue of our formerly pro-Iraq policies: "Ultraconservative Helms said that Iraq's ability to rapidly develop such a dangerous arsenal is attributable to 'unbelievable greed . . . and bureaucratic bungling'."

It's really invigorating to cheer on someone with whom you usually vehemently disagree. It causes you to check your pulse and then rejoice when you discover you're still alive. All I can say in this case is, "Go, Jesse, Go."

Here's another wonderful quote from a man who may very well have rehabilitated himself by living up to its spirit: "Always give your best, never get discouraged, never be petty; always remember, others may hate you. Those who hate you don't win unless you hate them. And then you destroy yourself." Richard Nixon said these eloquent words during his farewell address on August 8, 1974. What more wonderful advice could there be than to never hate back, and what better person to offer it than a man who was reviled by many at the time he said it, but who gained more respect through the adjusted lens of history?

Ronald Reagan succeeded not just on the issues, but because he presented a soaring spirit with his "morning in America" approach. In his first inaugural address on January 20, 1981, he proclaimed, "No arsenal or no weapon in the arsenals of the world is so formidable as the will and moral courage of free men and women." This is the kind of statement that truly inspires one to think about possibilities. For me, these mean possibilities other than war to achieve our aims. Reagan was far brighter than the left ever acknowledged.

My side does itself and the country a disservice when it positions itself as smarter than highly respected conservative icons like Ronald Reagan. We come off as intolerant and arrogant, everything a liberal isn't supposed to be.

Right Is Right on Reparations

Many of today's black Americans are from countries other than America, and many white taxpayers are not descendants of slave owners. There is an argument put forth by those who want recompense for slavery that we did the same thing for Japanese held in internment camps and Nazi-era slave laborers. But these monies went to the actual aggrieved parties and their families, not to people who happened to be the same race two hundred years later.

Many white Americans are descendants of those who fought and died to end slavery. Should they be compensated? Should we compensate women because of years of American misogyny? Indeed, if we're going to start compensating anyone, shouldn't we repay the American Indians for taking their land? How much money is going to make everything okay? Won't the cost of reparations take a huge amount of money out of our treasury that could be put to use for the good of all Americans, especially the most needy, many of whom are in the very group reparations purport to help?

And here is the overriding principle: according to the Convention for the Protection of Human Rights and Fundamental Freedoms, "Inheritance of the guilt of the dead is not compatible with the standards of criminal justice in a society governed by the rule of law."

Where Left Is Right and Right Is Left

Kathy Ireland may claim to be liberal about the rights of the unborn child, but I claim to be conservative on the abortion issue. Conservatives say they want less government, but they want to dictate what medical procedures a woman can have. They want to tell a woman that even if she is raped or the victim of incest, her body becomes a ward of the state for nine months. I'm conservative on abortion. I don't believe it's any of the government's business.

I'm also conservative on quotas and set-asides, but not affirmative action. They're too often lumped together, but the Supreme Court did a nice job of neatly separating them in the University of Michigan decision it reached during the 2003 term.

I'm for free trade. That's a conservative position. But it conforms to liberal ideals. Free trade promotes jobs for the poor and forces the hand of democracy in countries that would otherwise be more isolated. Protectionism reeks of special interests.

"The 'War' on Drugs"

Both liberals and conservatives are wrong on drugs. They should be legal. Insanity is defined as doing the same thing repeatedly and hoping for a different result. Our drug laws don't work. Never did; never will. And most politicians of both parties, with the courageous exception of former governor Gary Johnson of New Mexico, don't have the courage to admit this, because it's not politically correct. Legalizing drugs would take the profit motive out of the equation. Our resources could be better spent focusing on treatment rather than interdiction. It costs $30,000 a year to keep someone in jail, versus $20,000 for the most intensive drug treatment program. The social costs of drug abuse, like health care, incarceration and lost productivity, exceed $110 billion per year, and take fifty-two thousand American lives a year. U.S. drug users spend more than $63 billion annually to purchase drugs. Conservatives complain that liberals have a tendency to throw money at a problem and hope it will be solved. I'm against throwing money at a program that has proven not to work, "The 'War' on Drugs."

So call me a conservative. Amazingly, some of our viewers have done just that.

From: Dennis Y.
Sent: Friday, November 22, 2002 9:57 PM
To: Colmes
Subject: Are you a liberal?

I have been watching your show for 2 years but I have never heard you say anything that sounds all that liberal.

In what way are you a liberal?

Dennis

Dennis, there's a new book out I'd like you to read.

Right Is Right on America's Boundaries

The columnist Michelle Malkin has done some good work pointing out how vulnerable our borders are. It was Ms. Malkin who discovered that an illegal alien was able to secure a job putting up tents at the White House. This person worked there for two years, even after being tagged by the Immigration and Naturalization Service for deportation, hoodwinking both his employer and the Secret Service. Malkin has pointed out how easy it is to borrow or steal someone's identity and use it to create a life for oneself in the United States. I certainly don't agree with everything she says about illegal immigration. For example, foreign nationals contribute to our economy, particularly farming, and often take jobs Americans won't. They are responsible for the success of the $1.2 billion fruit industry in Washington State. In Georgia 99 percent of illegals are employed. I also believe they deserve certain services. After all, they are granted tax IDs by the IRS and pay $1 billion in taxes in New York State alone. That's why Ronald Reagan signed the 1986 Amnesty Act that gave residency status to immigrants who were here prior to 1972.

However, as Malkin pointed out in *National Review Online*, "The United States is one of the few industrialized countries in the world that has not tightened immigration and entrance policies in response to the Sept. 11 attacks. Temporary visas for Middle Eastern students, tourists, and businessmen remain plentiful; immigrant visas continue to be given away at random or for the right price; the borders remain porous; the welcome mat for illegal aliens is expanding; and the deportation system is in shambles."

Indeed, among the nineteen September 11 terrorists, two could have been denied entry because of prior visa violations, six should have been denied because they used false names, three were here longer than their visas allowed, two had student visas but didn't show up for class, and two were on an FBI watch list. This covers twelve of the terrorists, and some of these missteps apply multiple times to the same terrorists. But *this* is where our problems begin, and it underscores what should be our first line of offense against those who would do us harm.

Short of committing an enormous amount of resources, we can't fully control our borders. Do we post the military along both the Mexican and Canadian divides? I'm open to that idea. Of course, protecting American borders seems like a much better use of our military than invading Iraq or nation-building in Afghanistan, especially since it is the porous nature of our borders that make our country most vulnerable to infiltration. I don't think too many liberals are going to agree with me on this one.

It's not inconsistent to fight for humane treatment for everyone in America, both legal and illegal, while working to secure our borders for the safety of these very same people. Liberals can show they're bullish on security by drawing a line in the desert and acknowledging that it's time to stop the flow of illegal immigrants as conservatives have, but showing compassion for those already here. Republican Jeff Flake of Arizona favors granting guest worker status to illegals already here, allowing them to work toward citizenship. John Cornyn of Texas, another Republican, wants to give illegal aliens the opportunity to work here for three years if they are sponsored by employers, and then have their applications for permanent resident status expedited. Now *that's* compassionate conservatism. Or rational liberalism.

Left Plus Right Equals America

So sue me. I don't always agree with the party line. Truth is not the province of either side, and any thinking person will disagree with any other thinking person at least some of the time. Oscar Wilde said, "Whenever people agree with me, I always feel I must be wrong." I think this is quite a healthy attitude. We must always examine and reexamine our ideas and our feelings. That is the only way we can grow.

There's no reason for liberals to feel they *have* to disagree with conservatives simply because it hurts too much to admit they're right on some issues. Agreeing with the other side doesn't make you lose your liberal credentials. In fact, in the name of openness and tolerance, it strengthens them. Surely we can all agree that, left or right, we all want what's best for America; that we believe in the democratic ideals as laid out in the Constitution; that we owe a debt of gratitude to those who have sacrificed for America's honor; and that we should respect the office of the presidency along with the other branches of government. We recognize that these structures enable our democracy to flourish.

It's not important whether you're liberal or conservative. It's less important whether you're Democrat or Republican. It's most important that we're Americans. It is both conservative values and a liberal spirit that are the bedrocks of our nation, that sustain us with both a strong moral code and with liberty and justice for all.

For soaring words that capture the American spirit, it's hard to top what has become a conservative anthem, of sorts. Conservatives proudly embrace country music, and vice versa, but until America's first liberal country star emerges, I have to applaud Lee Greenwood, whose 1984 lyrics still make me quiver with love for my country:

> *I'm proud to be an American*
> *where at least I know I'm free,*
> *And I won't forget the men who died*
> *who gave that right to me,*
> *And I gladly stand up next to you*
> *and defend her still today,*
> *'Cause there ain't no doubt I love this land*
> *God Bless the U.S.A.*

TWELVE

Liberal Liberal Liberal Liberal

After Republicans gained control of Congress and swept a
majority of governorships in 1994, conservatives began
crowing that liberalism was dead. They've continued to try to realize
this prophecy by scheming to throw Bill Clinton out of office and,
having failed at that, attempting to pin just about every American
problem on our forty-second president in particular and on liberals
in general. They've ratcheted up the rhetoric to a level so shrill I
believe only canines have heard some of it. A generation ago, the
political adman Arthur Finkelstein began using the term *liberal* like
an epithet hurled by a schoolyard bully. He helped New York senator
Al D'Amato defeat New York state attorney general Robert Abrams
to win reelection in 1992 by calling Abrams "hopelessly liberal."
When George Pataki became New York governor by defeating
incumbent Mario Cuomo, it was with the help of Finkelstein's "too
liberal for too long" slogan. "Dangerously liberal," "embarrassingly
liberal," and "scarily liberal" became the mantras of Finklestein-
consulted candidates. Many of these candidates, like North

Carolina's Jesse Helms and Lauch Faircloth, New Hampshire's Bob Smith, South Carolina's Strom Thurmond, and Oklahoma's Don Nickles used Finkelstein's words to promote staunchly antigay platforms. No wonder Finkelstein is rarely photographed and never interviewed. It turns out he lives in Massachusetts with his gay lover and their two adopted children. It was humorous to hear senator and presidential candidate Bob Dole use Finklestein's tactics when he ran for president in 1996. Dole churlishly tossed the Finkelstein phrase at his opponent, Bill Clinton. Speaking at St. Louis University, Dole used the word *liberal* as a punch line for every public policy he opposed. As CNN reported,

> Dole fired up the crowd with some never-fail give-and-take:
>
> "What do you call someone who broke his promise and gave you the biggest tax increase in history?" he asked them.
>
> "A liberal!" they replied enthusiastically.
>
> "What do you call someone who tried to take over the nation's health care system and put the government in charge of it?" Dole asked.
>
> "A liberal!" cried the crowd.
>
> "What do you call someone who twisted arms in Congress to kill the balanced budget amendment?" Dole continued.
>
> "A liberal!" came the response.
>
> "What do you call someone who appointed a surgeon general who talked about legalizing drugs?"
>
> "A liberal!" the crowd replied once more.
>
> "You are right," Dole said. "Liberal-liberal-liberal Bill Clinton."

This is not only childish; it's also factually incorrect. The Center for Tax Justice asks, "Was the 1993 Tax Act 'the largest tax increase in history'?" Well, the Center points out that "the 1982 Tax Equity and Fiscal Responsibility Act (TEFRA) resulted in tax increases representing one percent of the GDP—half again bigger than the 1993 tax act."

Guess who voted for that tax bill? That's right, Bob Dole. Furthermore, Bill Clinton tried to give us national health care and didn't succeed, but it wasn't as though he personally "tried to take over the system." As for the balanced budget amendment, Republicans must be happy they don't have one now. And "liberal liberal liberal Bill Clinton" beat Dole in the 1996 presidential election. Badly.

Conservatives have done such a good job on the word *liberal* that in some quarters only one letter remains, and it's called "the 'L' word." We're called "the loony left," "lying liberals," or the diminutive and demeaning "lib." I don't hear liberals referring to their opposites as "cons," even though enough of them have served prison time. The left is just not as nasty to the right. The word *conservative* has not been reduced to the "C" word. Liberals don't possess the kind of mean-spiritedness that drives them to try to eviscerate the other side. Unfortunately, liberals have for too long taken this lying down. They've taken to calling themselves "progressive," "moderate," or "independent," or they'll duck the issue entirely and say, "Let's stop all this labeling." Rarely do conservatives run away from this kind of truth in advertising; conservatives display their label with pride. It's about time that liberals stood up proudly, declared that their views are deeply steeped in fine American tradition, and stopped running away from what they are. I'm a liberal. What are you going to make of it?

It's time for liberals to stand up and embrace the very word that represents the core of who they are and what they believe. The activist and comedian Dick Gregory called his 1964 autobiography *Nigger.* Dedicating the book to his mother, he wrote, "Dear Momma—Wherever you are, if ever you hear the word 'nigger' again, remember they are advertising my book." Gregory shuns the phrase "The 'N' Word" declaring, "It's not the N-word to me. It's nigger, nigger, nigger, nigger." If Gregory can be this bold about "nigger," refusing to allow that word to be the sole property of bigots, liberals of conviction should not settle for "the 'L' word" and proudly claim their liberalism.

The lack of self-consciousness among Republicans and conservatives has enabled them to do a better job of using the media and getting their message out, and liberals should learn from the conservative refusal to be cowed by the other side. Standing up for what you believe against a loud, dogmatic, well-organized opposition may seem forbidding, but it doesn't go unrecognized.

From: Peter
Sent: Saturday, February 15, 2003 12:04 AM
To: colmes
Subject: Allen. First a comment then Kudos to follow.

Allen,
thank you for speaking your mind and for giving me a voice in the cable news debate . . . it is encouraging to know i need only think it and soon you will speak it. Instead of exhausting myself through the many discussions i need only say "wanna know what i think? watch FOX's Hannity & Colmes and Pay close attention to the smart guy"

Peter
Derry, New Hampshire

In spite of today's incessant, denouncing rhetoric on the right, it's not difficult to understand liberal appeal. Liberals pride themselves—as they should—on being at the forefront of civil rights and gay rights, and of breaking through the glass ceiling that has held women back. Americans still perceive Democrats as being ahead on key issues. A CBS News poll conducted May 9–12, 2003, shows that Americans believe Democrats are better than Republicans at protecting the environment, making prescription drugs affordable, creating new jobs, improving health care, improving education, and even making sure our tax system is fair. Now, *that's* encouraging.

The American public may finally be recognizing the folly of the tax-cut cure-all for every fiscal woe. Conservatives call themselves fiscally responsible, but their one answer for every economic ill is a tax cut. When the economy was booming thanks to the Clinton years, Bush 43 rode his way to the presidency promising a tax cut. When the surplus evaporated and became a huge deficit, partly because of a failing economy, partly because of "The 'War' on Terror," and partly because of a tax rebate, the cure, according to the Bushies, was a tax cut. When I was a child at sleepaway camp, the doctor in the infirmary was famous for prescribing Sucrets. If you had a cold: Sucrets. Fever: Sucrets. Bad back: Sucrets. I'm glad Bush 43 is not an emergency room doctor. Sucrets might be good for a knife wound, but only if you've been stabbed in the throat.

Guess Who's Liberal

It shouldn't be surprising that Americans side with liberals on major issues. What were our forefathers if not liberals, fighting for freedom against tyranny, writing a Constitution that ensured basic human rights for all persons regardless of class, race, religion, gender, or sexual orientation. Indeed, our nation's founders were beyond liberal; they were revolutionaries. There is one thing they surely were not: conservative. Similarly, many legendary men and women who moved America forward on many fronts proudly wore the liberal label. Albert Einstein once referred to himself as "a Jew with liberal international convictions." I hope this self-description doesn't sit too poorly with my conservative friends, and that, armed with this information, they don't rush to deny that Dr. Einstein developed the theory of relativity.

Carl Sagan was one of our greatest scientists and visionaries. He played a major role in the development of our space program and won awards for his work analyzing the atmospheres of Mars and Venus. His book *Cosmos* became the best-selling science book in the

English language, ever, and the series of the same name on PBS was seen by a half billion people in sixty countries. He won a Pulitzer for his book *Dragons of Eden*, a seminal work on the evolution of the human brain. Sagan was a lifelong liberal who warned us about nuclear war and the "nuclear winter" that could result. Other Sagan passions included women's reproductive rights and social freedoms.

John Glenn, considered a hero to many, was the first American to orbit the earth. Even before this accomplishment brought him to international prominence, Glenn was a marine pilot who flew 59 combat missions in the South Pacific during World War II. Glenn then requested combat duty during the Korean conflict, where he flew another 63 missions. After a combined 149 missions in two wars, Glenn went to test pilot school, joined the Naval Air Test Center and, in 1957, set a speed record by flying from Los Angeles to New York in 3 hours, 23 minutes. As a senator, Glenn was the chief architect of the Nuclear Nonproliferation Act of 1978, which put strict controls on nuclear trade, helping to reduce the spread of nuclear weapons. Oh, and John Glenn was a member of that political party that has all those liberals in it.

Eleanor Roosevelt should be an inspiration for anyone who seeks to fight prejudice against groups that have been marginalized by society. She utilized the bully pulpit that comes with being First Lady to fight for women's rights, even holding news conferences just for female reporters. Roosevelt also conducted antilynching campaigns, advocated unions and fair labor practices, and battled for fair housing for minorities. It was Eleanor Roosevelt who made sure the New Deal programs her husband initiated were open to blacks as well as whites. She evolved a long way from the shy, lonely, young woman who once declared, "It was a wife's duty to be interested in whatever interested her husband." After her husband, President Franklin Delano Roosevelt, was gone, Harry Truman chose Eleanor to head the United Nations Human Rights Commission. She was instrumental in drafting the Declaration of Human Rights, stating that recognizing "the inherent dignity and . . . equal and inalienable rights of all members of the human family is the foundation of freedom, justice and peace in the world." While FDR proclaimed "The only thing we have to fear is fear itself," Eleanor Roosevelt applied this concept on a personal level. In her "If You Ask Me" newspaper column she wrote, "My greatest fear has always been that I would be afraid—afraid physically or mentally or morally and allow myself to be influenced by fear instead of by my honest convictions."

Eleanor Roosevelt is a wonderful example of someone who used the platform she had to make a difference. Another was the actor Gregory Peck. Peck's lifelong devotion to liberal causes was reflected not just in his personal actions, but also in the roles he played. As a member of the Hollywood Democratic Committee, he supported Roosevelt's liberal causes. Peck was named by actor Larry Parks as a Communist sympathizer to the House Un-American Activities Committee and signed a letter in 1947 denouncing this committee, at a time when many who spoke out were losing work because of their convictions. One of his most popular roles was that of the attorney Atticus Finch in the movie *To Kill a Mockingbird*. Released when the civil rights movement was in full bloom, Peck's Finch defends a black man falsely accused of rape in the 1930s rural south. "I put everything I had into it," Peck said of this role in 1989, "all my feelings and everything I'd learned in 46 years of living, about family life and fathers and children. And my feelings about racial justice and inequality and opportunity." Finch said a few things that could well improve today's political dialogue: "If you just learn a single trick," Atticus tells his daughter, "you'll get along a lot better with all kinds of folks. You never really understand a person until you consider things from his point of view . . . until you climb inside of his skin and walk around in it." In *Gentleman's Agreement*, Peck played a role his agent suggested he not take: a non-Jewish writer posing as a Jew to study anti-Semitism. Peck's character discovers the ugly truth about some of his own friends who, it turns out, weren't as liberal as they thought they were.

When he was president of the Academy of Motion Picture Arts and Sciences, Peck had the Oscar ceremony postponed after the death of Martin Luther King Jr. When he learned that six hundred thousand jobs at Chrysler could disappear during the automaker's financial woes in 1980, Peck agreed to do commercials for the company without compensation, hoping it would help put them in the black. When he was offered the Jean Hersholt Humanitarian Award by the Motion Picture Academy in 1968 he said, "I'm not a do-gooder. It embarrassed me to be classified as a humanitarian. I simply take part in activities that I believe in."

Tomorrow Is Now

Is it nature or nurture? Does God create liberals in the womb or can one's environment grow one to the left? Einstein, Sagan, Glenn, Roosevelt, and Peck were certainly products of their times. But did the times also make them the accomplished and outspoken liberals they were and are? Whether it was that, or congenital predispositions to fight for basic human decency, these Americans should be an inspiration for anyone who hopes to make a difference, especially at a time when an opposing point of view isn't always welcome and is, in fact, derided.

I'm grateful for the opportunity to conduct my career on platforms that enable my voice to be heard. Thankfully, we live in an America where you don't have to stay silent, even when your views don't represent the flavor of the month. In fact, it is *especially* important that dissenting and minority views always remain an essential part of our American fabric. The majority isn't always right, which is why we live in a constitutional republic that guarantees certain inalienable rights that can't be erased by majority rule. As Benjamin Franklin said, "Democracy is two wolves and a lamb voting on what to have for lunch. Liberty is a well-armed lamb contesting the vote!" And if you are a well-armed lamb, willing to participate in that contest, it won't be long before you find other like-minded lambs, perhaps enough to outnumber the wolves:

From: Mike
Sent: Friday, July 25, 2003 5:42 AM
To: Colmes
Subject: I'm Ticked

Mr Colmes,

When I first started watching your show I was, or thought I was,
a strict conservative. Your calm and commonsense
explanations . . . on events . . . have corrupted my once unshakable
conservatism. Each day I find myself becoming more liberal.
I don't know if I should be really mad at you for changing years of
consistent viewpoints or thank you for enlightening me to a
political philosophy I had previously considered to be "left-wing
wacko."

I should probably thank you. And will, thanks and keep up the
good work . . .

Mike
Hollywood, FL

On January 6, 1941, Franklin Delano Roosevelt delivered his
"Four Freedoms" address to Congress. More than half a century
later, it still represents the highest ideals for which this *liberal* nation
should aim:

In the future days, which we seek to make secure, we look forward to
a world founded upon four essential human freedoms. The first is
freedom of speech and expression—everywhere in the world. The
second is freedom of every person to worship God in his own way—
everywhere in the world. The third is freedom from want—which,
translated into world terms, means economic understandings which

will secure to every nation a healthy peacetime life for its inhabitants—everywhere in the world. The fourth is freedom from fear—which, translated into world terms, means a world-wide reduction of armaments to such a point and in such a thorough fashion that no nation will be in a position to commit an act of physical aggression against any neighbor—anywhere in the world.

Equally prescient was Eleanor Roosevelt. In her posthumously published book, *Tomorrow Is Now*, she wrote:

> Once more we are in a period of uncertainty, of danger, in which not only our own safety but that of all mankind is threatened. Once more we need the qualities that inspired the development of the democratic way of life. We need imagination and integrity, courage and a high heart. We need to fan the spark of conviction, which may again inspire the world as we did with our new idea of the dignity and worth of free men. But first we must learn to cast out fear. People who "view with alarm" never build anything.

It's remarkable how those words resonate today. In this period of uncertainty, liberals must stand strong against both our domestic adversaries who would compromise our freedoms and foreign forces that would destroy them, for once we give in to the former, we invite the latter. While holding our ground, however, we must extend our hands across political boundaries so we can walk the common ground that binds us together as Americans, in the name of shared love of country. We must look forward, not with fear, but with confidence in our convictions and the courage to stay true to our ideals. We must do so without delay, for tomorrow is now.

NOTES

Page

INTRODUCTION: WHY YOU NEED THIS BOOK

2 "One of the seminal . . .": John Rawls, *A Theory of Justice*. Cambridge: Harvard
   University Press, 1971.

5 "A Harris poll . . .": Humphrey Taylor, "Democratic Lead (Now Only Three Points)
   in Party Identification Has Declined to a New Low," The Harris Poll (Harris
   Poll #5), January 29, 2003.

ONE: RED, WHITE & LIBERAL

7 "The common thread . . .": "Brief History of the Democratic Party," Democratic
   National Committee, www.dnc.org.

19 "Not a one . . .": Thomas G. Paterson, Gary Clifford and Kenneth J. Hagan,
   American Foreign Relations: A History Since 1895, Lexington, VA: D.C. Heath
   Company, 1995, page 410.

23 "From a marketing . . .": Frank Rich, "Never Forget What?," *New York Times*,
   September 14, 2002.

23 "During the Gulf War . . .": Geoffrey Gray, "Bush's Little Shop of Horrors," *Village
   Voice*, March 12, 2002.

24 "But in June, 1997 . . .": United States General Accounting Office, Report on Gulf
   War Illness, June 1997, page. 8.

25 "After a year of stonewalling . . .": Paul M. Rodriguez, "Breakthrough on Gulf War
   Illness," *Insight*, April 19, 1999.

25 "Veterans' fears . . .": *Ibid.*

25 "Significant and potentially meaningful . . .": David Brown, "Defoliant Connected To
   Diabetes," *Washington Post*, March 29, 2000.

26 "For at least 50 years . . .": Pamela Hess, "Analysis: Army fears rebellion on Lariam,"
   United Press International, August 29, 2002.

26 "As recently as 1993 . . .": "Is Military Research Hazardous To Veterans' Health?
   Lessons Spanning Half A Century," Senate Committee on Veteran's Affairs,
   December 8, 1994.

27 "Persian Gulf veterans . . .": *Ibid.*

27 "President Bush has threatened . . .": Vernon Loeb, "Bush Threatens Veto of

Defense Bill; President Wants Costly New Disabled Military Pension Benefits Eliminated," *Washington Post*, October 7, 2002.

27   "This would divert . . .": *Ibid.*

28   "No other category . . .": *Ibid.*

28   "What prompted you . . .": *Hannity & Colmes*, Fox News Channel, June 26, 2002.

29   "Bellamy's granddaughter says . . .": *All Things Considered*, NPR, June 27, 2002.

30   "If there is a fixed star . . .": Justice Robert Jackson, *West Virginia State Board of Education v. Barnette* 319 U.S. 624 (1943).

30   "I can't think . . .": David Kertzer interview with author, August 7, 2003.

30   "I never use the words . . .": Martin Crutsinger, "Energy Lobbyist Loses Job After Writing to Watt," Associated Press, January 27, 1982.

31   "Their goal remains . . .": Gayle M.B. Hanson, "Time to Snap Out of Victim Culture," *Insight on the News*, January 3, 2000.

32   "When your country . . .": David Horowitz, "The Peace Movement Isn't About Peace," Frontpagemag.com, January 22, 2003.

TWO: "THE 'WAR' ON TERROR"

38   "George Bush was not . . .": David Frum, *The Right Man*. New York: Random House, 2003, p. 272–274.

39   "barely five hours . . .": "Plans for Attack Began on 9/11," Cbsnews.com, September 4, 2002.

39   "The British government . . .": President George W. Bush, State of the Union Address, January 28, 2003.

40   "Three senior administration . . .": Jonathan S. Landay, "White House Was Warned of Dubious Intelligence Used in Speech, Official Says," *Knight Ridder Newspaper*, June 13, 2003.

40   "Based on my experience . . .": Joseph C. Wilson, "What I Didn't Find in Africa," *New York Times*, July 6, 2003.

40   "Knowing all that we know . . .": Walter Pincus, "White House Backs Off Claim on Iraqi Buy," *Washington Post*, July 8, 2003.

40   "technically correct": Donald Rumsfeld, *Meet the Press*, NBC, July 13, 2003.

41   "First, CIA approved . . .": John Solomon, "Tenet Says CIA Erred in Letting Bush Make Iraq Nuclear Deal Allegations," Associated Press, July 11, 2003.

41   "We did not know . . .": Condoleezza Rice, *Meet the Press*, NBC, June 8, 2003.

42   "I was with Secretary Powell . . .": Condoleezza Rice, White House press briefing aboard *Air Force One*, July 11, 2003.

42   "had to go into bargaining mode . . .": Greg Miller, "CIA Names Bush Aide in Speech Scandal," *Los Angeles Times*, July 18, 2003.

42   "There is still a dispute . . .": David E. Singer and James Risen, "C.I.A. Chief Takes Blame in Assertion On Iraqi Uranium," *New York Times*, July 12, 2003.

43   "Saddam Hussein is actively . . .": Condoleezza Rice, *Late Edition*, CNN, September 8, 2002.

43   "considers it far more likely . . .": James Risen, David E. Sanger and Thom Shanker, "In Sketchy Data, Trying to Gauge Iraq Threat," *New York Times*, July 20, 2003.

43   "By themselves . . .": Joby Warrick, "Evidence on Iraq Challenged; Experts

Question If Tubes Were Meant for Weapons Program," *Washington Post*, September 19, 2002.

44   "I became dismayed . . .": Spencer Ackerman and John. B. Judis, "The First Casualty," *New Republic*, June 30, 2003.

44   "The administration ignored . . .": *Ibid*

44   "In Nashville . . .": *Ibid*

45   "Increasingly, we believe . . .": Dick Cheney, *Meet the Press*, NBC, September 8, 2002.

45   "It possesses and produces . . .": President George W. Bush, Remarks on Iraq, *Federal Document Clearinghouse*, October 7, 2002.

45   "Baghdad for now appears . . .": P. Mitchell Prothero, "Congress Debates Iraq Resolution," United Press International, October 8, 2002.

45   "The Central Intelligence Agency . . .": James Risen, "Terror Acts By Baghdad Have Waned, U.S. Aides Say," *New York Times*, February 6, 2002.

45   "We have sources . . .": President George W. Bush, Weekly Radio Address, *Federal Document Clearinghouse*, February 8, 2003.

45   "intelligence gathered . . .": President George W. Bush, Remarks, Washington, D.C., *Federal Document Clearinghouse*, March 17, 2003.

45   "we know where they are . . .": Donald Rumsfeld, *This Week with George Stephanopoulos*, ABC, March 30, 2003.

46   "no reliable information . . .": Esther Schrader, "Pentagon Agency Lacked Proof of Iraqi Chemical Arms," *Los Angeles Times*, June 7, 2003.

47   "There's no automaticity . . .": Maggie Farley and Maura Reynolds, "U.N. Measures on Iraqi Arms Near Passage," *Los Angeles Times*, November 8, 2002.

47   "six months away . . .": Remarks by President Bush and Prime Minister Blair to Press Pool at Camp David, *Federal Document Clearinghouse*, September 7, 2002.

47   "There's never been a report . . .": Joseph Curl, "Agency Disavows Report on Iraq Arms," *Washington Times*, September 27, 2002.

47   "But you know . . .": *Hannity & Colmes*, Fox News Channel, February 13, 2003.

48   "Yet despite . . ." David S. Cloud, "Bush's Efforts to Link Hussein to Al Qaeda Lack Evidence," *Wall Street Journal*, October 22, 2002.

49   "Zarqawi was not . . .": Dana Priest and Walter Pincus, "bin Laden-Hussein Link Hazy; U.S. Officials Qualify Statements on Possible Terrorist Ties," *Washington Post*, February 13, 2003.

49   "it's inconceivable . . .": *Ibid*.

49   "The CIA Director . . .": *Ibid*.

49   "At the Federal . . .": James Risen and David Johnston, "Threats and Responses: Terror Links; Split at C.I.A. and F.B.I. On Iraqi Ties to Al Qaeda," *New York Times*, February 2, 2003.

49   "Osama bin Laden . . .": James Risen, "Threats and Responses: CIA; Captives Deny Qaeda Worked with Baghdad," *New York Times*, June 9, 2003.

49   "spokesmen at the White House . . .": *Ibid*.

50   "Liberal democracy . . .": Greg Miller, "Showdown with Iraq: Democracy Domino Theory 'Not Credible'," *Los Angeles Times*, March 14, 2003.

50   "for missions . . .": Dana Millbank, "For Bush, Facts Are Malleable; Presidential Tradition Of Embroidering Key Assertions Continues," *Washington Post*, October 22, 2002.

50   "Blix disputed . . .": Judith Miller and Julia Preston, "The Inspector; Blix Says He
      Saw Nothing to Prompt a War," *New York Times*, January 31, 2003.

50   "I would call . . .": Remarks on Iraq by U.S. Secretary of State Colin L. Powell to the
      United Nations General Assembly, *Defense & Foreign Affairs Daily*, January 29,
      2003.

51   "It was a shock . . .": Jill Lawless, "British Government Admits It Erred in Not
      Crediting U.S. Academic's Work Copied in Iraq Dossier," Associated Press,
      February 7, 2003.

51   "If we don't stop extending . . .": Governor George W. Bush and Vice President Al
      Gore, Presidential Debate, *Federal Document Clearinghouse*, October 3, 2000.

52   ". . . shouldn't we be rising . . .": *Hannity & Colmes*, Fox News Channel, March 19,
      2003.

54   "Freedom's untidy . . .": Pamela Hess, "Rumsfeld: Looting Is Transition to
      Freedom," *United Press International*, April 11, 2003.

54   "Our efforts focus on . . .": Niko Price, "AP, in First Nationwide Tally of Iraqi Civilian
      War Deaths, Counts at Least 3,240," Associated Press, June 10, 2003.

54   "However, a five-week investigation . . .": *Ibid*.

55   "we can no longer . . .": Letter to President Clinton from the Project for the New
      American Century, January 26, 1998.

55   "Indeed, the United States . . .": Thomas Donnelly, Donald Kagan and Gary
      Schmitt, "Rebuilding America's Defenses: Strategies, Forces and Resources for
      a New Century," Project for the New American Century, September 2000,
      p. 14.

55   "We weren't attacked . . .": Molly Ivins, "Come out, come out, wherever you are,"
      Chicago Tribune, November 21, 2002.

55   "I want justice . . .": Martin Walker, "Dow Falls, bin Laden Wanted 'Dead or Alive',"
      United Press International, September 17, 2001.

55   "I truly am not . . .": Scott Lindlaw, "Bush Says Saddam Still a Menace, but Dismisses
      bin Laden as Nearly Irrelevant," Associated Press, March 14, 2002.

56   "The young members . . .": Patrick Tyler, "Fearing Harm, bin Laden Kin Fled from
      U.S.," *New York Times*, September 30, 2001.

56   "A spokesman for the Saudi Arabian . . .": Andrew Buncombe, "Fears of Reprisal
      Force bin Laden Family to Flee Their Homes," *Independent* (London),
      September 26, 2001.

56   "A Saudi diplomat . . .": Kevin Cullen, "Saudi Diplomat: I.D.s Were Stolen," *Boston
      Globe*, September 29, 2001.

57   "In late 2002 . . .": Ron Fournier, "War on Terrorism (Con't): Tops Bush's Re-
      election Agenda," *Associated Press*, December 28, 2002.

57   "We can go . . .": Jim Vertuno, "Rove Touts Republicans as Tougher on Terrorism,
      Drawing Sharp Rebuke from Democrats," Associated Press, January 18, 2002.

58   "You may want . . .": Tom Ridge, *The NewsHour with Jim Lehrer*, PBS, February 19,
      2003.

58   "As it happens 46 percent . . .": Cliff Radel, "Duct and Cover: Terrorists Are No
      Match for Our Tape," *Cincinnati Enquirer*, February 15, 2003.

58   "John Kahl, gave . . .": Center for Responsive Politics, www.opensecrets.org

58   "If we tried . . .": Bob Woodward, *Bush At War*. New York: Simon & Schuster, 2002,
      p. 84.

58   "war against Iraq . . ." *Ibid*.

59 "I am deeply . . .": Jim Abrams, "Senator Links Biological Shipments To Persian Gulf Illnesses," Associated Press, February 9, 1994.

59 "Among the people . . .": Michael Dobbs, "U.S. Had Key Role in Iraq Buildup; Trade in Chemical Arms Allowed Despite Their Use on Iranians, Kurds," *Washington Post*, December 30, 2002.

60 "In a September interview . . .": *Ibid.*

60 "On February 25, 2003 . . .": Report, the National Security Archive at George Washington University, February 25, 2003.

61 "14 consignments . . .": "Russia Denies Report It Helped Iraq Develop Biological Weapons; British Television Says United States Assisted Iraqi Arms Programs," *Baltimore Sun*, February 13, 1998.

61 "At least . . .": *Ibid.*

62 "$1.5 billion worth . . .": Henry Weinstein and William C. Rempel, "Iraq Arms: Big Help From U.S.; Technology Was Sold With Approval—And Encouragement—From the Commerce Department But Often Over Defense Officials' Objections," *Los Angeles Times*, February 13, 1991.

62 "advanced computers . . .": *Ibid.*

62 "sixty Hughes helicopters . . .": *Ibid.*

62 "We believe . . .": *Ibid.*

62 "In 1988 . . .": Henry Weinstein and William C. Rempel, "Iraq Arms: Big Help From U.S.; Technology Was Sold With Approval—And Encouragement—From the Commerce Department But Often Over Defense Officials' Objections," *Los Angeles Times*, February 13, 1991.

62 "The (American) helicopters . . .": Christopher Dickey and Evan Thomas, "How Saddam Happened," *Newsweek*, September 23, 2002.

63 "During last year's presidential campaign . . .": Colum Lynch, "Firm's Iraq Deals Greater Than Cheney Has Said; Affiliates Had $73 Million in Contracts," *Washington Post*, June 23, 2001.

63 "No, no, I had a firm policy . . .": Dick Cheney, *This Week*, ABC, July 30, 2000.

63 "No. No. I made the statement . . .": Dick Cheney, *This Week* ABC, August 27, 2000.

63 "signed contracts . . .": Colum Lynch, "Firm's Iraq Deals Greater Than Cheney Has Said; Affiliates Had $73 Million in Contracts," *Washington Post*, June 23, 2001.

64 "Let me cite to you . . .": White House Press Briefing, March 24, 2003.

65 "a quarter of the world's oil . . .": "There's Oil In Them Thar Sands," *Economist*, June 28, 2003.

65 "sixty thousand barrels a day . . .": H. Josef Hebert, "Clinton Asks Oil-Producing Countries for Increased Production," Associated Press, March17, 2000.

65 "Trying to eliminate . . .": George Bush and Brent Scowcroft, *A World Transformed*. New York: Knopf, 1998, p. 489.

66 "We should not . . .": *Ibid.*

66 "The Gulf War . . ." *Ibid.*

66 "America will become . . .": The U.S. Commission on National Security/21st Century, "Road Map for National Security: Imperative for Change," January 31, 2001, pp. 8, 19.

67 "contributed $1.6 million . . .": Center for Responsive Politics, www.opensecrets.org.

68 "was another beneficiary of Lilly's largess . . .": Jonathan D. Salant, "Doctors, Drug Companies Back Senator Frist," Associated Press, January 11, 2003.

69 "Do you support it?": *Hannity & Colmes*, Fox News Channel, November 19, 2002.

70   "Airlines failed to enforce . . .": Jonathan D. Salant, "Pre-9/11 Rules Barred Box Cutters," Associated Press, November 11, 2002.

70   "Most prominent . . .": David Firestone, "Domestic Security Bill Riles 9/11 Families," *New York Times*, November 26, 2002.

71   "two-lie answer": Molly Ivins, "Kissinger Back at His Game: Covering Up," *Chicago Tribune*, December 12, 2002.

72   "A year after September 11 . . .": Gary Hart and Warren Rudman, "America Still Unprepared, America Still in Danger," Special Taskforce Sponsored by the Council on Foreign Relations, October 2002, p. 9.

73   "that while 95 percent . . .": Editorial, "Secure All Hatches At America's Ports," *Newsday* (New York), March 16, 2003.

74   "I would argue that . . .": *Hannity & Colmes*, Fox News Channel, January 2, 2003.

76   "the United States was spending . . .": Tony Karon, "Why U.S. Soldiers Aren't Leaving Iraq Yet," *Time*, July 17, 2003.

76   "In November, the Afghan . . .": Frida Berrigan, "Afghan War Is Cheaper Than Peace," *San Diego Tribune*, December 12, 2002.

76   "Eric Margolis . . .": Eric Margolis, "Déjà Vu in Afghanistan," *Toronto Sun*, December 19, 2002.

76   "Afghanistan is a model . . .": Donald Rumsfeld, Department of Defense Briefing, August 9, 2002.

77   "But there is nothing . . .": Barton Gellman, "In U.S.; Terrorism's Peril Undiminished: Nation Struggles on Offense and Defense, and Officials Still Expect New Attacks," *Washington Post*, December 24, 2002.

78   "a new relationship based on . . .": Matthew Engel, "The Fall of Kabul: Missiles: Bush Tells Putin He Will Slash Warheads: Russian Leader Welcomes Offer but Fails to Match It," *Guardian*, November 14, 2001.

78   "I looked into his eyes . . .": Bennett Roth, "Bush Says Rift with Putin Can Be Mended; President Visits Russia, Aims to Ease Tensions," *Houston Chronicle*, June 1, 2003.

78   "Congress approved $1.5 billion . . .": David Firestone, "Administration to Delay Aid To Local Law Enforcement," *New York Times*, December 4, 2002.

THREE: UNCIVIL LIBERTIES

85   "We should not forget . . .": Noam Chomsky, *9–11*. New York: Seven Stories Press, 2002, p. 40.

85   "we have to examine . . .": "Punishment with Justice, but No Vengeance," *Agence France Press*, October 1, 2001.

86   "Let's get the . . .": Daniel Ellsberg, *Secrets: A Memoir of Vietnam and the Pentagon Papers*. New York, Viking Press, 2002, p. 432.

87   "It looks as if they're nervous . . .": *Public Citizen*, Press Release, December 20, 2001.

89   "In the twelve months ending . . .": Adam Clymer, "Government Openness at Issue As Bush Holds On to Records," *New York Times*, January 3, 2003.

89   "George Bush is getting money . . .": Leslie Wayne, "Elder Bush in Big G.O.P. Cast Toiling for Top Equity Firm," *New York Times*, March 5, 2001.

90   "The objective is to capture terrorists . . .": Seymour Hersh, "The Bush Administration's New Strategy in the War on Terrorism," *New Yorker*, December 23, 2002.

90 "They want to turn these guys . . .": *Ibid.*

91 "President Bush declared an 'extraordinary emergency' . . .": George Lardner and Peter Slevin, "Military May Try Terrorism Cases; Bush Cites 'Emergency'," *Washington Post*, November 14, 2001.

91 "to those who scare peace loving people . . .": John Ashcroft, Hearing of the Senate Judiciary Committee. *Federal News Service*, December 6, 2001.

91 "They that can give up . . .": John Bartlett, *Familiar Quotations*, 10th ed. 1919.

91 "I don't want to hear two messages . . .": John Ashcroft, Hearing of the Senate Judiciary Committee. *Federal News Service*, December 6, 2001.

91 "suspected terrorists were able to acquire guns . . .": Susan Page, "Terrorists Use Gun Shows, McCain Says," *USA Today*, November 28, 2001.

92 "We face a drastic shortage of linguists . . .": Margie Mason, "Military Boots Six Gay Arab Linguists Despite Shortage," Associated Press, November 15, 2002.

92 "In 1993, after the first World Trade Center bombing . . .": "Evidence Mounts That Sept. 11 Was Predictable," *USA Today*, October 15, 2001.

93 "Mr. Padilla is an American . . .": Joel Connelly, "Reagan-Appointed Judge Has Words for Ashcroft," *Seattle Post-Intelligencer*, July 15, 2002.

94 "Undiscriminating executions or punishments . . .": "We Are the War Criminals Now," *Independent* (London), November 29, 2001.

95 "They were denied access to community . . .": Megan Garvey, Martha Groves and Henry Weinstein. "Hundreds Are Detained After Visits to INS," *Los Angeles Times*, December 19, 2002.

95 "With a warrant, FBI agents may now enter . . .": Nat Hentoff, "The End of Privacy; The Patriot Act's Un-American Incursion on Liberty," *Washington Times*, June 3, 2002.

96 "if I was in charge, I would execute . . .": Philip Shenon, "Report on U.S. Antiterrorism Law Alleges Violations of Civil Rights," *New York Times*, July 21, 2003.

97 "Every purchase you make with a credit card . . .": William Safire, "You Are a Suspect" *New York Times*, November 14, 2002.

97 "made a very deliberate decision . . .": "Poindexter's Bombshells; Reagan Shielded on Diversion, Contradicted on Iran Deal; Admiral Says He Tore Up Signed Document," *Los Angeles Times*, July 15, 1987.

98 "Without due process, of which probable cause . . .": Andrew Napolitano, "Don't Tread on Freedom," *New Jersey Law Journal*, October 15, 2001.

99 "In a democracy, personal liberties . . .": *Ibid.*

100 "In Germany, they first . . .": Dale Turner, "Neutrality, Injustice in the Face of Wrong Crucify Jesus Anew," *Seattle Times*, April 12, 2003.

FOUR: THE MYTH OF THE LIBERAL MEDIA

101 "Any dictator would admire," Noam Chomsky.

101 "the national TV news appeared to be . . .": Mark Crispan Miller, "What's Wrong with This Picture?," *The Nation*, January 7, 2002.

102 "its stranglehold on the cultural life . . .": Stanley Kurtz, "Cultural Shift," *National Review Online*, January 11, 2002.

103 "I admit it: the liberal media . . ." *New Yorker*, May 22, 1995.

103   "The truth is, I've gotten fairer . . .": "Washington Insight/Campaign '96," *Los Angeles Times*, March 14, 1996.

105   "Two of these three major . . .": E.J. Dionne, "The Rightward Press," *Washington Post*, December 6, 2002.

105   "a preference for the values . . .": *Ibid.*

106   "the survey revealed that the nation's newspapers . . .": Greg Mitchel, "E&P/TIPP poll." *Editor and Publisher*, November 6, 2000.

106   "The *Editor & Publisher*/TIPP poll . . .": *Ibid.*

106   "how much would I have to pay you . . .": David Bauder, "Congressman Says GE's Jack Welch Spent Two Hours at NBC Decision Desk on Election Night," Associated Press, September 11, 2001.

106   "Congressman Waxman comes up with the shocking revelation . . .": Doug Halonen, "Waxman Still Critical of Welch's Actions," *Electronic Media*, September 17, 2001.

108   "As for talk radio, the numbers . . .": "Talk Radio Research Project," *Talkers*, May, 2003.

109   "The January 6 [2002] list was chock full . . .": Stanley Kurtz, "Cultural Shift," *National Review Online*, January 11, 2002.

109   "You singled out Fox News . . .": *Hannity & Colmes*, Fox News Channel, December 10, 2002.

111   "Indeed, in its August 13, 2003, edition . . .": Andrew Grossman, *Hollywood Reporter*, August 13, 2003.

111   "A Pew Research Center poll of 3,002 adults . . .": Mark Jurkowitz, "Survey Finds Americans Tuning Out World News," *Boston Globe*, June 10, 2002.

114   "The Media Research Center . . .": Stephen Dinan, "Inside Politics," *Washington Times*, June 26, 2002.

114   "I did find a big disparity . . .": Geoffrey Nunberg, *Fresh Air*, National Public Radio, March 19, 2002.

114   "Bob Somerby . . .": "Bugging Bernie," dailyhowler.com, January 12, 2002.

115   "I also choose not to . . ." Bernard Goldberg, *Bias: A CBS Insider Exposes How the Media Distorts the News*. New York: HarperCollins, 2001, p. 80.

115   "The 175-bed shelter in this city . . .": Bob Jamieson, "Slowdown of Economy Causing Number of Homeless to Rise," *ABC World News Tonight*, ABC, February 11, 2001.

115   "It's not just New York City . . ." Brian Palmer, "New York's Homeless Face Incredible Challenges," *CNN Saturday Morning News*, CNN, August 4, 2001.

116   "*Bias* should be taken seriously," Janet Maslin, "A Network Veteran Bites the Hands That Fed Him," *New York Times*, December 13, 2001.

116   "I would say ninety percent . . .": Jonathan Chait, "The Contradictions of Conservative Media Criticism," *New Republic*, March 18, 2002.

116   "During my service in the United States . . .": Al Gore, *Inside Politics*, CNN, March 9, 1999.

116   "was the leader in Congress on the connections . . .": Michelle Mittelstadt, "Republicans Pounce on Gore's Claim That He Created the Internet," Associated Press, March 11, 1999.

116   "If the Vice President created the Internet . . .": *Ibid.*

116   " 'Created' morphed to 'invented' . . .": "Inventing the Internet," *USA Today*, March 15, 1999.

117   "I called for a congressional investigation . . .": Hadley Pawlak, "Gore Moves Quickly to Explain Latest Exaggeration," Associated Press, December 1, 1999.

117   "Gore boasted about his efforts . . .": Ceci Connolly, "Gore Paints Himself As No Beltway Baby; On Stump in New Hampshire, Vice President Highlights Days As a 'Home Builder,' 'Soldier'," *Washington Post*, December 1, 1999.

118   "But to be fair, it is not true . . .": Jeff Jacoby, "The Real Meaning of Willie Horton," *Boston Globe*, January 20, 2000.

119   "We can clean up pollution . . .": Joann Lovigilio, "Gore Talks Energy Conservation in Philadelphia," Associated Press, June 27, 2000.

119   "Texas released more than . . .": The Environmental Laboratory Washington Report, June 10, 1999.

119   "During Bush's tenure with Harken . . .": Karin Meadows, "Bush Helped Lead Petroleum Company Slow to Clean Up Pollution," Associated Press, October 6, 2000.

120   "Energy Secretary Spencer Abraham met . . .": Dana Milbank and Mike Allen, "U.S. Court Upholds New Air Pollution Control Standards," *Washington Post*, March 31, 2002.

120   "The Bush administration . . .": Dana Milbank and Mike Allen, "Energy Contacts Disclosed; Consumer Groups Left Out, Data Show," *Washington Post*, March 26, 2002.

120   "federal agents to seize . . .": "A Degrading Energy Plan," *Boston Globe*, August 3, 2001.

121   "any potential benefit . . .": "Preserving Artic Paradise," *Boston Globe*, February 21, 2001.

121   "If you want to do . . .": Dick Cheney, *Hardball*, CNBC, March 21, 2001.

122   "Bill Burkett, a former lieutenant-colonel . . .": Tom Rhodes and Matthew Campbell, "Bush Holds Narrow Lead Despite Last Minute Row," *Sunday Times* (London), November 5, 2000.

122   "Bush himself, in his 1999 autobiography . . .": Walter Robinson, "1-Year Gap in Bush's Guard Duty; No Record of Airman At Drills 1972–73," *Boston Globe*, May 23, 2000.

122   ". . .both accounts . . .": *Ibid.*

122   "Lt. Bush has not been . . .": *Ibid.*

123   "I worked for Bill Clinton in 1992 . . .": Paul Begala, *UAW Legislative Conference*, February 6, 2001.

123   "Yes, I flew it,": Scott Lindlaw, "President on Board Aircraft Carrier Says 'Difficult Work' Remains in Iraq" Associated Press, May 1, 2003.

124   "Juanita Broaddrick's story became widely known . . .": Greg Pierce, "Inside Politcs," *Washington Times*, December 21, 1999.

124   "a modern-day Joan of Arc.": "Jones Advisor Denies She Is Seeking Book Deal," *Chicago Tribune*, October 27, 1997.

124   "no substantial and credible evidence . . .": Peter Yost, "Ray: 'No Credible Evidence' of Crimes Regarding GOP Files," Associated Press, March 16, 2000.

125   "Even if she does stake out . . .": "Getting the Message," *New Republic*, November 25, 2002.

125   "a disaster for the Democrats": "A New Face for Democrats," *Economist*, November 16, 2002.

126   "But Alan, you know that that outfit . . .": *Hannity & Colmes*, Fox News Channel, November 26, 2002.

126   "Between 1979 and 1997 . . .": "In Bush budget, tax cuts for top one percent are larger than health, education and all other initiatives combined." *Center on Budget and Policy Priorities*, March 2, 2001.

127   "The First Amendment . . . rests on the assumption . . .": Justice Hugo Black, *Associated Press v. United States*, 326 U.S. (1945).

FIVE: STRAW MEN, HYPOCRISY,
AND CONSERVATIVE LIES

129   "Conservatives are more likely . . .": Suzanne Fields, "Conservatives don nonchalance of understatement," *Washington Post*, January 9, 2003.

131   "I hope I never have . . .": *Larry King Live*, CNN, July 22, 1992.

131   "she'll take the child . . .": W. Dale Nelson, "Quayle Says He'd Support Daughter on Any Abortion Decision," Associated Press, July 23, 1992.

132   "didn't bet the milk money . . .": Jonathan Alter and Joshua Green, "The Man of Virtues Has a Vice," *Newsweek*, May 2, 2003.

133   "The House responded . . .": George W. Bush Participates in Welcome Ceremony, Trenton, New Jersey, *Federal Document Clearinghouse*, September 23, 2002.

133   "You tell those . . .": Jim Abrams, "Daschle Accuses President of Seeking to Politicize Debate over Iraq," Associated Press, September 25, 2002.

134   "What do Saddam . . .": Dana Milbank, "A Double-Barreled Attack on Daschle," *Washington Post*, November 9, 2001.

134   "Formerly admired . . .": Jimmy Carter, "The Troubling New Face of America," *Washington Post*, September 5, 2002.

135   "you'll hear more . . .": *Hannity & Colmes*, Fox News Channel, November 20, 2002.

136   "Jimmy Carter will probably not go down . . .": Doug Mellgren, "Nobel Laureate Jimmy Carter Urges Peace in a 'More Dangerous' World," Associated Press, December 10, 2003.

136   "It's now the Nobel . . .": *Hannity & Colmes*, Fox News Channel, October 15, 2002.

138   "democratic hemisphere": Text of Jimmy Carter speech broadcast to Cuban people, Associated Press, May 14, 2002.

138   "We knew he (bin Laden) . . .": Jamie Herzlich and Christian Murray, "Clinton: U.S. Should Increase Foreign Aid," *Newsday*, February 16, 2002.

139   "U.S. government representatives . . .": Letter to the Editor, *Vanity Fair*, December 7, 2001.

140   "By any measure available . . .": Barton Gellman, "Struggles Inside the Government Defined Campaign," *Washington Post*, December 20, 2001.

141   "The Sudan factory . . .": E-mail to author from Sandy Berger, July 23, 2003.

141   "We need to keep this country . . .": Terence Hunt, "Clinton: Fighting Terrorism 'a Long Hard Struggle,'" Associated Press, July 30, 1996.

142   "phony issue": Harry F. Rosenthal, International News, *Chicago Tribune*, July 30, 1996.

143   "A number of initiatives . . .": *CBS Evening News*, CBS, August 5, 2002.

143   "Once we were going . . .": Michael Elliott, "Could 9/11 Have Been Prevented?," *Time*, August 4, 2002.

144 "gave $43 million . . .": Editorial, "Bad Actors; Afghanistan's Taliban Regime Is Brutal and Harsh—So Why Does Washington Send It Aid?," *Newsday*, May 29, 2001.

144 "froze $254 million . . .": Mark Fineman, "Victims Lining Up to Tap Terrorists' Frozen Assets; Money: Those Injured in 1998 Embassy Bombings Have Filed Claims. Recent U.S. Victims Also Likely Will Seek Compensation," *Los Angeles Times*, October 12, 2001.

145 "What I am condemning . . .": Japan Mathebula, "Mandela Calls Bush Shortsighted and Arrogant for Iraq Policy," Associated Press, January 30, 2003.

145 "Questions are swirling . . .": "Clinton Behind Mandela's Bush-Bashing?," *Newsmax.com*, February 1, 2003.

146 "Why won't the same media . . .": Carl Limbacher, "Racist Cover-Up in Story of Clinton's 'Illegitimate Son'?," *Newsmax.com*, December 15, 1998.

147 "whether the FBI Lab's . . .": Carl Limbacher, "Clinton Paternity 'Test' Called Into Question," *Newsmax.com*, January 18, 1999.

147 "When he was elected . . .": Vital Statistics on the Presidency, *CQ Guide to U.S. Elections*, Federal Election Commission.

148 "A prominent conservative . . .": Robert Novak, "Daschle Could Not Get the Rebels to Abandon Their Rebellion, But Clinton Did," *Chicago Sun-Times*, January 19, 2003.

148 "I think there are a lot of reasons . . .": *Hardball*, MSNBC, November 20, 2002.

149 "The Bush camp . . .": Andrew Miga, "Campaign 2000: Electoral, Popular Vote Split Could Get Ugly," *Boston Herald*, November 3, 2000.

149 "I think we ought . . .": Dan Balz, "House GOP Sets Protest On Seating: Disputed Election in Indiana District Prompts Disruption," *Washington Post*, April 23, 1985.

150 "political and moral outrage . . ." *Ibid.*

150 "damned robbery": *Ibid.*

150 "We can also comfortably . . . : Kathleen Parker, "Hard to Forgive Democrats' Divisiveness," *Chicago Tribune*, November 29, 2000.

150 "Almost half . . .": Rep. Gene Taylor, "The Reagan Administration, Taxes, & Trust Funds," www.house.gov/genetaylor/, April 16, 2001.

150 "When Reagan assumed office in January 1981 . . .": United States Office of Management and Budget, *Statistical Abstract of the United States 2002*, Table #449, p. 305.

152 "the wealthiest 1 percent . . .": David E. Rosenbaum, "Selling Tax Breaks for the Wealthiest," *New York Times*, December 22, 2002.

152 "the increasing reliance . . .": *Ibid.*

153 "A federal tax rebate . . .": Bruce Bartlett, "Tax Rebates Won't Stimulate the Economy," *Wall Street Journal*, November 1, 2001.

153 "According to IRS data": Joel Friedman, "Who Belongs to the Investor Class?" *Center on Budget and Policy Priorities*, January 23, 2002.

154 "he offered $10 billion in new money . . .": President George W. Bush, State of the Union Address, January 28, 2003.

154 "Yes, I know all the bad things . . .": David Hoffman, "Visit 'Morally Right' Reagan Says of Bitburg: Reporters Are Blamed for Controversy," *Washington Post*, April 30, 1985.

154 ". . . in his 1965 autobiography . . .": Al Hunt, "The Non-Character Issue," *Wall Street Journal*, September 28, 2000.

155   "At the time of the 1963 tax cuts . . .": Thomas Oliphant, "A Shameless Misuse of JFK's Name," *Boston Globe*, March 27, 2001.

155   "It stretches decency a bit . . .": Marsha Mercer, "Bush Takes Tax Cut Plan to Key Foe's Turf," *Richmond Times Dispatch*, March 10, 2001.

155   "It is intellectually dishonest . . .": Dana Bash, "Senator Kennedy asks conservative group to stop using tapes of JFK," CNN.com, March 12, 2001.

156   "In his book . . .": Dinesh D'Souza, *The End of Racism: Principles for a Multicultural Society*. New York: Free Press, 1995, p. 113.

156   "compensatory consideration": Leonard Greene, "King's Legacy; Listen to His Whole Message," *New York Post*, January 20, 2003.

156   "A society that has done . . .": Kimberle Crenshaw, "Fighting the Post Affirmative Action War," *Essence*, July, 1998.

156   "proved to be the transmission . . .": Dinesh D'Souza, "The West's Secrets of Success," *Chicago Sun-Times*, April 28, 2002.

157   "If the question . . .": W. Dale Nelson, "Cannon Book Portrays Reagan as Strong Man, Weak Manager," Associated Press, April 22, 1991.

157   "Maybe I would have had a stronger . . .": David S. Broder, "Bush Asserts Vindication in Iran Affair; Says Key Facts Were Denied Him," *Washington Post*, August 6, 1987.

157   "According to a memo . . .": David S. Broder, "Two Would-Be Trumans Charge Into Fall Campaign; Clinton Challenges Press to Examine 'Veracity' of President on Iran-Contra," *Washington Post*, September 8, 1992.

157   "The Iran operations . . .": "Excerpts From the Iran-Contra Report: A Secret Foreign Policy," *New York Times*, January 19, 1994.

158   "Some of them are pathetic . . .": Jonathan Rauch, "Is There An Excuse for George Nethercutt?," *National Journal*, August 12, 2000.

158   "Your word . . .": John Hughes, "Northwest Lawmakers Take a Wait-and-See Attitude with Clinton," Associated Press, August 18, 1998.

159   ". . . a number of new developments . . .": Testimony Confirmation Spencer Abraham for Energy Secretary, Senate Energy and Resources Committee, *Federal Document Clearinghouse*, January 18, 2001.

160   "*expanded* the federal payroll by 61,000 . . .": Paul Hyde, "GOP Now Loves Big Government," *Greenville News*, January 31, 2003.

160   "Since the 1960s . . .": Jeffery Frankel, "Trading Places: Republicans' Economic Policy Is Now Closer to That Associated with the Democrats, and Vice Versa," *Financial Times*, September 13, 2002.

160   "Highlights include . . .": *Ibid.*

160   "Graham and other . . .": Paul Hyde, "GOP Now Loves Big Government," *Greenville News*, January 31, 2003.

160   "The era of big government . . .": Jeffrey H. Birnbaum, "The Return of Big Government; Federal Spending Is Skyrocketing, but Shockingly Little of It is Related to Sept. 11," *Fortune*, September 16, 2002.

161   "While $30 billion . . .": *Ibid.*

161   "A 1999 study . . .": Jeff Grabmeier, "Study Finds Unprecedented Delay In Appointing Federal Judges," *Ohio University Research News*, August 25, 1999.

162   "would be an unconscionable . . .": Suzanne Gamboa, "Controversy Emerges Around Next Bush Judicial Appointee," Associated Press, July 16, 2002.

162 "$8,600 from Enron . . .": Marianne Means, "Bush Overreacts to Failed
     Nomination," *Seattle Post-Intelligencer*, September 13, 2002.
163 "obtrusive": Todd S. Burroughs, "Rights Groups Oppose Bush's Court Nominee,"
     New Pittsburgh Courier, February 9, 2002.
163 "I did not spend . . .": Testimony Confirmation of Clarence Thomas for Supreme
     Court, Senate Judiciary Committee, September 11, 1991.
163 "If you are asking me . . .": *Ibid.*
163 "Senator, your question to me . . .": *Ibid.*
164 "he solicited letters of commendation . . .": R. Jeffrey Smith, "Judge's Fate Could
     Turn on 1994 Case," *Washington Post*, May 27, 2003.
164 "deliberate pattern of . . .": Jesse J. Holland, "Republican, Democrat Relations
     Breaking Down in Senate After Divisive Pickering Vote," Associated Press, March
     15, 2002.
165 "Determining which . . .": Sen. Orrin Hatch, "Judicial Activism: Usurping the
     Constitution and Legislative Powers," Address at the University of Utah,
     February 18, 1997.
165 "declared . . . he'd block": Jim Abrams, "Senator Accuses White House of Violating
     Pact on Recess Appointments," Associated Press, December 21, 1999.
166 "Senate Republican Leader . . .": E.J. Dionne, "Base Politics," *Washington Post*, May 14,
     2002.
166 "I would feel the same way . . .": John Bresnahan, "Senators Divided Over Gay
     Nominee," *Roll Call*, May 18, 1998.
167 "You should try to show . . .": Jim Abrams, "Senators Push for Gay Nominee Vote,"
     Associated Press, June 16, 1998.
167 "So you may . . .": *Meet the Press*, NBC, February 24, 2002.
167 "the Pentagon . . .": Matt Kelley, "Rumsfeld Says Pentagon Closing Heavily
     Criticized Office of Strategic Influence," Associated Press, February 26, 2002.
168 "And then there was . . .": Secretary Rumsfeld Media Availability En Route to Chile,
     November 18, 2002.
168 "The President began . . .": Rep. Tom Delay, "Removal Of United States Armed
     Forces From the Federal Republic of Yugoslavia," *Congressional Record*, April 28,
     1999.
168 "I normally . . .": *Ibid.*
168 "I'm saddened . . .": Ken Guggenheim, "Daschle: Bush Diplomacy Fails 'Miserably',"
     Associated Press, March 17, 2003.
169 "For us to call . . .": Rep. Tom DeLay, Floor Statement opposing resolution
     commending America's successful campaign in Kosovo, July 1, 1999.
169 "This is President . . .": Tim Weiner, "Crisis in the Balkans; The Debate: Try Harder
     To Win War, McCain Bill Would Urge," *New York Times*, May 4, 1999.
169 "A lackluster . . .": Alison Mitchell, "Kosovo Is Causing Breaks and Shifts in the 2
     Parties," *New York Times*, April 8, 1999.
169 "Bush, in Austin . . .": R.G. Ratcliffe, "Bush Toughens His Stance on NATO
     Bombing," *Houston Chronicle*, April 9, 1999.
170 "And I do think . . .": Helen Dewar, "Lott Retreats From Criticism of Airstrikes,"
     Washington Post, December 18, 1998.
170 "This president is shameless . . .": Wendy Koch and Judy Keen, "President's Timing
     Under Fire Some in GOP See Trust as the Issue," *USA Today*, December 17,
     1998.

170   "While I have been assured . . .": Tom Raum, "Lawmakers Support Airstrikes but
      Lott Questions Timing," Associated Press, December 16, 1998.

SIX: BILL CLINTON, OUR GREATEST PRESIDENT

175   "The federal government is balancing its budget . . .": Trent Lott, *Meet the Press*,
      NBC, March 26, 2000.

175   "I agree that Bill and Al are responsible . . .": Peter Baniak and Jack Brammer,
      "Clinton in Louisville to Boost Democrat's Race for Congress," *Lexington
      Herald Leader*, November 1, 2000.

175   "In order for us to have the security we all want . . .": George W. Bush, *Federal News
      Service*, July 15, 2002.

176   "a job-killer" and "one-way ticket to a recession . . .": Robert Dodge, "Clinton Tries
      to Sell Fiscal Plan to Public; Democrats Begin Rounding Up Votes," *Dallas
      Morning News*, August 4, 1993.

176   "The tax increase will kill jobs . . .": "The Clinton Budget," *Atlanta Journal-
      Constitution*, August 6, 1993.

176   "It's like a snakebite . . .": Gene Lyons, "Salvation from the Clinton Scandals; What
      Lieberman Brings to the Ticket," *Arkansas Democrat-Gazette*, August 9, 2000.

176   "April Fools' America . . .": Robert Dodge, "Senate OKs Deficit-Reduction Plan,"
      Dallas Morning News, April 2, 1993.

177   "This was happening against the backdrop . . .": Lee Davidson, "Is the Brady Bill
      doing enough?," *Deseret News (Salt Lake City, Utah)*, September 23, 2002.

178   "President Clinton will go down in history . . .": "Clinton: Enviros Praise President's
      Green Legacy," *Greenwire*, January 16, 2001.

178   "One of the top conservation presidents . . .": William Booth, "A Slow Start Built to
      an Environmental End-Run: President Went Around Congress to Build Green
      Legacy," *Washington Post*, January 13, 2001.

179   "giant sucking sound": Sara Fritz, "Perot Tactics May Be Too Unconventional to
      Have Impact," *Los Angeles Times*, October 7, 1992.

180   "I just hope and pray the decision that was made . . .": Dan Coates, News
      Conference, *Federal Document Clearing House*, August 20, 1998.

180   "There's an obvious issue that will be raised . . .": Guy Gugliotta and Juliet Eilperin,
      "Tough Response Appeals to Critics of President; Several Question Clinton's
      Timing of Raids," *Washington Post*, August 21, 1998.

180   ". . . there is a cloud over this presidency": *Ibid.*

180   "Once the fire from the retaliatory strike dies down . . .": Dana Rohrabacher, "A
      Quick Look at Reaction in Congress," CNN.com., August 28, 1998.

181   "Next year, just six . . .": *Hannity & Colmes*, Fox News Channel, December 5, 2002.

182   "as the Clintons left it . . .": Counter Clinton Library,
      www.counterclintonlibrary.com.

182   "The condition of the real property . . .": Christopher Newton, "GAO: No Evidence
      that White House Was Vandalized," Associated Press, May 18, 2001.

182   "So many fine people have come to find themselves . . .": "Text of Clinton's Letter to
      ROTC Director," Associated Press, February 13, 1992.

185   "I feel your pain, I feel your pain . . .": "Heckler Stirs Clinton Anger: Excerpts from
      the Exchange," *New York Times*, March 28, 1992.

185   "our first black president": Toni Morrison, *New Yorker*, October 1998.

186   "The United States government did something that was wrong . . .": Bill Clinton, *Federal Document Clearing House Political Transcripts*, May 16, 1997.

186   "Many thought that the African apology safari . . ." Jonah Goldberg, "Apologia Clintonia," *National Review Online*, November 23, 1999.

SEVEN: OJ IS INNOCENT

192   "Consider everything that Mr. Simpson would have had to have done . . .": Johnnie Cochran, *Closing Argument in O.J. Simpson Trial*, CNN, September 27, 1995.

192   "Problem, no match to anyone": Transcript of court proceeding, Sharon Rufo et al. vs. Orenthal James Simpson et al, Superior Court of Los Angeles, January 23, 1997. Available at www.courttv.com

193   "When he sees a 'nigger' (as he called it) . . .": "Letter from Kathleen Bell to O.J. Simpson's Lawyer," Associated Press, March 10, 1995.

193   ". . . he's probably gotten several tickets from policemen . . .": "Excerpts from Fuhrman Tapes," *USA Today*, August 30, 1995.

194   "I listen to liberals talk . . .": *Ibid.*

194   "They don't do anything . . .": Jim Newton and Bill Boyarsky, "Witnesses Tell Jury of Fuhrman's Racial Epithets," *Los Angeles Times*, September 6, 1995.

196   "had no firsthand knowledge of the group's views": Thomas Edsall, "Lott Renounces White 'Racialist' Group He Praised in 1992," *Washington Post*, December 16, 1998.

196   "I have made my condemnation of the white supremacist . . .": John Kifner, "Lott, and Shadow of a Pro-White Group," *New York Times*, January 14, 1999.

196   "The people in this room stand for the right principles . . .": *Ibid.*

196   "If racial discrimination in the interest of . . .": John Solomon, "Lott Advocated Tax Exemption for School that Banned Interracial Dating," Associated Press, December 12, 2002.

197   "I want to say this about my state . . .": Thomas Edsall, "Lott Decried For Part of Salute to Thurmond; GOP Senate Leader Hails Colleague's Run As Segregationist," *Washington Post*, December 7, 2002.

197   "All the laws of Washington and all the bayonets . . .": Jim Naughton, " 'Uncle Strom': The Pragmatist's Legacy; S.C's Thurmond, From Dixiecrat Fire-Eater to Patriarch of the GOP's Southern Strategy," *Washington Post*, November 2, 1988.

197   "A poor choice of words conveyed . . .": Jim Abrams, "Senate GOP Leader Apologizes for Remark," Associated Press, December 9, 2002.

197   "You know, if we had elected this man . . .": Thomas Edsall and Brian Faler, "Lott Remarks on Thurmond Echoed 1980 Words; Criticism Unabated Despite Apology for Comment on Former Dixiecrat's Presidential Bid," *Washington Post*, December 11, 2002.

197   "terrible" and that it was "a mistake of the head, not the heart": Jim Abrams, "Lott Expresses Regret for Remarks," Associated Press, December 11, 2002.

197   "I think he went as far as one could go . . .": Alan Colmes, *Hannity & Colmes*, Fox News Channel, December 11, 2002.

198   "I think there's too much piling on Trent Lott . . .": Alan Colmes, *The O'Reilly Factor*, Fox News Channel, December 13, 2002.

199   "Let's go over to Colmes . . .": *Ibid.*

200   "Any suggestion that the segregated past was acceptable . . .": Ron Fournier, "Bush Calls Lott's Remarks 'Offensive,' White House Says He Should Keep Senate Post," Associated Press, December 12, 2002.

200   "Something's going to have to change . . .": "Gov. Bush Says Lott's Statements Are 'Damaging' to Republicans," Associated Press, December 18, 2002.

200   "court documents show that a federal . . .": Dan Eggen and David A. Vise, "Ashcroft's Accuracy on Desegregation Challenged," *Washington Post*, January 18, 2001.

200   "charges that Ashcroft worked to suppress . . .": Nancy Gibbs and Michael Duffy, "The Fight for Justice; His Opponents Call John Ashcroft an Extremist. So Why Did George W. Bush Think He Was Picking an Attorney General Who'd Be a Cinch to Confirm?," *Time*, January 22, 2001.

201   "consummate conniver, manipulator and a liar": "Questions for Ashcroft," quoted in *Capital Times* (Madison, WI), January 16, 2001.

201   "Your magazine also helps set the record straight . . .": Derrick Jackson, "Ashcroft's Flirtations with the Racist Right," quoted in *Boston Globe*, January 10, 2001.

201   "In every stage of the bus boycott we have been oppressed . . .": Robert Caro, *Master of the Senate: The Years of Lyndon Johnson*. New York: Alfred A. Knopf, 2002, p. 767.

202   "Bad weather? No problem . . .": Bruce Alpert and Bill Walsh, "On the Hill; News from the Louisiana Delegation in the Nation's Capital," *Times-Picayune* (New Orleans, LA), December 29, 2002.

202   "Mary, if you don't respect us . . .": Katherine Seelye, "In Louisiana, a Democrat Wins a Tough Senate Race," *New York Times*, December 8, 2002.

203   "remember who changed your flag": James Salzer, "Perdue Savors Win, Courts Democrats," *Atlanta Journal-Constitution*, November 7, 2002.

204   "There are white niggers . . .": Robert Byrd, *Fox News Sunday*, Fox, March 4, 2001.

204   "We all make mistakes . . .": Susan Schmidt, "Sen. Byrd Apologizes for Racial Remarks," *Washington Post*, March 5, 2001.

204   "Conrad, how can you live back there . . .": "Senate Watch," *The Hotline*, October 21, 1994.

204   "Burns decried the dependence of America . . .": Al Kamen, "Burns's A List: African Americans, Arabs," *Washington Post*, March 12, 1999.

205   "In 1991, right after . . .": Ruth Marcus, "A Senator's Stunning Reference to Slaves; Burn's Remarks Followed Rights Bill Passage," *Washington Post*, November 13, 1991.

205   "[Connerly] concedes that in a few cases new . . .": William Jasper, "Battling Reverse Discrimination," *New American*, December 9, 1996.

205   "Supporting segregation need not be racist . . .": Bob Herbert, "Weirder and Weirder," *New York Times*, December 19, 2002.

206   "At their core, the Michigan policies amount . . .": Tom Ruam, "Republicans Sending Mixed Signals in Efforts to Reach Out to Blacks," Associated Press, January 15, 2003.

207   "It is important to take race into consideration if you must . . .": Condoleezza Rice, *Meet the Press*, NBC, January 19, 2003.

207   "I think they saw a person that they thought had potential . . .": *Ibid.*

207   "I think there's nothing wrong with that in the United States . . .": *Ibid.*

207   "Rosa Lopez, the maid who lived next door . . .": Andrea Ford and Jim Newton,

"The O.J. Simpson Murder Trial; Lopez Ends Her Testimony; 2 Simpson Lawyers Fined," *Los Angeles Times*, March 4, 1995.

208 "Mary Ann Gerchas, a jewelry store owner . . .": "Gerchas Arrested in False Statements on Car Loan," *Los Angeles Times*, February 12, 1995.

208 "Kary Mullis was going to testify . . .": Henry Weinstein, "The O.J. Simpson Murder Trial; Prosecutor Vows to Attack Defense DNA Expert . . . ," *Los Angeles Times*, March 28, 1995.

EIGHT: JESUS WAS A LIBERAL

211 "He was most likely . . .": *Hannity & Colmes*, Fox News Channel, December 4, 2002.

215 "the sacred principle . . .": James Madison, "The Detached Memoranda," quoted in Robert S. Alley, *James Madison on Religious Liberty*. Buffalo, N.Y.: Prometheus Books, 1985.

215 "would be not to profane . . ." quoted in Joseph Loconte, "James Madison and Religious Liberty," *Heritage Foundation Reports*, March 16, 2001.

215 "As the government . . .": quoted in Paul Galloway, "Founding Fathers More Pluralistic Than Christian," *Chicago Tribune*, June 30, 1995.

216 "Believing with you . . .": quoted in Derek Davis, "Thomas Jefferson and the 'Wall of Separation' Metaphor," *Journal of Church and State*, January 1, 2003.

216 "eternal hostility . . .": quoted in Sidney Goetz, "Commemorating Thomas Jefferson," *The Humanist*, May, 1993.

216 "The artificial structures . . .": quoted in Sidney Goetz, "Would the Freethinking Jefferson be Elected Today?," *The Humanist*, January 1, 2002.

216 "The problem . . .": Zachary Karabell, "Book Review: An Alternative to the Secular Myth of America's Creation," *Los Angeles Times*, January 12, 2002.

217 "Religion and government . . .": quoted in Nat Hentoff, "Vouchers: A Way to Subsidize Religion," *Washington Post*, July 11, 1998.

217 "During almost . . .": quoted in Steven Morris, "America's Unchristian Beginnings," *Los Angeles Times*, August 3, 1995.

217 "while Washington was very deferential . . .": Paul F. Boller, *Washington and Religion*. Dallas: Southern Methodist University Press, 1963, p. 82.

217 "That Jesus . . .": quoted in Steven Morris, "America's Unchristian Beginnings," *Los Angeles Times*, August 3, 1995.

217 "I have, with most of the . . .": *Ibid.*

219 "Do you think God chose . . .": *Hannity & Colmes*, Fox News Channel, July 11, 2002.

220 "I never prayed . . .": *Fresh Air*, National Public Radio, December 13, 2002.

220 "an ultra-liberal . . .": Gayle White, "Voice of Peace, A Complex Christian: A Man of Faith Who Lives What He Preaches," *Atlanta Journal-Constitution*, October 12, 2002.

220 "a biblical worldview": Michael Lind, "Deep in the Heart of Darkness: Under George W. Bush, the Worse of Two Texas Traditions Is Shaping America," *Washington Monthly*, January 1, 2003.

221 "If I go . . .": Ralph Z. Hallow, "GOP Ally's Threat Seen Cause for Party Concern; Dobson Vows to Pull Out 2.1 Million Members," *Washington Times*, February 17, 1998.

221 "estimated at 200 million . . .": Evelyn Nieves, "Family Groups Gear Up for Battle over Gay Marriage," *Washington Post*, August 17, 2003.

221   "But I think there is . . .": *Hannity & Colmes*, Fox News Channel, November 22, 2002.

222   "the Pagans . . .": *The 700 Club*, Christian Broadcasting Network, September 13, 2001.

222   "I want to tell you . . .": *Rivera Live!* CNBC, September 19, 2001.

222   "a very evil and wicked religion": Richard N. Ostling, "Evangelist Billy Graham Hasn't Quite Retired, but the Franklin Graham Era Has Begun," Associated Press, November 21, 2001.

222   "I do not believe . . .": Franklin Graham, "My View of Islam," *Wall Street Journal*, December 3, 2001.

223   "You believe Islam . . .": *Hannity & Colmes*, Fox News Channel, February 19, 2002.

223   "But is the religion itself . . .": *Hannity & Colmes*, Fox News Channel, August 5, 2002.

224   "The God of Islam . . .": *NBC Nightly News*, NBC, November 16, 2001.

224   "expelling all Muslims with visas . . .": Larry Witham, "Muslim Activist Won't Apologize to Evangelists," *Washington Times*, November 22, 2002.

224   "worse than the Nazis": *Ibid.*

224   "It is logical to assume . . .": Pat Robertson, *Bring It On*. Nashville: W Publishing Group, 2002, p. 264.

224   "The fact is . . .": *The 700 Club*, Christian Broadcasting Network, February 21, 2002.

225   "a wild-eyed fanatic . . .": *Hannity & Colmes*, Fox News Channel, September 18, 2002.

225   "Liberals always lie": *Ibid.*

226   "I know you are a very strong . . .": *Hannity & Colmes*, Fox News Channel, April 10, 2002.

226   "Islam is a religion . . .": Cal Thomas, "Men of Faith in Washington, D.C., Need Our Prayers," crosswalk.com.

229   "Young lady . . .": Dan Balz, "Democratic Candidates Vow To Protect Abortion Rights," *Washington Post*, January 22, 2003.

229   "Like all propagandists . . .": Ann Coulter, *Slander*. New York: Crown, 2002, p. 166.

229   "I believe in a president . . .": Edwin M. Yoder, "Stained-Glass Blather," *Washington Post*, August 9, 1986.

229   "You cannot be America's president . . .": Sidney Goetz, "Would the Free-Thinking Jefferson be Elected Today?," *The Humanist*, January 1, 2002.

229   "because he changed . . .": Stephen Buttry, "Candidates Focus on Christian Beliefs," *Des Moines Register*, December 15, 1999.

230   "Not big enough": James Harding, "Preaching to the Converted," *Financial Times*, January 12, 2003.

230   "Liberals hate . . .": Ann Coulter, *Slander*. New York: Crown, 2002, p.194.

230   "rounding up . . .": *Ibid.*, p. 196.

230   "But it also prohibits . . .": Peter Gomes, "Homophobic? Read Your Bible," *New York Times*, August 17, 1992.

231   "The same Bible . . .": *Ibid.*

231   "militant homosexuals . . .": Myra MacPherson, "Big-Time Politics from the Pulpit of Old-Time Religion," *Washington Post*, September 27, 1984.

232   "The character . . .": "Parents Alert: Tinky Winky Comes Out of the Closet," *National Liberty Journal*, February, 1999.

232   "As a Christian . . .": David Reed, "Falwell's Newspaper Outs Teletubbies' Character," Associated Press, February 9, 1999.

232   "he declared that the Antichrist": Andrew Petkofsky, "Solution Spiritual, Falwell

Says, Anti-Christ May Be Alive Now," *Richmond Times-Dispatch*, January 16, 1999.

233   "What are liberals . . .": Ray Dubuque, "What Are Liberals Anyway?," www.liberalslikechrist.org

NINE: CONSERVATIVES SAY THE DARNDEST THINGS

235   "a black, a woman . . .": Helen Thomas, "Upbeat White House Ends Year Anticipating Early 1984 Announcement that Reagan Will Run Again," United Press International, December 19, 1983.

236   "There ought to be . . .": Michael Holmes, "B.U.S.H BEAT: Governor Rips Web Site Parody," Associated Press, May 21, 1999.

236   "I told all four . . .": "President-elect George W. Bush Holds Media Availability with Congressional Leaders," *Federal Document Clearinghouse*, December 18, 2000.

237   "If you set aside . . .": "Washington Wire," *Wall Street Journal*, May 25, 2001.

237   "If people don't . . .": David E. Rosenbaum, "No Strong Voice Is Heard On Bush's Economic Team," *New York Times*, July 21, 2002.

237   "Companies come . . .": H. Josef Herbert, "Cabinet Members Say They Didn't Inform Bush About Enron Calls for Help," Associated Press, January 13, 2002.

237   "Able-bodied adults . . .": Amity Shlaes, "Republicans Sample the Rhetoric of Confidence: Remarks by Treasury Secretary Paul O'Neill Show an Administration Now Confident Enough to Spread Its Wings," *Financial Times*, May 22, 2001.

238   "Absolutely. In economic . . .": William Greider, "The Man From Alcoa: Treasury Secretary Paul O'Neill Is Turning Out To Be a Dangerous Crank," *The Nation*, July 16, 2001.

238   "If we win . . .": Martin Kasindorf and Wendy Koch, "Opponents Seize on Gun Lobby's Hopes for Bush," *USA Today*, May 5, 2000.

238   "I had other priorities . . .": George C. Wilson, "Cheney Believes Gorbachev Sincere; But Defense Chief Says Cutting West's Forces Would Be Premature," *Washington Post*, April 5, 1989.

238   "a triple draft dodger": Carl P. Leubsdorf, "Clinton Leads Tribute to Airmen, Cites Today's Goals," *Dallas Morning News*, June 5, 1994.

238   "Our young men and women . . .": Debate Between the Ten Republican Candidates for President, Manchester, New Hampshire, *Federal Document Clearinghouse*, October 11, 1995.

239   "what was left . . .": Donald Rumsfeld, Department of Defense Press Briefing, *Federal Document Clearinghouse*, January 7, 2003.

240   "We should invade . . .": Ann Coulter, "This Is War," anncoulter.com, September 12, 2001.

240   "girly boys": Howard Kurtz, "*National Review* Cans Columnist Ann Coulter," *Washington Post*, October 2, 2001.

240   "We should require . . .": Ann Coulter, "Where's Janet Reno When We Need Her," anncoulter.com, September 20, 2001.

240   "Congress could . . .": *Ibid.*

240   "My only regret . . .": George Gurley, "Coultergeist," *New York Observer*, August 23, 2002.

241　"just turn [the sheriff] . . .": "Lawmaker Tries to Explain Remark; Rep. Chambliss, a
　　　Senate Hopeful, Commented on Muslims," *Washington Post*, November 21, 2001.
241　"If I see someone . . .": Eli Sanders, "Understanding Turbans," *Seattle Times*,
　　　September 27, 2001.
241　"Look at who runs . . .": "Coble And Myrick Are Criticized By Advocacy Groups For
　　　Remarks," *Winston-Salem Journal*, February 6, 2003.
241　"Some probably . . .": *Ibid.*
242　"We have been . . .": *Politically Incorrect*, ABC, September 17, 2001.
243　"they're reminders . . .": Ari Fleischer, White House Press Briefing, White House
　　　Press Releases, September 26, 2001.
243　"make the United States . . .": Daniel Pipes, "It Matters What Kind of Islam
　　　Prevails," *Los Angeles Times*, July 22, 1999.
244　"every fundamentalist Muslim . . .": Daniel Pipes, "Bin Laden Is a Fundamentalist,"
　　　Nationalreviewonline.com, October 22, 2001.
244　"My anger . . .": Robert Jensen, "U.S. Just as Guilty of Committing Own Violent
　　　Acts," *Houston Chronicle*, September 26, 2001.
244　"radical leftist . . .": Tracy Breton, "Campus Critics of U.S. Policy Barraged with
　　　Hate Mail," *Providence Journal-Bulletin*, October 21, 2001.
245　"Without a hearing . . .": Stuart Taylor, "It's Time to Junk the Double Standard on
　　　Free Speech," *Atlantic*, January 25, 2002.
245　"If a group establishes . . .": Tanya Schevitz, "Professors Want Own Names Put On
　　　Mideast Blacklist; They Hope to Make It Powerless," *San Francisco Chronicle*,
　　　September 28, 2002.
248　"Where are you liberal?" *Hannity & Colmes*, Fox News Channel, July 10, 2002.
249　"Well, we have a system . . .": *Hannity & Colmes*, Fox News Channel, September 30,
　　　2002.
250　"We would like for the right-to-life . . .": Christopher Scanlan, "Elders: I'm Willing
　　　to Be Lightning Rod; Surgeon General Candidate an Activist," *Houston
　　　Chronicle*, December 17, 1992.
251　"more than a hundred people released . . .": Amnesty International,
　　　www.amnestyusa.org/abolish

TEN: CONSERVATIVES ARE DOWNRIGHT MEAN

253　"If I could prove . . .": Edward Walsh, "Burton Remark Splits House Panel; Waxman
　　　Criticizes Plan to Release Hubbell Prison Tapes," *The Washington Post*, April 22,
　　　1998.
258　"I always see . . .": Suzanne Gamboa, "Top Texans Spar Over Armey Comments on
　　　Jews and Liberals," Associated Press, September 24, 2002.
258　"You can go back . . .": Juliet Eilperin, "Two Lawmakers Assail Armey For
　　　Comments About Jewish Voters,"*Washington Post*, September 25, 2002.
258　"Barney Fag": Mary Ann Akers, "Armey calls Rep. Frank 'Barney Fag'," United Press
　　　International, January 27, 1995.
260　". . . liberals are always . . .": Ann Coulter, *Treason*. New York: Crown, 2003, p. 16.
260　"Are you prepared . . .": *Hannity & Colmes*, Fox News Channel, June 25, 2003.
262　"savagely cruel bigots . . .": Ann Coulter, *Slander*. New York: Crown, 2002, p. 205.
264　"I know what you were . . .": Peggy Noonan, "No Class," *Wall Street Journal*'s
　　　Opinion Journal, November 1, 2002.

267   "I want my party . . .": David Espo, "Kasich to Withdraw from GOP Race, Smith
        Quits Party," Associated Press, July 13, 1999.

268   "Santorum has told . . .": Jim Vanhei, "GOP Looks to Move Its Social Agenda; Hill
        Push to Include Abortion Curbs, 'Faith-Based' Programs," *Washington Post*,
        November 25, 2002.

268   "If the Supreme Court . . .": Lara Jakes Jordan, "Santorum Says Homosexual Acts Are
        Threat to American Family," Associated Press, April 22, 2003.

269   "I have no problem . . .": *Ibid.*

269   "almost 13% . . .": "The Non-Taxpaying Class," Editorial, *Wall Street Journal*,
        November 20, 2002.

269   "If you include . . .": Paul Krugman, "Hey, Lucky Duckies!," *New York Times*,
        December 3, 2002.

270   "Only 2.3 percent . . .": "Welfare Rolls Lowest in Three Years," Associated Press,
        August 23, 2000.

271   "Marriage holds the place . . .": Joan Lowy, "Uncle Sam Says: Save Sex For
        Marriage," *Scripps Howard News Service*, March 6, 1999.

271   "give preference . . .": Robert Pear, "Human Services Nominee's Focus on
        Married Fatherhood Draws Both Praise and Fire," *New York Times*, June 7,
        2001.

272   "Welfare rolls dropped . . .": Joseph H. Brown "Welfare Reform Is a Work in
        Progress," *Tampa Tribune*, August 26, 2001.

272   "remained poor": Nina Bernstein, "In Control Group, Most Welfare Recipients Left
        the Rolls Even Without Reform," *New York Times*, February 20, 2002.

272   "All right, you—": *Hannity & Colmes*, Fox News Channel, January 14, 2003.

ELEVEN: WHERE RIGHT IS RIGHT

287   "A Harris poll . . .": Humphrey Taylor, "Democratic Lead (Now Only Three Points)
        in Party Identification Has Declined to a New Low," The Harris Poll (Harris
        Poll #5), January 29, 2003.

291   "Ultraconservative Helms said that Iraq's ability . . .": Henry Weinstein and William
        Rempel, "Iraq Arms: Big Help from U.S.; Technology Was Sold with
        Approval—and Encouragement—from the Commerce Department but Often
        over Defense Officials' Objections," *Los Angeles Times*, February 13, 1991.

292   "Always give your best, never get discouraged . . .": "Nixon's Words," *Seattle Times*,
        April 23, 1994.

292   "No arsenal or no weapon in the arsenals . . .": Lou Cannon, "Inaugural Address:
        Evocative Version of Campaign Message; The Inaugural Address: Enunciating
        a Basic Creed," *Washington Post*, January 21, 1981.

295   "It was Ms. Malkin . . ." *Hannity & Colmes*, Fox News Channel, January 4, 2003.

295   "The United States is one of the few industralized countries . . .": Kathryn Jean
        Lopez, " 'What Would Mohammed [Atta] Do?'," *National Review Online*,
        September 18, 2002.

TWELVE: LIBERAL LIBERAL LIBERAL LIBERAL

299   "hopelessly liberal,": Bob Keeler, "Abrams' Day; Claims Victory over Ferraro in
        Seesaw Race," *Newsday* (New York), September 16, 1992.

299   "too liberal for too long": Tom Precious, "Flush with Victory Pataki Charges Ahead; Instead of Taxes and Crime He Focuses on Government Reform a Day After His Primary Win," *Times Union* (Albany, NY), September 15, 1994.

300   "What do you call someone who broke his promise . . .": Curt Anderson, "Dole Says He'll Prove Clinton Is a 'Liberal with a Hidden Plan'," Associated Press, September 25, 1996.

300   "Was the 1993 Tax Act . . .": Citizens for Tax Justice, CTJ's Presidential Candidate Tax Policy Scorecard, www.ctj.org.

302   "A CBS News poll . . .": "Poll: Economy Remains Top Priority," cbsnews.com, May 13, 2001.

304   "it was a wife's duty": "American Experience: Eleanor Roosevelt," PBS, 2000.

304   "the inherent dignity": Universal Declaration of Human Rights, adopted by the General Assembly of the United Nations, December 10, 1948.

305   "My greatest fear has always been that I would be afraid . . .": Eleanor Roosevelt, *If You Ask Me*. New York: Hutchinson, 1948, p. 112.

305   "I put everything I had into it . . .": Mike Clark, "Gregory Peck's Days of Glory," *USA Today*, June 13, 2003.

306   "I'm not a do-gooder . . .": "Peck on Peck," *Dallas Morning News*, June 13, 2003.

307   "In the future days . . .": President Franklin D. Roosevelt, Address to Congress, January 6, 1941.

308   "Once more we are in a period of uncertainty . . .": Eleanor Roosevelt, *Tomorrow Is Now*. New York: HarperCollins, 1966, p. xvii.

INDEX